Applesoft BASIC
Subroutines
& Secrets

A Collection of Programming Tips, Tricks, and Techniques

Jeanette Sullivan & Dave Sullivan

Hayden Book Company

A DIVISION OF HAYDEN PUBLISHING COMPANY, INC.
HASBROUCK HEIGHTS, NEW JERSEY / BERKELEY, CALIFORNIA

Acquisitions Editor: KAREN PASTUZYN
Production Editor: LORI WILLIAMS
Design: JOHN M-RÖBLIN
Illustrations: PETER BONO
Compositor: McFARLAND GRAPHICS AND DESIGN

Library of Congress Cataloging-in-Publication Data

Sullivan, Jeanette.
    Applesoft BASIC subroutines & secrets.

    1. Apple II (Computer)—Programming.   2. Basic
(Computer program language)   I. Sullivan, Dave (Dave
Leonard)   II. Title.   III. Title: Applesoft BASIC
subroutines and secrets.
QA76.8.A662S85   1985   005.36'5   85-13976
ISBN 0-8104-6756-9

Apple is a registered trademark of Apple Computer Inc., which is
not affiliated with Hayden Book Company.

Printed in the United States of America

	2	3	4	5	6	7	8	PRINTING
85	86	87	88	89	90	91	92	93	YEAR

PREFACE

This book has been written for the users of the Apple II computers who are familiar with BASIC and would like to enhance their ability to write interesting, innovative, and professional-looking programs. The programs can be used with the Apple II Plus, IIe, and IIc computers.

Once you have learned how to write programs in BASIC, you may want to add special features, sound, or graphics to your programs. This book is a collection of tips and tricks that can be easily incorporated into your programs. The ideas are either in a program or subroutine format. You can use the RENUMBER program on the System Master disk to renumber the subroutines or programs to fit into your programs. You can then use the MERGE feature of the RENUMBER program to merge the subroutine into your program. This is explained in the first chapter.

Chapter 1 also provides ways to enter and edit programs and to improve access to your programs or files on disk. Chapter 2 assists you in data entry and error checking and shows you how to include commas and colons in entries, as well as how to disable both the CONTROL C and the RESET keys. Chapter 3 presents various ways of displaying the output on the screen in a format that makes it easy for the user to interpret it, then introduces several ways to erase the screen.

Chapter 4 includes special effects for printing a message in a diamond shape, strobing the keyboard, and text animation. Chapter 5 presents techniques for sorting, searching, and scrambling.

Chapters 6 and 7 provide both low and high resolution graphics routines to get instant backgrounds, draw warps, and scroll the screen. Chapters 8 and 9 demonstrate how to draw circles and spirolateral-type designs and then present a poor man's slide show of your graphics pictures.

Chapter 10 enables you to use the Apple speaker to produce special sound effects and musical tunes. The Appendixes include the ASCII code chart; the Apple memory map; color charts for graphics; a list of commonly used PEEK, POKE, and CALL commands; and a summary of commands to save graphics or text.

The ideas in this book can be accessed in random order. A few sections, however, are more easily understood if you read the section in its entirety. These sections are "Low Resolution Special Effects with Machine Language Routines" (Chapter 6); "Bit Mapping" and "High Resolution Special Effects with Machine Language Routines" (Chapter 7); and all of Chapter 10. In order to understand Chapter 8, first read the introductory pages of that chapter along with the explanation for the Circle program.

EQUIPMENT NEEDED

To use the programs in this book, you will need the following equipment:

- An Apple II (with Applesoft), II Plus, IIe, or IIc with 48K minimum
- A disk drive
- A monitor or TV (color recommended)
- Paddles, joystick, or track ball for the following programs: Paddle Adjustment 0-N, Paddle Adjustment A-N, Laser Shoot, Lores Paddle Demo, Hires Paddle Demo

CONTENTS

3. OUTPUT FORMAT   43

PROGRAM ENTRY AND DISK ACCESS

This chapter presents some techniques to aid in program entry and editing along with hints on how to speed program execution.

The System Master disk has many useful programs. One of these is RENUMBER, which will not only renumber a program but will also merge two programs.

The search for the perfect HELLO program is a never-ending task. Just when you think your HELLO program has every feature you can imagine, you see another HELLO program with some new function. This chapter presents a few additional features to add to your "almost perfect" HELLO program.

This chapter also contains techniques to personalize your disk to read a heading of your selection in place of the words "DISK HEADING," to use the ampersand utility as a shorthand notation for some of the system commands, and to protect your files. It also includes the PEEK commands to enable you to copy a binary file without the program FID from the System Master.

PRINT STATEMENT SPACING

This shows you how to avoid splitting words when using the PRINT statement.

EXPLANATION

Often a word will be split when you use the PRINT statement. You could use different PRINT statements for every 39 characters or you could use the following method. Enter the PRINT statement either with the ? or the command PRINT and make sure that there is a space under the first quotation mark. You might have to add several spaces to avoid splitting a word.

The following two statements show how this spacing works. Each statement shows how the statement was entered, how it looks when you list it, and how it looks when you run it.

Sample 1:

Statement Entry
```
]10 PRINT "THIS IS A TEST OF THE APPLE'S
    PRINT    STATEMENT."
```

LIST
```
]LIST
10 PRINT "THIS IS A TEST OF THE
    APPLE'S PRINT    STATEMENT.
    "
```

RUN
```
]RUN
THIS IS A TEST OF THE APPLE'S PRINT
STATEMENT.
```

Sample 2:

Statement Entry
```
]10 ? "THIS STATEMENT DEMONSTRATES SPACIN
G ON   THE APPLE COMPUTER."
```

LIST
```
]LIST
10  PRINT "THIS STATEMENT DEMONST
    RATES SPACING ON   THE APPLE
    COMPUTER."
```

RUN
```
]RUN
THIS STATEMENT DEMONSTRATES SPACING ON
THE APPLE COMPUTER.
```

CLEARING THE SCREEN

GR:HOME or HGR:HOME

The following statements clear the text portion of a graphics screen.

EXPLANATION

The GR or HGR command sets the computer in the low resolution or high resolution mode with a text window of four lines below the graphics screen. The HOME command after the GR or HGR command clears the text screen.

If you want to use the window to write a message, then either use a few PRINT statements or VTAB 21.

```
10 GR:HOME
20 VTAB 21
```

or

```
10 HGR:HOME
20 VTAB 21
```

TEXT:HOME

This command starts the program with a standard-sized screen that is clear of graphics and text.

EXPLANATION

You will often see a program begin with the TEXT command.

```
10 TEXT:HOME
```

Text has several effects:

1. Sets the screen to full screen window.
2. Gets out of graphics mode and into text mode.
3. Sets the cursor to last line of the text screen.

If the program uses graphics or the program that you previously ran uses graphics, then use the TEXT command to set the screen to text mode in case the new program has a title or directions in text.

If your program or a previous program uses the POKE commands that adjust the screen windows, then the command TEXT returns the screen to normal default size of 24 rows and 40 characters per row. Chapter 4 will explain the POKE commands to adjust the screen size.

The HOME command clears the screen and places the cursor at the upper left corner or home position.

Many of the programs in this book are short demonstrations and consequently do not always use TEXT:HOME. It is advisable to use TEXT:HOME on your finished program.

CLEARING MEMORY

CLEAR

This command clears the variables and resets the dimension of the arrays to the default value.

EXPLANATION

When you run a program, the variables and arrays are cleared. The numeric and integer variables and arrays are set to zero, and the string variables and arrays are set to contain the empty string represented by " ". Sometimes within a program you want to clear the variables without starting the program at the beginning. The CLEAR command will help you clear the memory.

Often you will see the following statement either at the start of a program or within a program:

```
10 TEXT:CLEAR:HOME
```

CLEAR has several effects:

1. Resets all numeric variables and numeric arrays to zero.
2. Resets all the integer variables and integer arrays to zero.
3. Resets all string variables and string arrays to the null or empty string.
4. Resets the dimensions of numeric, integer, and string arrays to the default value of 10. This lets you access the array elements 0-10.
5. Clears the microprocessor's stack of return addresses and values.

FRE(0)

This command returns the amount of memory available and can be used to clean up unused string variables.

EXPLANATION

The command PRINT FRE(0) returns the amount of memory available. If the memory is expressed as a negative number, add 65536 to obtain the positive equivalent. The number 65536 is the maximum amount of memory available on a 64K Apple and is obtained by raising 2 to the 16th power, since two bytes are necessary to address any memory location.

```
PRINT FRE(0) + 65536
```

or

```
? FRE(0) + 2 ^ 16
```

CLEARING UNUSED STRING VARIABLES

The command X = FRE(0) clears the unused string variables so you won't run out of computer memory because of lack of sufficient string storage. String variables are stored in a special area of random access memory (RAM).

Any number can be used for the argument. You will often see zero used. The variable name X can be replaced by any legal numeric variable name. This command can be used periodically in a program that uses strings.

```
100 X = FRE(0)
```

SPEED OF PROGRAM EXECUTION

The following are some ideas to speed up the execution of a program.

1. Use colons to put several related statements on the same line. This way the computer does not have to look up the additional line numbers. The following example groups the set of commands to fill in the background in low resolution graphics.

```
10 COLOR = 6:FOR X = 0 TO 39:HLIN 0,39 AT X:NEXT X
```

2. Choose meaningful variable names and reuse them in the program.
3. Use subroutines for sets of commands that will be used several times in a program. This also improves the readability of the program and makes the program flexible for future changes.
4. Put the most often used subroutines at the lowest line numbers. When the computer encounters instructions to branch to a line number, it starts looking at the very beginning of the program and searches sequentially through the program until it finds the line.
5. Put often-used DATA statements at the beginning of the program for the same reason as subroutine placement.
6. Omit the index variable in a FOR. . .NEXT statement. The program does not have to take time to verify that you entered the correct index. It keeps track of these indices in a stack.

```
50 NEXT:NEXT
```

7. Omit the REM statements. One version can be documented and the other version can be used for speed.
8. Use variables in place of constants. It takes less time for the computer to look up the value of a variable than to convert a constant to a real number. Variables also provide more flexibility in a program. Rather than change each occurrence of that constant, merely change the value of the variable or let the user enter the value of the variable.
9. Use the FRE (0) statement periodically to clean up the string storage area of memory if your program uses many variables.

EDITING PROGRAM STATEMENTS

This section explains the technique for editing a program statement. Sometimes it is easier to edit the statement, while other times it is more convenient to retype a new statement. Whether to edit or retype depends on the length of the statement and the type of error.

EXPLANATION

You can use the ESC key and I, J, K, and M to edit a line on the Apple II Plus/IIe. If you have an Apple IIe/IIc, you can also use the four arrow keys.

To edit a line in a program:

1. List the program line. If the program is short you can list the program. If the program is lengthy, it is easier to list only the line or set of lines to be edited.
2. Press the ESC key.
3. Press I to move up, J to move left, K to move right, and M to move down. If you have an Apple IIe/IIc, you can use I, J, K, and M, or press the appropriate arrow key.
4. Move to the first digit of the number of the line to be modified.
5. Press the space bar to exit the mode that moves you around the screen.
6. Move over to the character to be changed using the right arrow key.
7. Change the character or characters and copy the rest of the line if necessary, or press the right arrow key until you are at the end of the statement.
8. List the line to be sure that the error was corrected.

EDITING WITH ESC KEY

Tables 1-1 and 1-2 summarize the ESC key commands for editing. You only have to press the ESC key once to get into the moving aspect of the editing mode. Use the appropriate keys (I, J, K, or M) or the four arrows to move. Press any key other than I, J, K, or M on the Apple II/II Plus or any key other than I, J, K, M, E, F, or the four arrow keys on the Apple IIe/IIc, to get out of the moving mode and start editing the statement.

TABLE 1-1. ESC KEY EDITING FOR APPLE II / II PLUS	
Key	**Effect**
ESC I	Cursor moves up one line
ESC J	Cursor moves left one character
ESC K	Cursor moves right one character
ESC M	Cursor moves down one line
ESC E	Clears text from cursor to end of line
ESC F	Clears text from cursor to end of page

TABLE 1-2. ESC KEY EDITING FOR APPLE IIe / IIc

Key	Effect
ESC I or ESC ↑	Cursor moves up one line
ESC J or ESC ←	Cursor moves left one character
ESC K or ESC →	Cursor moves right one character
ESC M or ESC ↓	Cursor moves down one line
ESC E	Clears text from cursor to end of line
ESC F	Clears text from cursor to end of page

CONTROL COMMANDS

The control commands can be used in program entry or execution.

EXPLANATION

Table 1-3 displays some control commands that you can use either when entering or executing a program.

TABLE 1-3. CONTROL COMMANDS

CONTROL Command	Effect
CONTROL C	Stops program and displays line number where the stop occurred
	If program was expecting keyboard input, you will have to press the RETURN key after CONTROL C
	Continue the program where it left off with command CONT
CONTROL G	Rings bell
	Must be within quotes in the program
CONTROL H	Moves cursor back one space/character
	Same as left arrow
CONTROL J	Line feed without carriage return
	Moves cursor down one line
CONTROL M	Carriage return (cr)
	Same as RETURN key
CONTROL S	Stops listing and sometimes program execution
	Any key will continue listing or program
CONTROL U	Moves cursor right one space/character
	Same as right arrow
CONTROL X	Deletes current line

INITIALIZING A BLANK DISK WITH A HELLO PROGRAM

This section provides a simple HELLO program and demonstrates how to initialize a blank disk.

EXPLANATION

Before a blank disk can be used, it must first be prepared to receive data. This preparation is called initializing or formatting the disk. During initialization, whatever program is in the computer's memory becomes the greeting or HELLO program.

In order for the computer to recognize disk drive commands and act upon them, a special program called DOS, which stands for disk operating system, must be in the computer's memory. When you insert an initialized disk in the disk drive and turn on the computer, a copy of DOS is written into the computer's memory. Since different brands of computers use different disk operating systems, the same disk cannot be used interchangeably on any computer to save or run programs. Apple II, II Plus, IIe, and IIc all use the same DOS, and the same disk can be used interchangeably with each of these computers.

The following steps show you how to initialize a blank disk with a HELLO program.

1. Boot DOS. The process of loading a copy of DOS into the computer's memory is called "booting DOS." You can boot DOS by inserting an initialized disk or the System Master into drive 1, closing the door, and turning on the computer.
2. Insert the blank disk. Remove the initialized disk and insert the blank disk you want to initialize.
3. HELLO program. Type in NEW to erase any program in memory and then enter the following HELLO program. This program becomes your greeting program or HELLO program when you boot the disk, since this is the first program that the computer runs after it boots DOS.

```
5   REM  === HELLO PROGRAM ===
10  TEXT : NORMAL : HOME
20  PRINT  CHR$ (4)"CATALOG"
30  NEW
99  END
```

Line 20 issues a CONTROL D command, which is represented by CHR$ (4), in order to execute the DOS command CATALOG from within a BASIC program.
4. INIT HELLO. When you initialize a disk, you are erasing the disk completely. Do not initialize any disk containing programs that you want to save.

Do not run the program. Type INIT HELLO and press the RETURN key. You will hear a whirring and clanking noise. This is normal at this time. The in-use disk drive light will go on. The INIT command puts a copy of DOS on the blank disk. Within a minute, the in-use light will go out, the noise will stop, and the cursor will reappear on the screen to indicate that the computer is waiting for your next command.

The name of the greeting program can be any legal name, but traditionally programmers use the name HELLO.
5. Test HELLO program. Test the HELLO program by either typing PR#6 or RUN HELLO. If you have an Apple IIe/IIc, you can also press the CONTROL (open apple) and RESET keys simultaneously for a warm boot. The disk should spin and produce a catalog of the disk contents. At this time, only the HELLO program is present.

6. LOCK HELLO. It is a good idea to lock your HELLO program so you do not accidentally erase it at a later time. Type LOCK HELLO and press the RETURN key. The catalog listing will show an asterisk before the A (for Applesoft program).

CHANGING HELLO PROGRAM AT A LATER TIME

If you find a better HELLO program and want to change yours at a later time, unlock the HELLO program, type NEW, enter or load the new HELLO program, and type SAVE HELLO.

Do not type INIT HELLO, as this will erase your entire disk. You cannot easily change the name of your HELLO program once the disk is initialized, so future greeting programs on that disk should also use the same name.

PERSONALIZED DISK VOLUME HEADING

This routine replaces the name DISK VOLUME in the upper left corner of the screen with a heading of your choice when you boot a disk, run HELLO, or type CATALOG. This name can be your name or can indicate the contents of the disk such as TIPS/TRICKS, GAMES, or UTILITIES.

EXPLANATION ═══

The routine at lines 1000–1030 personalizes the disk volume heading to a heading of your choice that is 12 characters or less.

```
5    REM   === HELLO/CHANGE DISK HEADING ===
10   GOSUB 1000
20   TEXT : NORMAL : HOME
30   PRINT  CHR$ (4)"CATALOG"
40   NEW
99   END
995  REM   === CHANGE DISK HEADING ===
997  REM   --- A$ HOLDS NEW HEADING OF 12 CHARACTERS OR L
ESS ---
1000 A$ = "TIPS/TRICKS":L =  LEN (A$)
1005 REM   --- PAD A$ WITH SPACES FOR LENGTH OF 12 CHARA
CTERS ---
1010 A$ = A$ +  CHR$ (32):L = L + 1: IF L < 12 THEN 1010

1015 REM   --- POKE HEADING INTO MEMORY ---
1020 FOR X = 45999 TO 46010: POKE X, ASC ( MID$ (A$,L,1
)) + 128:L = L - 1: NEXT X
1030 RETURN
```

If you have used the HELLO program given earlier, then unlock your HELLO program, enter the following program, and save it as your new greeting program with the command SAVE HELLO.

The old HELLO program will be replaced with this program, which includes the routine to change the volume heading. Lock the new HELLO program with LOCK HELLO.

If you have a different HELLO program than the one presented, add a GOSUB statement at the beginning of the HELLO program to insert this routine and add the routine at lines 1000–1040.

Select any name of 12 characters or less for A$ in line 10. The value of A$ will then be substituted for the standard name DISK VOLUME.

If the name is more than 12 characters, then the program will not work properly. If the name contains less than 12 characters, then the program pads the name with blanks to obtain a length of 12.

Line 20 pokes the new heading one character at a time into memory locations 45999–46010, which are reserved for the disk heading.

Be sure to run HELLO at least once in order to enter the proper POKE commands to personalize your disk. Then you only need to type CATALOG to see your special heading appear on the screen.

If you reboot a different disk, the heading will be of that new disk.

You can include this routine in your HELLO program when you initialize your disk or you can add it to an existing HELLO program.

When you boot your disk or run HELLO, the following catalog listing will appear.

CATALOG

TIPS/TRICKS 254

*A 003 HELLO

RENUMBERING A PROGRAM

You can use the RENUMBER program on your System Master disk to renumber all or part of a BASIC program. The programs and subroutines in this book can be renumbered to fit your programs.

EXPLANATION ══

You can renumber the entire program or part of a program.

1. Run the RENUMBER program.
2. Load the program to be renumbered and list it.

The first command must be the ampersand sign (&). Table 1-4 lists parameters to consider.

TABLE 1-4. PARAMETERS FOR RENUMBERING

Parameters	Explanation	Default Value
F or FIRST	First new line number of new program	10
S or START	Starting at this line number of old program	0
I or INC	Incrementing by this number for the new program	10
E or END	Ending with this line number of old program	63999

ENTIRE PROGRAM TO DEFAULT PARAMETERS

If you want to take the default parameters as listed in Table 1-4, then enter the ampersand symbol and press the RETURN key.

&

PART OF A PROGRAM

You can renumber part of a program as well as the entire program. Press the RETURN key after entering the ampersand symbol and the parameters needed.

&F100,I10,S25,E490

The above command set the first new line number at 100. The numbering will be in increments of 10 and start at line 25 of the old program and end at line 490 of the old program.

Since you are taking the default of 10 for the increment, the increment parameter can be omitted:

&F100,S25,E490

The parameters can be in any order but must be separated by a comma. If you take the default value, you need not enter that parameter. Do not press the RESET key during the renumbering of a program or your program will be destroyed.

The line numbers can be any decimal number from 0 to 63999. RENUMBER will change the line number references in commands such as GOTO, ON A. . .GOTO, ON A. . .GOSUB, IF. . .THEN, GOSUB, LIST, RUN, and DEL. RENUMBER will not renumber any reference that is in a remark or enclosed in quotation marks.

RENUMBER FIX FOR APPLE II/II PLUS USERS ONLY

There is a small bug in the RENUMBER program on the System Master for the Apple II Plus computer. If you have a System Master for IIe or IIc, then this bug has been remedied. If you have the original System Master DOS 3.3 for an Apple II or II Plus, then the following POKE commands will debug the RENUMBER program.

EXPLANATION

If your program has statements that multiply constants, with the constant to the right of the asterisk, then unwanted renumbering may occur in the mathematical formula.

If the integer part of a constant that appears to the right of the asterisk is the same in value as an "old" line number, then the constant is also changed when the line number is changed.

Here's an example of the bug in RENUMBER. If you enter this program:

```
5 N = 1
7 A = N * 5
9 PRINT N,A
```

and renumber it with the & command, you get:

```
&
10 N = 1
20 A = N * 10
30 PRINT N,A
```

when what you really wanted is:

```
10 N = 1
20 A = N * 5
30 PRINT N,A
```

Take the following steps to avoid this problem.

1. Load the RENUMBER program.
2. POKE 4789,172.
3. POKE 4790,171.
4. Save the RENUMBER program to another disk, since System Master is write-protected.
5. Lock the RENUMBER program.
6. Run the RENUMBER program to test it.

MERGING TWO PROGRAMS

The RENUMBER program also merges two separate programs into one. This is intended for incorporating a subroutine into a program or merging two programs.

EXPLANATION

You need to use two commands to merge two programs. The first command, &H, stores the first program in a separate portion of memory. The second command, &M, merges the first program with the second program. You can now save this new program with any legal name.

To merge two files or programs, either on the same or separate disks, follow this procedure:

1. Run the RENUMBER program.
2. Load the first program into memory.
3. List the program and renumber if necessary.
4. &H will put the first program on hold.
5. Load the second program into memory.
6. List and renumber if necessary.
7. &M will merge the two programs.
8. Save the merged program.

Do not press RESET during the merging or your program(s) will be destroyed. Avoid duplicate line numbers. The program will list both line numbers if a duplicate occurs.

AMPERSAND SHORTCUT TO CATALOG, RUN, OR LIST

You can shorten the number of keystrokes for any of the system commands such as CATALOG, LIST, or RUN to a one-character entry, namely the ampersand symbol.

EXPLANATION

Three sets of POKE commands are provided for replacing the commands CATALOG, LIST, or RUN with the ampersand. Since only one set of POKE commands can be used at a time, decide which command you want to be represented by the ampersand symbol and enter the appropriate POKE commands either in the immediate mode or in a program.

These commands can be added to your HELLO program as a permanent feature. Remember to either boot your disk or run the HELLO program to activate the ampersand utility.

If you want to deactivate the ampersand utility, return the three memory locations to their default (standard) values. Enter the following line either in the immediate mode or program mode.

```
POKE 1013,76: POKE 1014,88: POKE 1015,255
```

CATALOG WITH &

Include the following POKE commands in your HELLO program so &RETURN will catalog your disk.

```
POKE 1013,76
POKE 1014,110
POKE 1015,165
```

LIST WITH &

These POKE commands will allow &RETURN to list the program.

```
POKE 1013,76
POKE 1014,165
POKE 1015,214
```

RUN WITH &

Put these three POKE commands in the beginning of a program so &RETURN will run the program.

```
POKE 1013,76
POKE 1014,18
POKE 1015,217
```

PROTECTING FILES FROM UNAUTHORIZED ACCESS

This procedure protects your files from unauthorized access.

EXPLANATION

One method is to include a CONTROL key in the name of the file when you save it on the disk. The control character will not show up on the screen when you catalog your disk. Then you can load or run the program only if you enter the proper control character and at the proper place in the filename.

SAVE MYSTERY   (include a CONTROL key in the filename)

MODIFICATION

More than one control character can be used in the name.

FINDING CONTROL CHARACTER IN FILENAME OR STRING VARIABLE

The following program helps you find the control character in a filename as well as control characters in string variables. Perhaps you saved your program with a control chraracter and have now forgotten which control character you used or where you placed it. This program will enable you to locate the hidden character.

EXPLANATION

To find a control character in a file or program name or in a string variable, run the following program, catalog the disk, and any control characters in a program name will flash.

Load and list a program you suspect has control characters embedded in string variables and the control characters will flash.

To reinstate the normal printout, type PR#0.

```
5   REM  === FIND CONTROL CHARACTER ===
10  TEXT : HOME
20  FOR A = 768 TO 768 + 27
30  READ V: POKE A,V: NEXT A
40  POKE 54,0: POKE 55,3: CALL 1002
99  END
100  DATA  201,141,240,21,201,136
110  DATA  240,17,201,128,144,13
120  DATA  201,160,176,9,72,132
130  DATA  53,56,233,64,76,249
140  DATA  253,76,240,253
```

BINARY FILE ADDRESS

The following PEEK commands return the starting address and length of a binary file in memory. This is useful if you are working with shape tables, graphic pictures, game programs, or any other binary file and want to copy the binary file to another disk, but do not have a System Master disk handy.

BACKGROUND

In order to copy a binary file from one disk to another, you must know the starting address and the length. The copy procedure cannot be done with the regular LOAD and SAVE commands, since a binary file is a machine language file and is located at a specific address. If you have the System Master handy, you can use FID. But there are times when you may not have access to a System Master.

EXPLANATION

The address and length of the binary file each requires two bytes. The following two PEEK commands return the starting address and length of any binary file in memory in decimal form.

First load the binary file with the command BLOAD filename. You do not need the starting address or length when loading a file with the BLOAD command. The computer will load the binary file starting at the same address at which it was previously saved with a BSAVE command. Enter the following commands either in the immediate mode or within a program.

```
PEEK(43634) + PEEK(43635) * 256    > returns starting address
PEEK(43616) + PEEK(43617) * 256    > returns length
```

SAVING A BINARY FILE TO ANOTHER DISK

Do the following to save a binary file to another disk without using the program FID on the System Master.

EXPLANATION

Load the binary file with the command BLOAD filename and enter the PEEK commands listed previously to find the starting address and the length. Then insert the second disk and enter the following command to save the file, where the starting address and the length are represented in decimal notation. The new name can have the same name as the old filename or a different one.

```
BSAVE filename,Astarting address,Llength
```

ALTERNATING DISK DRIVES

The following statement demonstrates how to alternate between two disk drives.

EXPLANATION

If you have two disk drives, often you will want to access drive 2 while linked to drive 1 and the converse. When you boot your disk, you automatically access drive 1. This is often stated as "logged onto" drive 1. You can then log onto drive 2 to access programs on that disk drive either in the immediate or program mode.

To access the "other" drive in the immediate mode, add a comma and the letter D followed by the number of the drive you want to access. This works with commands such as CATALOG, RUN, LOAD, BRUN, BLOAD, and BSAVE. For example, the following commands can access drive 2 when logged onto drive 1, where filename represents the name of the file or program you want to access.

```
RUN filename,D2
```

If you want to use one of the commands listed above from within a BASIC program, then you must add a CONTROL D or CHR$(4) and quotes. The comma, letter D, and drive number (1 and 2) must be enclosed in quotes.

The following statements present some examples on switching disk drives, where filename represents the name of the file or program to be accessed, starting address represents the starting address of the binary file, and length stands for the length of the binary file.

If you are logged onto disk drive 1 and want to access drive 2, enter the following statement:

```
10 PRINT CHR$(4);"RUN filename,D2"
```

or

```
10 A$ = "filename"
20 ? CHR$(4);"BLOAD";A$",D2"
```

or

```
20 PRINT CHR$(4);"BSAVE";A$;",Astarting address,Llength,D2"
```

If you are logged onto disk drive 2 and want to access drive 1, enter the following statement:

```
10 PRINT CHR$(4);"RUN filename,D1"
```

or

```
10 A$ = "filename"
20 ? CHR$(4);"BLOAD";A$",D1"
```

or

```
20 PRINT CHR$(4);"BSAVE";A$;",Astarting address,Llength,D1"
```

CHANGING DISK DRIVES

This command changes the disk drive that the computer is logged onto.

EXPLANATION

The following command allows you to switch from drive 1 to drive 2 and vice versa. The general format is the following command, where n is the number of the drive that you want the computer to log onto:

```
POKE 43264,n
```

This command is useful when you are logged onto a disk drive and want to access the "other" drive: for example, if you load a program from one drive and it needs to load binary files from the "other" drive. Instead of entering a disk command such as CATALOG,Dn, where n is the number of the drive that you want to access, you can POKE location 43264 with the number of the drive that you want. This command immediately changes the drive that you are logged onto.

DATA ENTRY AND ERROR TRAPPING

The term "user-friendly" has become a cliché these days. However, it conveys an important programming concept. Your program should be written to enable the user to enter the necessary data with few keystrokes and minimal effort.

The program should clearly explain what type of answer the computer is requesting from the user and attempt to trap errors before the program continues. This chapter includes programs that aid in making data entry a user-friendly process.

Do you want to avoid the EXTRA IGNORED reply when the user enters commas or colons in his reply with the INPUT command? If you use the GET command, you can allow the user to enter commas and colons as part of his reply.

The GET command is very useful but can cause problems when a DOS (disk operating system) command follows. Several ways of avoiding this pitfall are explained.

Have you ever wanted to disable the CONTROL C command or the RESET key for program privacy? This chapter provides the necessary commands to protect your program along with providing password protection.

EVEN/ODD NUMBER CHECK

The following program determines if a number is even or odd.

EXPLANATION

The statements 30 and 40 divide a number X by 2 and check for a remainder. If there is no remainder, then the number is even. If a remainder exists, then the number must be odd. The INT function returns only the whole number portion of a number.

```
5   REM   === EVEN/ODD NUMBER ===
10    HOME
20    INPUT "ENTER A NUMBER ";X
30    IF X / 2 =   INT (X / 2) THEN   PRINT X" IS EVEN"
40    IF X / 2 <   >   INT (X / 2) THEN   PRINT X;" IS ODD"
99    END
```

TEST FOR FACTOR

This program determines if B is a factor of A.

EXPLANATION

If A divided by B has no remainder, then B is a factor of A. If a remainder exists, then B is not a factor of A.

```
5   REM    === TEST FOR FACTOR ===
10    HOME
20    INPUT "ENTER TWO NUMBERS ";A,B
30    IF A / B =   INT (A / B) THEN   PRINT B" IS A FACTOR O
F "A
40    IF A / B <   >   INT (A / B) THEN   PRINT B" IS NOT A F
ACTOR OF "A
99    END
```

ONE-KEYSTROKE ENTRY AND ERROR TRAPPING

Most replies from the user can be one-key answers such as Y for yes or N for no. However, when the program asks a yes/no question, the user may be unsure whether he should answer with a Y or YES or with an N or NO reply. Furthermore, the user may mistakenly enter an inappropriate reply such as Q or X.

The program must provide for this dilemma by displaying the type of answer expected, disregarding an incorrect answer, and repeating the question if an incorrect answer is given.

Trap invalid entries before printing them to the screen if possible. If the program is expecting a Y or N reply, don't even print an incorrect or inappropriate answer on the screen or erase it after it is typed and ask the question again.

The next three programs offer a variety of ways of error trapping an invalid keypress and only allowing the valid keypress to remain printed on the screen.

GET COMMAND

This program checks the validity of a one-character reply by using the GET command.

EXPLANATION

The GET command accepts a one-character response but does not print it to the screen. You can check the validity of the keypress and, if correct, you can print the character. If an invalid key is entered, you can send the computer back to the GET statement without printing the invalid response.

```
5   REM  === CONTINUE WITH GET COMMAND ===
10    HOME
20    VTAB 22
30    PRINT "CONTINUE Y/N? ";
40    GET A$
50    IF A$ = "Y" THEN  PRINT A$: GOTO 80
60    IF A$ = "N" THEN 999
70    GOTO 40
80    HOME : PRINT "REST OF PROGRAM"
999   END
```

INPUT COMMAND

This program checks the validity of a one-character keypress by using the INPUT command and a CALL command.

EXPLANATION

The INPUT command and CALL −868 can be used instead of the GET command to validate the keypress. The CALL −868 command is a machine language routine built into BASIC that clears the line from the cursor to the right edge of the screen. This is useful for erasing an invalid entry.

```
5   REM  === CONTINUE WITH INPUT COMMAND ===
10  HOME
20  VTAB 22: CALL  - 868
30  INPUT "CONTINUE Y/N ";A$
40  IF  LEFT$ (A$,1) = "Y" THEN 70
50  IF  LEFT$ (A$,1) = "N" THEN 999
60  GOTO 20
70  HOME : PRINT "REST OF PROGRAM"
999  END
```

MODIFICATIONS

1. The command CALL −875 or CALL −958 can be used in place of CALL −868. CALL −875 clears the entire text line.

   ```
   20 VTAB 23: CALL -875
   ```

2. The command CALL −958 clears the text line from the cursor to the bottom of the page. This is useful if the entry takes more than one line.

   ```
   20 VTAB 23: CALL -958
   ```

PEEK(37)

This program uses the PEEK(37) command along with the INPUT command to check the validity of the reply when the reply occurs at various positions on the screen.

EXPLANATION

The PEEK(37) command identifies the vertical position of the cursor, since this entry may not always occur at row 23. It returns the current vertical position of the cursor in the range 0–23 rather than the tabbing range of 1–24. The command PEEK(36) returns the current horizontal position of the cursor in the range of 0–39 rather than the tabbing range of 1–40. When you use the tab functions and PEEK(37), you must tab over or down one more place than the value of the cursor position returned with PEEK(36) or PEEK(37) commands.

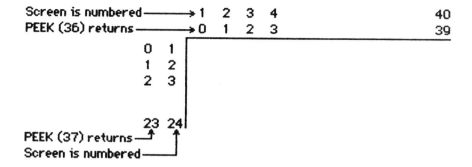

This program prints a random set of blank lines to simulate the occurrence of the input at various rows on the screen.

```
5    REM  === ERROR TRAP PEEK ===
10   TEXT : HOME
20   FOR X = 1 TO  INT ( RND (1) * 10) + 1: PRINT : NEXT
X
30   PRINT "WOULD YOU LIKE TO TRY AGAIN (Y/N) ";
40   CALL  - 958
50 C =  PEEK (36):R =  PEEK (37): REM  COLUMN AND ROW
60   INPUT A$
70   IF  LEFT$ (A$,1) = "Y" THEN 10
80   IF  LEFT$ (A$,1) = "N" THEN 100
90   VTAB R + 1: HTAB C + 1: GOTO 40
100   HOME : VTAB 12: HTAB 18: PRINT "THE END"
199   END
```

Y/N TRICK

This program makes it easy for the user to answer a yes/no question with a one-character response of Y for yes or N for no, by putting the cursor in a set of parentheses that allows room for only a one-character reply. This idea works for true/false or north/south type answers as well.

EXPLANATION

The command PEEK(36) returns the horizontal position of the cursor in the range 0–39. The screen is numbered in the range 1–40. See the Explanation in the PEEK(37) section.

The command CALL −875 clears the entire text line. This command is used to erase an incorrect response and print the question again.

This program prompts the user to enter either a Y for yes or N for no and places the cursor in parentheses while waiting for the keypress. It uses a GET command to accept the entry. If the entry is correct, the program prints the character pressed and continues with the program. If the entry is incorrect, then the program erases the data entry line, reprints the line, and waits for the correct keypress.

Line 140 checks the current position of the cursor and stores that value as X. It then subtracts one from X and tabs to that new position. Actually the program is adding 1 to X for the tab position and subtracting 2 in order to get the cursor within the quotes. HTAB $X + 1 - 2$ is the same as HTAB $X - 1$.

```
5   REM  === YES/NO TRICK ===
100   HOME
110   VTAB 23
120   CALL  - 875
130   PRINT "ENTER Y OR N ( )";
140 X =  PEEK (36): HTAB X - 1: GET A$
150   IF A$ <  > "Y" AND A$ <  > "N" THEN  PRINT : GOTO 1
10
160   HTAB X - 1: PRINT A$
```

WHICH LETTER?

This program uses a one-line mathematical technique to determine which subroutine to execute. This idea can be used for a menu or set of selections within a game such as an adventure game.

BACKGROUND

Often a menu is used to list the options the user can choose from. The program must identify the correct line to execute in order to carry out the requested selection. For example, a menu of selections such as E-ENTER, C-CHANGE, S-SEARCH, P-PRINT, or Q-QUIT can be presented to the user.

Rather than use a series of IF. . .THEN statements that are space- and time-consuming, you can use a one-line mathematical statement to determine which line is to be executed.

EXPLANATION

In the following program, line 40 replaces four IF. . .THEN statements. The expressions on line 40 are evaluated as true or false. A true expression is converted to a 1, and a false expression is converted to a 0. The program uses the GET command to accept only the first letter of the selection.

If N is selected, then $X = 1 + 0 + 0 + 0$
$$X = 1$$
If S is selected, then $X = 0 + 1*2 + 0 + 0$
$$X = 2$$
If E is selected, then $X = 0 + 0 + 1*3 + 0$
$$X = 3$$
If W is selected, then $X = 0 + 0 + 0 + 1*4$
$$X = 4$$

```
5    REM   === WHICH LETTER? ===
10   HOME
20   PRINT "N)ORTH  S)OUTH  E)AST  W)EST"
30   PRINT "WHICH DIRECTION: ";: GET D$
40 X = (D$ = "N") + (D$ = "S") * 2 + (D$ = "E") * 3 + (D
$ = "W") * 4
50   ON X GOTO 100,300,500,700
60   PRINT "NOT A VALID DIRECTION": PRINT : GOTO 20
99   END
100   HOME : PRINT "NORTH": END
300   HOME : PRINT "SOUTH": END
500   HOME : PRINT "EAST": END
700   HOME : PRINT "WEST": END
```

NULL OR EMPTY STRING <> BLANK STRING

This demonstrates the difference between the null or empty string and the blank string.

EXPLANATION

The null or empty string A$ is expressed as A$ = "" with the two quotes immediately next to each other. A$ has a length of zero.

The blank string B$ is expressed as B$ = " " with a space between the two quotes. B$ has a length of 1. This is used for inserting a space.

The null or empty string is <u>not</u> the same as the blank string.

```
5   REM  === NULL STRING <> BLANK STRING ===
10   TEXT : HOME
20  A$ = ""
30  B$ = " "
40   IF A$ = B$ THEN  PRINT "THE EMPTY STRING EQUALS THE
BLANK STRING"
50   IF A$ <  > B$ THEN  PRINT "THE EMPTY STRING DOES NOT
 EQUAL THE     BLANK STRING."
60   PRINT
70   PRINT "THE LENGTH OF THE NULL STRING A$ IS "; LEN (A
$)
80   PRINT "THE LENGTH OF THE BLANK STRING B$ IS "; LEN (
B$)
99   END
```

NULL ENTRY CHECK

Sometimes the user makes a null entry, that is, presses the RETURN key without first answering the question. These routines only accept a nonempty reply.

EXPLANATION

The following routines represent two different techniques for locating a null entry and repeat the question if only the RETURN key is pressed. If a null entry is made, then N$ is a null string with a length of zero.

Line 20 generates a random number to place line 30 at a random row on the screen. Line 30 requests the user to enter his/her name.

1. Check for empty string. Line 40 has two quotes next to each other with no space between them. PEEK(37) returns the current vertical cursor position. CALL −958 clears the screen from the cursor to the bottom of the page.

```
5   REM   === NULL ENTRY CHECK (A) ===
10   TEXT : HOME
20   VTAB  INT ( RND (1) * 23) + 1
30   INPUT "ENTER YOUR NAME PLEASE ";N$
40   IF N$ = "" THEN  VTAB  PEEK (37): CALL  - 958: GOTO
     30
50   PRINT "HI ";N$;" I AM HERE TO SERVE YOU"
99   END
```

2. Check for empty string with a length of zero. Line 40 checks the length of N$. An empty string has a length of zero.

```
5   REM   === NULL ENTRY CHECK (B) ===
10   TEXT : HOME
20   VTAB  INT ( RND (1) * 23) + 1
30   INPUT "ENTER YOUR NAME PLEASE ";N$
40   IF  LEN (N$) = 0 THEN  VTAB  PEEK (37): CALL  - 958:
     GOTO 30
50   PRINT "HI ";N$;" I AM HERE TO SERVE YOU"
99   END
```

ENTERING COMMAS IN DATA STATEMENTS

This program allows you to enter commas as part of the data in the DATA statement.

EXPLANATION

Commas are used as separators of data items in the DATA statements. If you want to include commas within the data elements, then enclose the elements in quotes.

```
5   REM  === COMMAS IN DATA STATEMENTS ===
10  HOME : PRINT
20  PRINT "NAME","ADDRESS": PRINT
30  READ N
40  FOR X = 1 TO N
50  READ N$(X),A$(X)
60  PRINT N$(X),A$(X)
70  NEXT X
99  END
100  DATA 3: REM    NUMBER OF NAMES/ADDRESSES
110  DATA JONES,"THOUSAND OAKS, CA"
120  DATA SMITH,"SMITHTOWN, NY"
130  DATA BROWN,"FREEHOLD, NJ"
```

ENTERING COMMAS AND COLONS IN USER REPLY

A common programming problem is that of providing a way for the user to include commas and colons in his reply. As you have probably found, the INPUT command will not accept commas or colons. Instead, it returns an EXTRA IGNORED error message and invalidates the comma or colon and everything thereafter. There are several techniques to solve this problem. Two methods are presented: the first uses the INPUT command and a leading quote; the second way uses the GET command. This is especially useful for entering the city, state, and zip code for a mailing label.

WITH INPUT COMMAND

This technique allows the user to enter commas and colons in his reply.

EXPLANATION

To include commas and colons in a reply to any INPUT command, start the reply with a leading quote. The commas and colons will then be included in the string. The trailing quote can be omitted.

RUN
ENTER CITY AND STATE "CHICAGO, ILLINOIS

The disadvantage of this method is that it can only be used if the user is familiar with computers or someone instructed him to use a leading quote when including commas and colons in his reply.

WITH GET COMMAND

This program allows the user to enter commas and colons in his reply by using the GET command.

EXPLANATION

This program uses the GET command in a routine that gets each character, one at a time, and concatenates (adds to) the characters into one string that permits commas and colons as valid entries.

It uses the CHR$(13), which is the RETURN keypress, to check for the end of the entry. It then concatenates the individual characters into one string variable that can be stored and printed to the screen.

You cannot back up when entering data in this manner for the computer will record the extra keystrokes.

```
5   REM  === COMMAS/COLONS OK ===
10   HOME
20 CS$ = "": REM  NULL STRING
30   PRINT "ENTER CITY, STATE AND ZIP"
40   GET A$
50   IF A$ =  CHR$ (13) THEN 90
60   PRINT A$;
70 CS$ = CS$ + A$
80   GOTO 40
90   PRINT
100  PRINT "YOUR ADDRESS IS ";CS$
```

DOS COMMANDS AFTER A GET COMMAND

This tip avoids the pitfall of a DOS command after a GET command.

BACKGROUND ===

The GET command is indeed very useful. However, it can cause problems when a DOS command follows. A DOS command must be preceded by a carriage return, but the GET command does not produce a carriage return. Of course, there are ways to avoid the problem by adding a carriage return between a GET command and a DOS command.

EXPLANATION ===

The following programs offer three different methods to avoid the GET pitfall.

```
5   REM  === GET/DOS COMMAND (ERROR) ===
10   TEXT : HOME
20   PRINT "PRESS <Q> TO QUIT"
30   PRINT "PRESS <C> TO CATALOG ";
40   GET A$
60   IF A$ = "Q" THEN  END
70   IF A$ = "C" THEN  PRINT  CHR$ (4)"CATALOG": GOTO 90
80   IF A$ <  > "Q" AND A$ <  > "C" THEN 10
90   PRINT : PRINT "NEXT COMMAND GOES HERE"
```

In this example, the word CATALOG will be printed to the screen rather than the command CATALOG executed.

Method 1: Add line 50 to insert a carriage return between the GET command and the DOS command.

```
5   REM   === GET/DOS COMMAND (A) ===
10   TEXT : HOME
20   PRINT "PRESS <Q> TO QUIT"
30   PRINT "PRESS <C> TO CATALOG ";
40   GET A$
50   PRINT
60   IF A$ = "Q" THEN  END
70   IF A$ = "C" THEN  PRINT  CHR$ (4)"CATALOG": GOTO 90
80   IF A$ <  > "Q" AND A$ <  > "C" THEN 10
90   PRINT : PRINT "NEXT COMMAND GOES HERE"
```

Method 2: Omit line 50 and precede the CONTROL D command with a carriage return, which is represented by the character string of 13 in line 70.

```
70 IF A$ = "C" THEN PRINT CHR$(13)CHR$(4)"CATALOG"
```

```
5   REM     === GET/DOS COMMAND (B) ===
10   TEXT : HOME
20   PRINT "PRESS <Q> TO QUIT"
30   PRINT "PRESS <C> TO CATALOG ";
40   GET A$
60   IF A$ = "Q" THEN   END
70   IF A$ = "C" THEN   PRINT  CHR$ (13); CHR$ (4);"CATALO
G": GOTO 90
80   IF A$ <  > "Q" AND A$ <  > "C" THEN 10
90   PRINT : PRINT "NEXT COMMAND GOES HERE"
```

Method 3: At the beginning of the program, define a string such as D$ to represent the carriage return concatenated to the CONTROL D command. Omit line 50, add line 7, and change line 70.

```
5   REM       === GET/DOS COMMAND (C) ===
7 D$ =  CHR$ (13) +  CHR$ (4)
10   TEXT : HOME
20   PRINT "PRESS <Q> TO QUIT"
30   PRINT "PRESS <C> TO CATALOG ";
40   GET A$
60   IF A$ = "Q" THEN   END
70   IF A$ = "C" THEN   PRINT D$;"CATALOG": GOTO 90
80   IF A$ <  > "Q" AND A$ <  > "C" THEN 10
90   PRINT : PRINT "NEXT COMMAND GOES HERE"
```

ONERR GOTO Command

When the computer encounters errors that it can recognize such as overflow, illegal quantity error, or division by zero, the program stops execution and displays the appropriate reply.

Some errors can be handled by the program if the the problem has been anticipated and programming instructions have been provided. A range error such as plotting outside of the legal screen limits or an overflow error such as a number too large for the computer to handle can be handled by the ONERR GOTO command.

The ONERR GOTO command traps an error before the computer displays the error message and abruptly halts the program execution.

```
10 ONERR GOTO 1000
```

Line 10 instructs the computer to branch or jump to line 1000 whenever an error occurs. The ONERR command is usually placed at the start of the program or the routine where an error might occur.

When an error occurs, the computer places a numeric code in memory location 222. This code corresponds to the type of error. You can examine this code with a single PEEK command and act accordingly.

The RESUME command causes a branch back to the beginning of the statement where the error occurred.

To disable the ONERR GOTO command and return the program to its automatic error detection and halt method, use the statement:

```
POKE 216,0
```

The following programs demonstrate a few of the ways that the ONERR GOTO command can be used to trap errors.

OVERFLOW ERROR

This program shows one way that the ONERR GOTO command can be used to trap and handle an error before the computer halts execution. It traps an overflow error when calculating powers of an inputted number.

EXPLANATION

Error code 69 represents an overflow error that occurs when the answer exceeds the limits of the computer. Use the following program to determine the upper limits of the computer.

```
5   REM  === ONERR OVERFLOW DEMO ===
10   ONERR  GOTO 1000
20   HOME
30   INPUT "ENTER A NUMBER ";N
40   PRINT
50   PRINT N"^2=";N ^ 2
60   PRINT N"^3=";N ^ 3
70   PRINT N"^10=";N ^ 10
80   PRINT
90   GOTO 30
99   END
1000 E = PEEK (222)
1010 IF E = 69 THEN  PRINT "NUMBER TOO LARGE": PRINT :
GOTO 30
1020 RESUME
```

APPLESOFT ERROR CODES

Table 2-1 shows the error codes for Applesoft BASIC error messages.

Code	Error Message
TABLE 2-1. APPLESOFT	
ERROR MESSAGES	
0	NEXT without FOR
16	Syntax error
22	RETURN without GOSUB
42	Out of data
53	Illegal quantity
69	Overflow
77	Out of memory
90	Undefined statement
107	Bad subscript
120	Redimensioned array
133	Division by zero
163	Type mismatch
176	String too long
191	Formula too complex
224	Undefined function
254	Bad response to INPUT statement
255	CONTROL C interrupt attempted; can't continue error

DOS Error Codes

Table 2-2 shows the error codes for DOS error messages.

TABLE 2-2. DOS ERROR MESSAGES

Code	Error Message
1	Language not available
2,3	Range error
4	Write-protected
5	End of DATA
6	File not found
7	Volume mismatch
8	I/O error
9	Disk full
10	File locked
11	Syntax error
12	No buffers available
13	File type mismatch
14	Program too large
15	Not direct command

ILLEGAL QUANTITY

This program traps a range error in low resolution graphics.

EXPLANATION

The ONERR GOTO command does not allow this program to be stopped with a CONTROL C command. Instead, a CONTROL C entry reruns the program. If a number less than 0 or greater than 39 is entered, the program asks for a reentry from the user and CALL —1052 rings a bell. Only when 40,40 is entered will the program end.

```
5    REM  === ERROR FOR ILLEGAL QUANTITY ===
10   ONERR  GOTO 995
20   GR : HOME
30   VTAB 21
40   PRINT "ENTER 40,40 TO QUIT PROGRAM"
50   VTAB 23
60   POKE 34,22
70   PRINT "PRESS ANY KEY TO BEGIN ";
80   GET A$: PRINT
90   COLOR= 6
100  N = 1
110   VTAB 23: CALL  - 958
120   PRINT N;". ENTER X,Y COORDINATES ";
130   INPUT "";X,Y
140   IF X = 40 AND Y = 40 THEN  POKE 34,20: HOME : GOTO
199
150   PLOT X,Y
160  N = N + 1
170   GOTO 110
```

```
199   END
995   REM   --- ERROR HANDLING ROUTINE ---
1000  E =  PEEK (222): REM   IDENTIFY ERROR CODE
1010  IF E = 53 OR E = 254 THEN   CALL  - 1052: GOTO 110
1020  IF E = 255 THEN   RUN
1030  RESUME
```

DISABLING CONTROL C

CONTROL C AND RESUME

This program disables the CONTROL C command to provide program protection and prevent other users from seeing your program.

EXPLANATION

Pressing CONTROL C or CONTROL C RETURN stops the program execution, which permits the user to list your program. One way to achieve program protection is to disable the CONTROL C command with the ONERR GOTO command.

The following program prints numbers from 1 to 100 and their square roots. If you try to stop the program with a CONTROL C command, the computer will respond with an appropriate message and resume the program execution.

```
5    REM   === DISABLE CONTROL C AND RESUME ===
10   ONERR  GOTO 1000
20   HOME
30   FOR X = 1 TO 100
40   PRINT X, SQR (X)
50   NEXT X
99   END
995  REM   --- DISABLE CONTROL C ---
1000 E =  PEEK (222)
1010  IF E = 255 THEN   HOME : VTAB 10: PRINT "CAUGHT YOU
 TRYING THE CONTROL C COMMAND": FOR Z = 1 TO 1000: NEXT
 Z: HOME : RESUME
```

CONTROL C AND GOTO N

By changing line 1010, the program can be restarted whenever your press the CONTROL C command.

```
5    REM   === DISABLE CONTROL C AND GOTO N ===
10   ONERR  GOTO 1000
20   HOME
30   FOR X = 1 TO 100
40   PRINT X, SQR (X)
50   NEXT X
99   END
995  REM   --- DISABLE CONTROL C ---
1000 E =  PEEK (222)
1010  IF E = 255 THEN   HOME : VTAB 10: PRINT "CAUGHT YOU
 TRYING THE CONTROL C COMMAND": FOR Z = 1 TO 1000: NEXT
 Z: HOME : GOTO 30
```

DISABLING CONTROL C AND RESET KEYS

This program disables both the CONTROL C and the RESET keys.

BACKGROUND

If you tried to break the previous two programs with a CONTROL C or CONTROL C RETURN, you instead received a message from the programmer. However, you could have passed the RESET key and broken into the program.

EXPLANATION

By adding three POKE commands, you can also disable the RESET key, so that RESET, instead of stopping the program, runs the program.

The POKE commands in line 15 should be used with care. First enter and run the program without the POKE commands. Then enter the three POKE commands and save the program on a disk before you run the program.

If you run the program and let it complete its loop, all is well. However, if you try to interrupt with a RESET keypress, then the program will run from the beginning. Along with this desired result comes an undesirable effect. You cannot access the disk unless you reboot it.

To enable the RESET key, return the POKE commands to their default values by entering the following three POKE commands either in the program or immediate mode.

```
POKE 1010,191: POKE 1011,157: POKE 1012,56

5   REM  === DISABLE CONTROL C AND RESET ===
10  ONERR  GOTO 1000
13  REM  --- DISABLE RESET ---
15  POKE 1010,102: POKE 1011,213: POKE 1012,112
20  HOME
30  FOR X = 1 TO 100
40  PRINT X, SQR (X)
50  NEXT X
60  PRINT : PRINT
70  PRINT "REBOOT DISK IF YOU PRESSED CONTROL RESET"
99  END
995  REM  --- DISABLE CONTROL C ---
1000 E =  PEEK (222)
1010  IF E = 255 THEN  HOME : VTAB 10: PRINT "CAUGHT YOU
 TRYING THE CONTROL C COMMAND": FOR Z = 1 TO 1000: NEXT
 Z: HOME : GOTO 30
```

PASSWORD PROTECTION WITH RESET DISABLED

These three programs provide password protection for a program. They are not foolproof, since they work only when your program has been run. If someone is able to list your program, they can find the necessary password.

SIMPLE PASSWORD

There is great concern about privacy of data and illegal access to programs or data. You, of course, would like to protect your programs from unauthorized access after you have slaved hours to get them debugged and running perfectly.

One method is to require the user to enter a password to start your program. The CONTROL C and RESET keys must be disabled, so the user cannot press CONTROL RESET to exit from your program and list it.

The following program provides some protection of your best program yet. Once the program is run, no one can peek at the listing. However, once the program has ended or has initially been loaded, rather than run from the disk, there is still the possibility of a sneak preview of your hard work. At least this is a start toward protecting your ideas.

EXPLANATION ═══

The GET command is used to request the correct password before entry into your program. This program accepts a two-character password with a limit of three attempts, and it traps CONTROL C or CONTROL RESET attempts to stop the program and perhaps view the program or password.

CONTROL C RETURN is interpreted as a password attempt and counts as one of your tries. CONTROL RESET restarts the program at the first line. It is like a RUN command.

The three POKE commands in line 10 should be used with care. Enter the program, test it, add line 10, but do not run the program. Save the program and then run it. If you try to save the program or catalog your disk after running the program and interrupting it with a RESET keypress, you will have difficulty as the computer hangs.

Change the password in line 20 from JS to a two-character password of your choice.

```
5    REM   === PASSWORD ===
10   POKE 1010,102: POKE 1011,213: POKE 1012,112
20  PW$ = "JS"
30   HOME
40  T = 0
50   VTAB 3: HTAB 1: CALL  - 868
60   PRINT "ENTER PASSWORD TO CONTINUE: ";
70   GET P$,W$
80  A$ = P$ + W$: IF A$ = PW$ THEN 110
90  T = T + 1: IF T = 3 THEN 199
100   GOTO 50
110   HOME : PRINT "PAGE 2": END
199   VTAB 12: PRINT : PRINT "THE END": END
```

CONTROL CHARACTERS IN PASSWORD

Your password can be composed of any letter, digit, or special character such as an asterisk (*), number sign (#), or exclamation mark (!). You may wish to use one or more control characters in your password.

By changing line 20 of the previous program, you can use CONTROL J and CONTROL S as the password. See Appendix A for the list of control characters and their respective ASCII codes.

```
5   REM  === PASSWORD/CONTROL CHARACTER ===
10  POKE 1010,102: POKE 1011,213: POKE 1012,112
20 PW$ =  CHR$ (10) +  CHR$ (19): REM  CONTROL J  CONTRO
L S
30   HOME
40 T = 0
50   VTAB 3: HTAB 1: CALL  - 868
60   PRINT "ENTER PASSWORD TO CONTINUE: ";
70   GET P$,W$
80 A$ = P$ + W$: IF A$ = PW$ THEN 110
90 T = T + 1: IF T = 3 THEN 199
100   GOTO 50
110   HOME : PRINT "PAGE 2": END
199   VTAB 12: PRINT : PRINT "THE END": END
```

To further protect your program, change line 199 to read:

```
199 VTAB 12: PRINT : PRINT : "THE END": NEW
```

Be sure to save your program before you change line 199 to avoid losing your program.

Now the user cannot complete your program and list it. He can still load your program and list it if he has access to your disk.

ANY SYSTEM COMMAND RESULTS IN RUN

The command presented here causes any system command to run the program in memory. This provides further protection by not allowing the listing of your program.

EXPLANATION

The command POKE 214,255 causes any system command such as LIST, CATALOG, or PR#6 to run the program in memory. A listing of the program is not available.

Use this command with care. Do not run your program with this command until you have first saved the program. Once you activate this command, the only way to deactivate it is to turn off the computer. Test your program, debug it, add the POKE command, and save it.

This command is added to the simple password program PASSWORD. It can be added to any other program that you want to protect from being listed by a friend, foe, or competitor.

```
5    REM  === PASSWORD WITH AUTO-RUN ===
10   POKE 1010,102: POKE 1011,213: POKE 1012,112
13   REM  --- ANY SYSTEM COMMAND RUNS PROGRAM ---
15   POKE 214,255
20 PW$ = "JS"
30   HOME
40 T = 0
50   VTAB 3: HTAB 1: CALL  - 868
60   PRINT "ENTER PASSWORD TO CONTINUE: ";
70   GET P$,W$
80 A$ = P$ + W$: IF A$ = PW$ THEN 110
90 T = T + 1: IF T = 3 THEN 199
100    GOTO 50
110    HOME : PRINT "PAGE 2": END
199    VTAB 12: PRINT : PRINT "THE END": END
```

OUTPUT FORMAT

Another aspect of your program you may wish to make "user-friendly" is the screen display. A screen that is clear and uncluttered can be easily viewed and quickly understood. There are several ways of making an attractive yet functional display. One way is to center or right-justify messages. Another way is to use two, three, or four columns depending on the length of the data. Commas automatically give three columns, so tab commands will be used to obtain different numbers of columns. A method for entering numbers down the screen one column at a time is presented.

You will want the result of a mathematical calculation to be rounded off to different places depending on the problem. For a score or grade, you might want the answer to the nearest whole number, whereas, for a batting average, you will want the answer rounded to the nearest thousandth. Methods of rounding off are not built into BASIC but must be added by the user. The formulas are presented in this chapter.

There may be times when you wish to have the information in money format. There is no automatic function to round off your answers to the nearest hundredth of a cent, add the trailing zero or zeros on $25 or $12.5, or line up the decimal points for easy viewing of the results. Two different methods for aligning numbers and adding trailing zeros are explained in this chapter.

Borders and various window sizes can add variety to the screen display so certain items can be highlighted or outlined. Programs to obtain these effects are given.

Once the user is ready for the next screen, there are also several ways of erasing the old screen besides using the standard command to clear the screen.

AVOIDING ERROR WHEN RAISING TO A POWER

This technique shows you how to avoid a slight round-off error when raising to a power.

EXPLANATION

There are some slight inaccuracies when you use exponents in a BASIC program on the Apple. For example, when you raise 7 to the second power, the computer returns 49.0000001 instead of the expected 49. This same problem occurs with other integers raised to other powers and is a result of the way the computer handles exponents. The inaccurate answer will always contain nine digits. This can cause inaccuracies in your program or expected answers.

Table 3-1 shows some inaccuracies when the computer raises to a power.

TABLE 3-1. RAISING NUMBERS TO A POWER		
Problem	Expected Answer	Computer Answer
7 ^ 2	49	49.0000001
3 ^ 4	81	81.0000001
6 ^ 5	7776	7776.00001

To avoid this error, use either of the following statements, where X is the number being squared, P is the power or exponent, and N% or N is the Pth power of X:

```
N% = X^P
```

or

```
N = INT(X^P)
```

N% stores only the integer portion of the number and is called an integer variable.

Dividing Two Numbers

To Get Whole-Number Remainder

This program shows you how to divide two numbers and get the quotient and the remainder expressed as whole numbers. This is useful in math quizzes that test division skills.

EXPLANATION

This program divides A by B and stores the answer as Q with the whole number remainder R.

```
5   REM   === DIVIDE WITH INTEGER REMAINDER ===
10   HOME
20   INPUT "ENTER A AND B ";A,B
30 Q =   INT (A / B)
40 R = A - (B * Q)
50   PRINT A"/"B" = "Q" REMAINDER "R
99   END
```

You will notice that semicolons were not used in line 50. The computer will default to the semicolon format and squeeze the output together if the comma or semicolon are not used. For clarity, you may choose to use some semicolons in your PRINT statements.

If there is a possibility that A and B might be mixed numbers, then add line 45 to check for a fractional remainder.

```
45 IF R < 1 THEN R = 0
```

MODIFICATION

If you want only the remainder, then you can combine lines 30 and 40 and omit line 40:

```
30 R = A - INT(A/B) * B
50 PRINT R
```

To Get Fractional Remainder

This program divides two numbers and expresses the remainder as a decimal fraction.

EXPLANATION

This program returns the decimal remainder R after dividing A by B.

```
5   REM   === DIVIDE WITH FRACTIONAL REMAINDER ===
10   HOME
20   INPUT "ENTER A AND B ";A,B
30 Q = A / B
40   IF Q >  = 0 THEN R = Q -   INT (Q)
50   IF Q < 0 THEN R =   INT (Q) - Q
60   PRINT "REMAINDER ";R
99   END
```

Numbers Counting Up and Down Simultaneously

1 to N and N to 1

This program helps you count from 1 to N and from N to 1 simultaneously. This is useful in graphics and in working with arrays.

EXPLANATION

The loop counts from 1 to 10 in the first column and from 10 to 1 in the second column, since N = 10.

```
5   REM  === COUNT 1-N AND N-1 ===
10  N = 10
20  HOME
30  FOR A = 1 TO N
40  B = (N + 1) - A
50  PRINT A,B
60  NEXT A
99  END
```

MODIFICATIONS

1. Change the value of N on line 10 to end the counting at a number other than 10.
2. The program can be modified to start counting at any number other than 1 by changing the 1 in line 30 to the new starting number.

CRISSCROSS MESSAGE

This program prints every other letter of a message from left to right and fills in the missing letters from right to left simultaneously.

EXPLANATION

This program uses the counting idea in the program count 1-N and N-1 and modifies it to do some crisscross printing.

Enter your message as A$ in line 10. The variable EO, which represents even/odd, is 1 when the length of A$ is even and 0 when the length is odd. The center of the screen is calculated and stored as H.

Line 60 prints every other character from left to right. At the same time, line 80 fills in the missing letters from right to left as line 70 calculates the position of the missing characters.

The value of X ranges from 1 to LEN(A$) in increments of 2. When the length of A$ is an odd number, the value of N ranges from LEN(A$) − 1 to 2 in increments of 2. When the length of A$ is an even number, the value of N ranges from LEN(A$) to 0 in increments of 2.

For example, the following set of numbers represents the values of X and N when the length of A$ is 8, which is even, and 7, which is odd.

When LEN(A$) = 8, then as X goes from $1 \to 3 \to 5 \to 7$
N goes from $8 \to 6 \to 4 \to 2$

When LEN(A$) = 7, then as X goes from 1 → 3 → 5 → 7
N goes from 6 → 4 → 2 → 0

The IF. . .THEN statement on line 70 is necessary, since you cannot take the midstring of A$ starting at 0.

```
5    REM    === CRISSCROSS MESSAGE ===
10 A$ = "THIS MESSAGE WILL CRISSCROSS THE SCREEN"
20 EO = ( LEN (A$) / 2 =  INT ( LEN (A$) / 2))
30 H = 20 -  LEN (A$) / 2
40   HOME
50   FOR X = 1 TO  LEN (A$) STEP 2
60   VTAB 12: HTAB H + X: PRINT  MID$ (A$,X,1);
70 N =  LEN (A$) - X + EO: IF N = 0 THEN 99
80   HTAB H + N: PRINT  MID$ (A$,N,1);
90   NEXT X
99   VTAB 23: END
```

0 TO N AND N TO 0

This program helps you count from 0 to N and from N to 0 simultaneously.

EXPLANATION

The loop counts from 0 to 10 in the first column and from 10 to 0 in the second column, since N = 10.

```
5    REM   === COUNT 0-N AND N-0 ===
10 N = 10
20   HOME
30   FOR A = 0 TO N
40 B = N - A
50   PRINT A,B
60   NEXT A
99   END
```

MODIFICATIONS

1. Change the value of N on line 10 to end the counting at a number other than 10.
2. The program can be modified to start counting at any number other than 0 by changing the 0 in line 30 to the new starting number.

X MARKS THE SPOT

This program draws an X in low resolution graphics.

EXPLANATION

This program uses the idea in Count 0–N and N–0 to draw an X in low resolution graphics.

The values of both the X and Y coordinates in line 50, and the value of the X coordinate in line 60 increase from 0 to 39. Simultaneously, the value of the Y coordinate in line 60 decreases from 39 to 0. The colors alternate between red and blue.

```
5   REM   === X MARKS THE SPOT ===
10   GR : HOME
20   FOR X = 0 TO 39
30   IF X / 2  =  INT (X / 2) THEN  COLOR= 1
40   IF X / 2 < >  INT (X / 2) THEN  COLOR= 2
50   PLOT X,X
60   PLOT X,39 - X
70   NEXT X
99   END
```

RECTANGLES IN

This program draws rectangles starting from the outer edge and moving inward.

EXPLANATION

This program uses the idea in Count 0–N and N–0 to draw progressively smaller rectangles. The routine at line 40–100 determines the points to be plotted. The program starts plotting in the upper left and lower right corners.

```
5   REM   === RECTANGLES IN ===
10   GR : HOME
20 S = 2
30   COLOR= 1
40   FOR Y = 0 TO 19 STEP S
50   FOR X = Y TO 39 - Y
60   PLOT X,Y
70   PLOT 39 - X,39 - Y
80   PLOT Y,X
90   PLOT 39 - Y,39 - X
100   NEXT X,Y
199   END
```

1. You can change the step size by changing line 20:

```
20 S = 1
```

or

```
20 S = 3
```

2. For random colors, omit line 30 and add line 55:

```
55 COLOR = INT(RND(1)*15) + 1
```

RANDOM NUMBER RANGE

The following statements enable the computer to generate any range of random numbers.

0 TO N − 1 RANGE

The following statement returns a random number from 0 to N − 1, where N is any positive integer.

```
R = INT(RND(1)*N)
```

1 TO N RANGE

This statement returns a random number from 1 to N, where N is any positive integer.

```
R = INT(RND(1)*N) + 1
```

A TO B RANGE

This statement returns random numbers from A to B, where A and B are integers and $A < B$. The quantity $B - A + 1$ represents the number of numbers in the range A to B, and A represents the starting number.

```
R = INT(RND(1)*(B-A+1)) + A
```

For example, to get the following ranges, use the following statements:

Range Desired	Random Number Statement
−1 to 1	R = INT(RND(1)*3) − 1
13 to 19	R = INT(RND(1)*7) + 13
12 to 44	R = INT(RND(1)*33) + 12

JUSTIFYING THE MESSAGE

CENTERING

This program centers any message of 39 characters or less and prints a series of dashes above and below the message. This can be used for a heading or title.

EXPLANATION

Line 40 computes the starting tab position, where L represents the length of the message.

```
5   REM  === CENTER MESSAGE/DASHES ===
10  S$ = "-"
20  A$ = "DREARY DUNGEON"
30  L =  LEN (A$)
40  M = 20 -  INT (L / 2)
50   HOME
60   HTAB M
70   FOR A = 1 TO L: PRINT S$;: NEXT A: PRINT
80   HTAB M
90   PRINT A$
100   HTAB M
110   FOR A = 1 TO L: PRINT S$;: NEXT A: PRINT
199   END
```

MODIFICATION

The message for A$ can be inputted by the user. Change line 20 and add the following statements to enter the message and check that the message is 39 characters or less.

```
15  HOME
20  INPUT "ENTER MESSAGE ";A$
35  IF L = 39 THEN M = 1:GOTO 50
37  IF L > 39 THEN PRINT "MESSAGE TOO LONG": PRINT:GOTO 20
```

RIGHT-JUSTIFYING

This program right-justifies a message and prints a series of dashes above and below the message.

EXPLANATION

The calculation of the tabbing position is done in line 50, where L represents the length of the message.

```
5   REM  === RIGHT JUSTIFY MESSAGE/DASHES ===
10 S$ = "-"
20 A$ = "DREARY DUNGEON"
30 L =  LEN (A$)
40   HOME
50 H = 40 - L
60   HTAB H
70   FOR A = 1 TO L: PRINT S$;: NEXT A: PRINT
80   HTAB H
90   PRINT A$
100  HTAB H
110  FOR A = 1 TO L: PRINT S$;: NEXT A: PRINT
199  END
```

MODIFICATION

The user can input the message. Change line 20 and add lines 15, 35, and 37. Lines 35 and 37 check the length of the message.

```
15 HOME
20 INPUT "ENTER MESSAGE ";A$
35 IF L = 39 THEN H = 1:GOTO 60
37 IF L > 39 THEN PRINT "MESSAGE TOO LONG": PRINT:GOTO 20
```

ALIGNING COLUMNS

FOUR COLUMNS SIMULTANEOUSLY

This program prints an array of elements in four columns instead of the standard three columns obtained by using commas. This can be used with output such as grades, scores, or averages.

EXPLANATION

N represents the number of items to be printed. NC represents the number of columns, and NN stands for the number of items per column. Statements 80–110 determine which data element is to be printed. Either PRINT TAB( ) or HTAB can be used.

```
5    REM  === FOUR COLUMNS ===
10   HOME
20   HTAB 14: PRINT "THE NUMBERS": PRINT
30   N = 80:NC = 4
40   DIM A(N)
50   FOR X = 1 TO N:A(X) = X: NEXT X
60 NN = N / NC
70   FOR X = 1 TO NN
75   REM  --- DETERMINES ELEMENT -
80   PRINT A(X);
90   HTAB 10: PRINT A(X + NN);
100  HTAB 20: PRINT A(X + 2 * NN);
110  HTAB 30: PRINT A(X + 3 * NN)
120  NEXT X
199  END
```

SAMPLE OUTPUT

THE NUMBERS

1	21	41	61
2	22	42	62
3	23	43	63
4	24	44	64
5	25	45	65
6	26	46	66
7	27	47	67
8	28	48	68
9	29	49	69
10	30	50	70
11	31	51	71
12	32	52	72
13	33	53	73
14	34	54	74
15	35	55	75
16	36	56	76
17	37	57	77
18	38	58	78
19	39	59	79
20	40	60	80

THREE COLUMNS ONE AT A TIME

This program prints the output one column at a time. This is useful if the data is in alphabetical or numerical order.

EXPLANATION

This program enters the numbers 1–60 into array A(X) and prints the output in three columns down the page starting with the first column. Line 100 increments the row counter V. When the row counter equals 23, the row counter is reset to 3 and the horizontal tab counter V is incremented by 13 for the next column.

Either PRINT TAB( ) or HTAB can be used. If more than 60 items are to be printed, you will need a second page. String variables can be used by replacing A(X) with AS(X).

```
5   REM   === THREE COLUMNS ===
10  N = 60
20   DIM A(N)
30   FOR X = 1 TO N:A(X) = X: NEXT X
40   HOME
50  V = 3:H = 1
60   PRINT  TAB( 12)"THE RESULTS": PRINT
70   FOR X = 1 TO N
80   VTAB V: HTAB H
90   PRINT A(X)
100 V = V + 1: IF V > 22 THEN V = 3:H = H + 13
110   NEXT X
120   VTAB 23
199   END
```

SAMPLE OUTPUT

                    THE RESULTS

1	21	41
2	22	42
3	23	43
4	24	44
5	25	45
6	26	46
7	27	47
8	28	48
9	29	49
10	30	50
11	31	51
12	32	52
13	33	53
14	34	54
15	35	55
16	36	56
17	37	57
18	38	58
19	39	59
20	40	60

PRINTING LIST OF MORE THAN 24 ITEMS

This program prints a list of items 20 at a time and waits for the user to enter a keypress before continuing with the next 20 items. This is useful for viewing long lists of information.

BACKGROUND

The screen display on the Apple holds a maximum of 24 rows of information. This poses a problem when printing more than 24 items. One alternative is to separate the list into segments and display one section at a time, allowing the reader to view the data at his own pace.

EXPLANATION

The following program fills an array of 100 elements with a random number from 1 to 100. The routine at 50–80 prints the elements 20 at a time. When you press any key, it continues with the printout. The program segment starting at line 50 can be used with any printout of numeric or string array elements. If your list contains string variables, change the numeric array A(X) to a string array AS(X).

```
5    REM   === LIST OF ITEMS ===
10   N = 100
20   DIM A(N)
30   HOME
40   FOR X = 1 TO N:A(X) =  INT ( RND (1) * 100) + 1: NEX
T X
50   FOR X = 1 TO N
60   PRINT X;". ";A(X)
65   REM  -- CHECKS FOR MULTIPLE OF 20 --
70   IF X / 20 =  INT (X / 20) THEN  VTAB 23: PRINT "PRES
S ANY KEY TO CONTINUE";: GET A$: HOME
80   NEXT X
99   END
```

MODIFICATIONS

1. Line 70 can be replaced with the following PEEK command, which returns the vertical position of the cursor in the range of 0–23.

   ```
   70 IF PEEK(37) = 20 THEN VTAB 23: PRINT "PRESS ANY KEY TO
      CONTINUE";:GET A$:HOME
   ```

2. The value 20 in line 70 can be changed to another number provided it is less than 23.

ROUNDING OFF THE ANSWER

The following statements round X off to the nearest specified place.

EXPLANATION

Since BASIC has no built-in function to round off numbers, you must use a mathematical formula to round off to the appropriate place. After you have the number X, add one of the following lines to your program depending on how you want the number X rounded off.

TO THE NEAREST INTEGER

To ones place:	$I = INT(X + .5)$
To tens place:	$T = INT(X / 10 + .5) * 10$
To hundreds place:	$H = INT(X / 100 + .5) * 100$
To thousands place:	$TH = INT(X / 1000 + .5) * 1000$

TO THE NEAREST DECIMAL

To tenths place:	$T = INT(X * 10 + .5) / 10$
To hundredths place:	$H = INT(X * 100 + .5) / 100$
To thousandths place:	$TH = INT(X * 1000 + .5) / 1000$

DOLLAR-AND-CENT ALIGNMENT

When the numerical result is a number that represents money, you may want the answer to be in money format. The computer does not automatically round numbers off to the nearest hundredth, retain the zero to print $12.50, or align decimal points.

When the computer does a mathematical computation, it returns the answer with nine or less significant digits and ignores any trailing zeros when storing and displaying the final calculation. Thus, an answer of 12.50 is stored and printed on the screen as 12.5. In addition, it left-justifies all numbers.

There are subroutines that can be added to your program to round the answer off to the nearest hundredth of a cent, allow the trailing zeros to be be added, and adjust the output so the decimal points line up.

The programs below offer two different ways of making sense out of cents. Use the method that you prefer.

EXPLANATION

The following two programs ask you to enter five numbers. Each program rounds the numbers off to the nearest cent, pads the cents with zeros if necessary, and aligns the number in dollars-and-cents format at the top of the screen. You can change the positioning of the output by changing the tabbing command.

The number is entered as a numeric variable, then converted and printed as a string variable.

PRINT USING SIMULATOR

This program presents a method to round off a money answer to the nearest cent, add trailing zeros, and align the decimal points and the dollar signs.

EXPLANATION _____

This program lets the user enter five numbers and determines the largest number and stores it as MAX. The subroutine from 1000 to 1080 puts the answer in money format and prints the number at line 130.

A subroutine rounds off the answer to the nearest cent in line 1000 and converts the number (array element) to a string M$ in line 1010. Lines 1020–1060 determine the position of the decimal point represented by DP and pads the number accordingly in lines 1040 and 1050. Lines 1070–1080 determine the number of spaces (SP) between the dollar sign and the first digit of the number.

The tabbing in line 130 can be changed by changing 20 to a different number.

The subroutine in lines 1000–1080 can be replaced by the Dollars and Cents subroutine presented in the next program.

```
5    REM  === PRINT USING SIMULATOR ===
10   MAX = 0:H = 20:H = H - 1
20   N = 5: DIM A(N)
30    HOME
40    PRINT  TAB( 10)"PRINT USING SIMULATOR": PRINT
45    REM   -- ENTER NUMBERS --
50    FOR X = 1 TO N
60    PRINT "ENTER MONEY AMOUNT ";X;: INPUT " ";A(X)
70    IF A(X) >  = MAX THEN MAX = A(X)
80    NEXT X
90   H$ =  STR$ ( INT (MAX))
100   PRINT : PRINT
105   REM   --- FORMAT AND PRINT MONEY ---
110   FOR X = 1 TO N
120   GOSUB 995"DOLLAR/CENT FORMATTER"
130   PRINT  TAB( 20 -  LEN (H$))"$"; SPC( SP);M$
140   NEXT X
199   END
995   REM $$$$$$$$$$$$$$$$$$$$$$$$$$$$$
996   REM $ DOLLAR/CENT FORMAT   $
997   REM $$$$$$$$$$$$$$$$$$$$$$$$$$$$$
998   REM   -- ROUNDING TO NEAREST CENT --
1000 A(X) =  INT (A(X) * 100 + .5) / 100
1010 M$ =  STR$ (A(X))
1015  REM   --- FIND POSITION OF DECIMAL POINT ---
1020  FOR DP = 1 TO  LEN (M$)
1030  IF  MID$ (M$,DP,1) <  > "." THEN  NEXT DP
1040  IF DP - 1 =  LEN (M$) THEN M$ = M$ + ".00"
1050  IF DP + 1 =  LEN (M$) THEN M$ = M$ + "0"
1060 A$ =  STR$ ( INT ( VAL (M$)))
1065  REM   --- DETERMINE # OF SPACES BETWEEN $ AND NUMBE
R ---
1070  IF  VAL (A$) = 0 THEN SP =  LEN (H$): RETURN
1080 SP =  LEN (H$) -  LEN (A$): RETURN
```

PRINT USING SIMULATOR

```
ENTER MONEY AMOUNT 1 12.5
ENTER MONEY AMOUNT 2 .975
ENTER MONEY AMOUNT 3 1000
ENTER MONEY AMOUNT 4 43.976
ENTER MONEY AMOUNT 5 13.998


           $   12.50
           $     .98
           $1000.00
           $   43.98
           $   14.00
```

or

PRINT USING SIMULATOR

```
ENTER MONEY AMOUNT 1 12.3333333
ENTER MONEY AMOUNT 2 10.6666667
ENTER MONEY AMOUNT 3 .996
ENTER MONEY AMOUNT 4 18500
ENTER MONEY AMOUNT 5 199.5


           $   12.33
           $   10.67
           $    1.00
           $18500.00
           $  199.50
```

DOLLARS AND CENTS

This program presents another method to obtain the money format.

EXPLANATION

The program reads in a list of five numbers from DATA statements in lines 30–60, uses the subroutine at lines 1000–1080 to put the number in the money format, and prints the number at line 120.

Line 50 finds the largest number of the list and stores it as MAX. Line 70 converts the largest number to a string H$. The subroutine at lines 1000–1080 puts the number in money format. It rounds off the number in line 1000 and converts it to the string M$ in line 1010. Lines 1020–1060 find the position of the decimal point in the number to determine whether it should add a decimal point, zero, or two zeros. Lines 1070–1080 determine the number of spaces between the dollar sign and the first digit of the number.

The tabbing in line 120 can be adjusted to print in a different column by changing the 20 to a different number.

The PRINT USING simulator routine at lines 1000–1080 can be used interchangeably with the Dollars and Cents subroutine in the previous program.

```
5   REM  === DOLLARS & CENTS ===
10  MAX = 0:H = 20:H = H - 1
20  N = 5: DIM A(N)
25  REM  --- READ MONEY INTO ARRAY ---
30  FOR X = 1 TO N
40  READ A(X)
50  IF A(X) > = MAX THEN MAX = A(X)
60  NEXT X
70  H$ =  STR$ ( INT (MAX))
75  REM  --- FORMAT AND PRINT MONEY ---
80  HOME
90  PRINT  TAB( 13)"DOLLARS & CENTS": PRINT
100  FOR X = 1 TO N
110  GOSUB 996"DOLLAR/CENT FORMATTER"
120  PRINT  TAB( 20 -  LEN (H$))"$"; SPC( SP);M$
130  NEXT X
199  END
995  REM  $$$$$$$$$$$$$$$$$$$$$$$$$
996  REM  $ DOLLAR/CENT FORMAT $
997  REM  $$$$$$$$$$$$$$$$$$$$$$$$$
998  REM  -- ROUNDING TO NEAREST DECIMAL --
1000 A(X) = ( INT (A(X) * 100 + .5)) / 100
1010 M$ =  STR$ (A(X))
1015  REM  --- FIND POSITION OF DECIMAL POINT ---
1020  IF  INT (A(X)) = A(X) THEN M$ = M$ + ".00": GOTO 1
060
1030  IF  LEN (M$) = 2 THEN 1050
1040  IF  MID$ (M$, LEN (M$) - 2,1) = "." THEN 1060
1050 M$ = M$ + "0"
1060 A$ =  STR$ ( INT ( VAL (M$)))
```

```
1065  REM  --- DETERMINE # OF SPACES BETWEEN $ AND NUMBE
R ---
1070  IF  VAL (A$) = 0 THEN SP =  LEN (H$): RETURN
1080 SP =  LEN (H$) -  LEN (A$): RETURN
2000  DATA  25,19.98,.985,1234.4,99.997
```

```
                    DOLLARS & CENTS

                    $   25.00
                    $   19.98
                    $     .99
                    $1234.40
                    $ 100.00
```

INSTANT INVERSE SCREEN

This program enters a machine language routine to quickly change the screen to full inverse mode.

EXPLANATION ═══

L represents the starting memory location for the machine language routine, since this routine is relocatable. See the memory map in Appendix B for the free memory locations. ' Line 20 reads the data items and uses the POKE command to place them into the memory locations. The data items in line 30 represent the machine commands to instantly display the screen in inverse. Once the routine is entered into memory it can then be called in line 40.

```
5    REM  === INSTANT INVERSE TEXT SCREEN ===
10 L = 768
20   FOR X = 0 TO 22: READ V: POKE L + X,V: NEXT
30   DATA 160,0,132,6,169,4,133,7,162,4,169,32,145,6,200,
208,251,230,7,202,208,246,96
40   CALL L
50   VTAB 12: HTAB 18: PRINT "INVERSE"
60   VTAB 23
99   END
```

WINDOW ADJUSTMENT AND APPLICATIONS

WINDOW SIZE

Table 3-2 provides the ranges of the four POKE commands that adjust the size of the text window. You can obtain special effects such as freezing a heading or simulating a television screen or you can highlight messages with these POKE commands.

EXPLANATION

Table 3-2 indicates the memory locations, explains which dimension on the screen is affected, and lists the range of values that can be poked into each location along with the default values.

Poking these locations with the default values returns the screen to the standard dimensions. The command TEXT and the RESET key also return the screen to standard format.

Use the command TEXT:HOME to first obtain a standard blank screen. Then issue the desired POKE commands and again issue the HOME command to start the cursor in the new home position.

TABLE 3-2. TEXT SCREEN POKE COMMANDS

Command	Explanation	Range	Default
POKE 32,L	Left edge of window	0–39	POKE 32,0
POKE 33,W	Window width	1–40	POKE 33,40
POKE 34,T	Top edge of window	0–23	POKE 34,0
POKE 35,B	Bottom edge of window	1–24	POKE 35,24

USING POKE 33,33 TO EDIT A LINE

The command POKE 33,33 can be used to edit a line containing a string in quotes, a DATA statement, or a REM statement without getting the extra spaces.

EXPLANATION

To avoid the unwanted extra spaces when editing a program line that contains quotes, a REM statement, or a DATA statement, first type POKE 33,33. This command reduces the screen to 33 characters across instead of 40.

Then use the ESC key along with I, J, K, M, or the four arrow keys on the Apple IIe/IIc and move up to the line to be edited and make the changes. Refer to "Editing Program Statements" in Chapter 1 for an explanation of the editing commands if necessary.

When you are through editing, type either POKE 33,40 or TEXT to bring the screen size back to 40 characters across. The RESET key will also return the screen to standard dimensions.

FREEZE INVERSE HEADING

This program highlights a message in a border and freezes the heading. The rest of the screen scrolls up under the message.

EXPLANATION ═══

Line 10 sets the screen to standard values. Line 120 pokes in the value to change the top margin of the screen. The command HOME in line 120 sets the cursor to the new home position. A message is scrolled under the title 100 times for demonstration purposes.

The percent (%) symbol in lines 30, 40, and 50 can be replaced by any symbol other than quotation marks.

The POKE 32,0 command, the TEXT command, or the RESET key will return the screen to normal format.

```
5    REM  === FREEZE INVERSE HEADING ===
10   TEXT : HOME
20   INVERSE
25   REM  -- 40 SYMBOLS --
30   S1$ = "%%%%%%%%%%%%%%%%%%%%%%%%%%%%%%%%%%%%%%%%"
40   S2$ = "%                                      %"
50   S3$ = "%"
60   PRINT S1$;S2$;
70   PRINT S3$; TAB( 13)"PROGRAMS UNLIMITED"; TAB( 40)S3$
  ;
80   PRINT S2$;
90   PRINT S3$; TAB( 8)"BY THE GREATEST PROGRAMMER"; TAB(
  40)S3$;
100  PRINT S2$;S1$
110  NORMAL
120  POKE 34,8: HOME
130  FOR X = 1 TO 100: PRINT  TAB( 19)X: NEXT X
199  END
```

BORDER SUBROUTINE

This subroutine draws a border on the screen.

EXPLANATION

The subroutine starting at line 1000 draws a border around the screen. If you want to write within the border, then you must use HTAB and VTAB commands. The command PRINT TAB( ) will erase the left border.

```
5    REM  === BORDER SUBROUTINE ===
10   HOME
20 S$ = "%": GOSUB 1000"BORDER SUBROUTINE"
30   VTAB 12: HTAB 16
40   PRINT "THE END"
50   VTAB 23: HTAB 1
999  END
1000  FOR X = 1 TO 40: PRINT S$;: NEXT X
1010  FOR X = 1 TO 21
1020  HTAB 1: PRINT S$;: HTAB 40: PRINT S$;
1030  NEXT X
1040  FOR X = 1 TO 40: PRINT S$;: NEXT X
1050  RETURN
```

SAMPLE OUTPUT

```
%%%%%%%%%%%%%%%%%%%%%%%%%%%%%%%%%%%%%%%%
%                                      %
%                                      %
%                                      %
%                                      %
%                                      %
%                                      %
%                                      %
%                                      %
%                                      %
%                                      %
%                                      %
%                                      %
%                THE END               %
%                                      %
%                                      %
%                                      %
%                                      %
%                                      %
%                                      %
%                                      %
%                                      %
%                                      %
%%%%%%%%%%%%%%%%%%%%%%%%%%%%%%%%%%%%%%%%
```

FROZEN BORDER SUBROUTINE

The previous Border subroutine is modified to freeze the border in place while the rest of the text scrolls up the screen.

EXPLANATION

Line 1050 contains the four POKE commands to freeze the border. Line 1060 resets the new home position.

Either the HTAB or PRINT TAB( ) commands can be used with this program.

```
5    REM   === FROZEN BORDER SUBROUTINE ===
10   TEXT : HOME
20   S$ = "%": GOSUB 1000"BORDER SUBROUTINE"
30   VTAB 12: HTAB 16
40   PRINT "THE END"
50   VTAB 20: HTAB 1
999  END
1000  FOR X = 1 TO 40: PRINT S$;: NEXT X
1010  FOR X = 1 TO 21
1020  HTAB 1: PRINT S$;: HTAB 40: PRINT S$;
1030  NEXT X
1040  FOR X = 1 TO 40: PRINT S$;: NEXT X
1045  REM  -- ADJUST WINDOW SIZE --
1050  POKE 32,2: POKE 33,36: POKE 34,2: POKE 35,21
1060  HOME
1070  RETURN
```

CLEARING TEXT SCREEN FROM LEFT MIDDLE

This program clears the text screen from the left middle by using the window POKE commands. This provides an interesting way of clearing the screen.

EXPLANATION

The subroutine starting at line 1000 uses the window commands to clear the screen starting at row 12, clearing up and down simultaneously.

```
5    REM   === CLEAR TEXT LEFT MIDDLE ===
10   TEXT : HOME
20   FOR X = 1 TO 23
30   PRINT X;" CLEAR TEXT FROM LEFT MIDDLE"
40   NEXT X
50   GET A$
60   GOSUB 1000
99   END
995  REM  --- CLEAR TEXT ---
1000  FOR X = 1 TO 12
1010  POKE 34,12 - X
1020  POKE 35,12 + X
1030  POKE 33,3 * X + 4
1040  HOME
1050  FOR T = 1 TO 10: NEXT T
1060  NEXT X
1070  RETURN
```

GR COMMANDS WITHOUT GR COMMAND

The graphics commands VLIN, HLIN, and PLOT can be used in a text program without the commands GR and COLOR=. You will not get the color but you will get a variety of standard, flashing, and inverse characters on the text screen.

When the screen is in the GRaphic mode of low resolution graphics and you issue the TEXT command, the screen prints characters in standard, flashing, and/or inverse mode. The computer is trying to interpret the graphics commands as text. The following programs will use this idea to draw borders easily and erase the screen in yet another way.

POKE HLIN/VLIN DEMONSTRATION

This program demonstrates the results of using HLIN and VLIN commands without the commands GR and COLOR=. It draws a vertical line and two horizontal lines using the 255 possible values as characters.

EXPLANATION

This program pokes a value into memory location 48 to determine which character will be used in the horizontal and vertical lines. The values 0–255 are poked in one at a time. Memory location 48 holds the value of the low resolution graphics color times 17.

Two horizontal lines must be drawn, since two HLINs of graphics equal one line of text. The graphics screen is 40 dots across and the text screen is 40 characters across. However, the graphics screen is 48 characters down, if you use full screen low resolution graphics, while the text screen holds 24 rows of symbols or characters. Thus, it takes two rows of the graphics screen to equal one row of text screen.

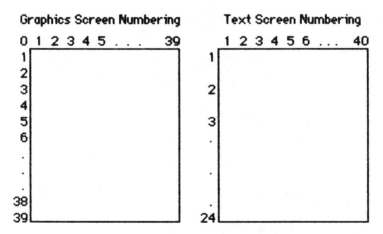

You can display characters on the 24th row with the VLIN and HLIN commands but not with the PRINT command, since the PRINT command issues a line feed instruction. If you tab to the 24th row and print a message, the computer prints on the 24th row, issues a line feed command to move everything on the text screen up one row, and displays the cursor on the 24th row.

```
5    REM   === POKE HLIN/VLIN DEMO ===
10   HOME
20   FOR X = 0 TO 255
30   POKE 48,X
40   VTAB 8: HTAB 20
50   PRINT "X= ";X
60   HLIN 0,39 AT 20: HLIN 0,39 AT 21
70   VLIN 0,39 AT 30
80   GET A$
90   NEXT X
99   END
```

SAMPLE OUTPUT ══

```
                                          $
                                          $
                                          $
                                          $
                                          $
                                          $
                                          $
                    X= 164                $
                                          $
                                          $
 $$$$$$$$$$$$$$$$$$$$$$$$$$$$$$$$$$$$$$$$$$$$$$$$$
                                          $
                                          $
                                          $
                                          $
                                          $
                                          $
                                          $
                                          $
                                          $


                                          +
                                          +
                                          +
                                          +
                                          +
                                          +
                                          +
                    X= 171                +
                                          +
                                          +
 ++++++++++++++++++++++++++++++++++++++++++++++
                                          +
                                          +
                                          +
                                          +
                                          +
                                          +
                                          +
                                          +
                                          +
```

Table 3-3 helps to determine which value to poke into location 48 for a particular character.

TABLE 3-3. SCREEN CHARACTER POKE VALUES

Text Character	Inverse	Flashing	Normal	Text Character	Inverse	Flashing	Normal
@	0	64	128	space	32	96	160
A	1	65	129	!	33	97	161
B	2	66	130	"	34	98	162
C	3	67	131	#	35	99	163
D	4	68	132	$	36	100	164
E	5	69	133	%	37	101	165
F	6	70	134	&	38	102	166
G	7	71	135	'	39	103	167
H	8	72	136	(	40	104	168
I	9	73	137	)	41	105	169
J	10	74	138	*	42	106	170
K	11	75	139	+	43	107	171
L	12	76	140	,	44	108	172
M	13	77	141	—	45	109	173
N	14	78	142	.	46	110	174
O	15	79	143	/	47	111	175
P	16	80	144	0	48	112	176
Q	17	81	145	1	49	113	177
R	18	82	146	2	50	114	178
S	19	83	147	3	51	115	179
T	20	84	148	4	52	116	180
U	21	85	149	5	53	117	181
V	22	86	150	6	54	118	182
W	23	87	151	7	55	119	183
X	24	88	152	8	56	120	184
Y	25	89	153	9	57	121	185
Z	26	90	154	:	58	122	186
[	27	91	155	;	59	123	187
\	28	92	156	<	60	124	188
]	29	93	157	=	61	125	189
^	30	94	158	>	62	126	190
—	31	95	159	?	63	127	191

This program draws a border around the text screen using some of the graphics commands.

EXPLANATION

The graphics commands HLIN and VLIN without the GR and COLOR= commands draw two vertical and two horizontal lines to obtain a border. Lines 30 and 50 draw a set of adjacent horizontal lines in graphics to get one text line.

```
5   REM  === TEXT BORDER WITH GR COMMANDS ===
10  TEXT : HOME
20 K = 36: POKE 48,K
30  HLIN 0,39 AT 0: HLIN 0,39 AT 1
40  VLIN 0,47 AT 0: VLIN 0,47 AT 39
50  HLIN 0,39 AT 46: HLIN 0,39 AT 47
60  POKE 32,2: POKE 33,34: POKE 34,2: POKE 35,22
70  HOME
80  VTAB 12: HTAB 16
90  PRINT "THE END"
99  END
```

SAMPLE OUTPUT

ERASING THE SCREEN WITH GRAPHICS COMMANDS

FROM UPPER LEFT CORNER

This program uses the HLIN and VLIN commands to fill and then to clear the text screen starting at the upper left corner. The clearing routine can be used whenever you have a screen full of text and want to clear the screen in a novel way.

EXPLANATION

Lines 30-50 use HLIN and VLIN commands to quickly fill the screen with a character. Refer to Table 3-3 for the values and their corresponding characters. Line 20 pokes in the character M in inverse. The routine at lines 70-110 clears the screen by drawing horizontal and vertical lines composed of the space character. The lines start at the upper left corner.

```
5    REM   === CLEAR SCREEN UPPER-LEFT ===
7    REM   -- FILL SCREEN --
10   HOME
20   POKE 48,13
30   FOR X = 0 TO 39
40   VLIN 0,47 AT X: HLIN 0,39 AT X
50   NEXT X
60   GET A$
65   REM   -- CLEAR SCREEN --
70   POKE 48,160
80   FOR X = 0 TO 39
90   VLIN 0,47 AT X: HLIN 0,39 AT X
100   FOR Z = 1 TO 25: NEXT Z
110   NEXT X
199   END
```

FROM LOWER RIGHT CORNER

This program uses the HLIN and VLIN commands to fill and then to clear the text screen starting at the lower right corner. The clearing routine is a variation of the previous program.

EXPLANATION

This program also uses HLIN and VLIN commands to quickly fill the screen with the character M in inverse at lines 20-50. The clearing routine at lines 70-110 start drawing the vertical and horizontal lines in the lower right corner.

```
5    REM   === CLEAR SCREEN LOWER-RIGHT ===
7    REM   -- FILL SCREEN --
10   HOME
20   POKE 48,13
30   FOR X = 0 TO 39
40   VLIN 0,47 AT X: HLIN 0,39 AT X
50   NEXT X
60   GET A$
65   REM   -- CLEAR SCREEN --
70   POKE 48,160
80   FOR X = 47 TO 0 STEP  - 1
90   VLIN 0,47 AT X * 39 / 47: HLIN 0,39 AT X
100   FOR Z = 1 TO 25: NEXT Z
110   NEXT X
199   END
```

WARP ERASE

This program uses the HLIN and VLIN commands to fill the screen and then to erase the screen with a warp effect. The clear routine can be used whenever you have a screen full of text to be erased and want a different effect.

EXPLANATION

Subroutine 100 fills the screen with a random character. The routine from 50 to 70 clears the screen by drawing rectangles of decreasing size. Line 40 selects the normal space as the character to erase the screen.

Line 60 adjusts for the rectangular screen by drawing 48 horizontal lines and 40 vertical lines.

```
5    REM   === WARP ERASE TEXT SCREEN ===
10   HOME
20   GOSUB 100"FILL SCREEN"
30   GET A$
35   REM   --- ERASE SCREEN ---
40   POKE 48,160
50   FOR X = 0 TO 21
60   HLIN 0,39 AT X: HLIN 0,39 AT 47 - X: VLIN 0,47 AT X:
 VLIN 0,47 AT (39 - X * 39 / 47)
70   NEXT X
99   END
100   POKE 48, INT ( RND (1) * 256): FOR X = 0 TO 47: HLI
N 0,39 AT X: NEXT X: RETURN
```

SCROLLING THE TEXT SCREEN

The standard way of clearing the screen for the next display is to instantly erase it with the HOME or CALL −936 commands. This chapter has introduced several other techniques to erase the screen. It is also possible to have the old display scroll up slowly for another effect.

ERASING THE SCREEN STARTING AT BOTTOM LINE

This program erases one text line at a time starting at the bottom of the screen.

EXPLANATION ═══

The command CALL −868 clears the text line starting at the cursor. CALL −998 moves the cursor up the screen one line.

```
5    REM  === ERASE TEXT SCREEN FROM BOTTOM ===
10   HOME
15   REM  -- FILL SCREEN --
20   FOR X = 1 TO 20
30   PRINT X;" THIS IS AN EXAMPLE OF  SCROLLING"
40   NEXT X
50   GET A$
55   REM  -- ERASE SCREEN --
60   FOR X = 1 TO 24
70   CALL  - 868: CALL  - 998
80   NEXT X
90   VTAB 1: PRINT "PAGE 2"
99   END
```

MODIFICATION ═══

A delay loop can be added to adjust the scrolling effect:

```
75 FOR Z = 1 TO 50:NEXT Z
```

SCROLLING UP THE SCREEN

This program scrolls the text up the screen and can be used as an end-of-text-page routine.

EXPLANATION

The program fills the screen on lines 20–40 and waits for the user to enter a keypress. The routine at lines 60–80 uses the command CALL −912 to scroll up the screen. The command CALL −912 moves the cursor down the screen one line.

```
5   REM  === SCROLL TEXT SCREEN ===
10   HOME
15   REM  -- FILL SCREEN --
20   FOR X = 1 TO 20
30   PRINT X;" THIS IS AN EXAMPLE OF SCROLLING"
40   NEXT X
50   GET A$
55   REM  -- ERASE SCREEN --
60   FOR X = 1 TO 24
70   CALL  - 912
80   NEXT X
90   VTAB 1: PRINT "PAGE 2"
99   END
```

MODIFICATIONS

1. Line 70 can be replaced by one of the following statements. CALL −922 moves the cursor down the screen one line.

   ```
   70 CALL -922
   ```

   or

   ```
   70 PRINT
   ```

2. The text can be scrolled up the screen at the desired speed by using a delay loop within the scrolling loop to scroll slowly.

   ```
   75 FOR Z = 1 TO 50:NEXT Z
   ```

The SPEED command can be used to slow down the scrolling by adding the following lines rather than the delay loop:

```
55 SPEED = 100
70 PRINT
85 SPEED = 255
```

The SPEED command works in conjunction with a PRINT command and therefore cannot be used with either CALL −912 or CALL −922, i.e., line 70 must be a PRINT command.

Special effects can be obtained by using the tab commands, string functions such as MID$, the ASCII code to obtain special characters or keys, or by strobing the keyboard.

This chapter introduces several ways to repeat the characters of a word in an interesting fashion. Pyramids, diamonds, and mirror image designs are printed.

The characters obtained by using their ASCII code provide access to keys such as the ESC key, space bar, arrow keys, and the DELETE and TAB keys on the Apple IIe/IIc.

There are times when you want the computer to execute a routine and continually check for an input from the user. The keyboard strobe provides this service without printing the cursor to the screen. You can wait for a certain amount of time for a reply from the user or you can wait indefinitely for a reply.

The tab commands and string functions can be used to animate the screen by sliding words and characters across. A message can be printed repeatedly across the screen to simulate a billboard effect.

String Manipulations for Output

Reverse Message

This program reverses the order of any word, number, or message that is entered.

EXPLANATION

Line 20 sets the string R$ to the null or empty string. The loop at lines 50-70 steps through the characters of the inputted string A$ one character at a time starting at the last character. Each character is then concatenated (added) to R$, which will hold the reverse string.

```
5   REM  === REVERSE MESSAGE ===
10  HOME
20 R$ = "": REM  NULL STRING
30  INPUT "ENTER A WORD OR NUMBER ";A$
40  PRINT
50  FOR X =  LEN (A$) TO 1 STEP  - 1
60 R$ = R$ +  MID$ (A$,X,1)
70  NEXT X
80  PRINT A$,R$
99  END
```

SAMPLE RUN

```
]RUN
ENTER A WORD OR NUMBER REVERSE

REVERSE          ESREVER

]RUN
ENTER A WORD OR NUMBER ROBOT

ROBOT            TOBOR
```

Pyramid

This program prints a word in a pyramid shape that is formed by two triangles of characters. The design is symmetric both vertically and horizontally. The length of the message is limited to 19 characters or less.

EXPLANATION

The string functions can be used to produce interesting designs with the characters of a string or digits of a number. Two loops are needed: the outer loop steps through each character of A$ one at a time, and the inner loop determines how many times the particular character will be printed. The routine at 130-200 is similar to the routine at 50-120 except that it steps through the characters of A$ in reverse order.

```
5    REM  === PYRAMID ===
10   HOME
20   INPUT "ENTER A WORD ";A$
30   IF  LEN (A$) > 19 THEN 20
40   HOME
43   REM  --- PRINT ROUTINE ---
45   REM  --- TOP TRIANGLE ---
50   FOR X = 1 TO  LEN (A$)
60   FOR Y = 1 TO X
70 T = 20 - X
80 M$ =  MID$ (A$,X,1)
90   PRINT  TAB( T)M$;" ";
100   NEXT Y
110   PRINT
120   NEXT X
125   REM  --- BOTTOM TRIANGLE ---
130   FOR X =  LEN (A$) TO 1 STEP  - 1
140   FOR Y = 1 TO X
150 T = 20 - X
160 M$ =  MID$ (A$,X,1)
170   PRINT  TAB( T)M$;" ";
180   NEXT Y
190   PRINT
200   NEXT X
299   END
```

SAMPLE OUTPUT ══

ENTER A WORD REFLECTION

```
                R
               E E
              F F F
             L L L L
            E E E E E
           C C C C C C
          T T T T T T T
         I I I I I I I I
        O O O O O O O O O
       N N N N N N N N N N
       N N N N N N N N N N
        O O O O O O O O O
         I I I I I I I I
          T T T T T T T
           C C C C C C
            E E E E E
             L L L L
              F F F
               E E
                R
```

MIRROR IMAGE DIAMOND

DESIGN 1

This program prints a mirror image diamond. The design is symmetric both vertically and horizontally. This program prints a space after each character. A maximum of 10 characters is permitted.

EXPLANATION ═══

Line 80 takes the word or message M$ apart and stores each character as an array element. Line 90 prints the first character in the center of the screen. Lines 100-180 use three loops to print out the characters. The outer loop steps through the remaining characters one at a time. The first inner loop at lines 110-130 prints the left side of the design and the second inner loop at lines 140-160 prints the right side of the design. The routine at lines 190-290 is similar to the routine at lines 70-180, but it steps through the characters in reverse order.

```
5   REM   === DIAMOND DESIGN 1 ===
10    DIM A$(20)
20    HOME
30    INPUT "ENTER A WORD ";M$
40    IF  LEN (M$) > 10 THEN 30
50    HOME
60 T = 20
70    REM   --- TOP ---
80    FOR X = 1 TO  LEN (M$):A$(X) =  MID$ (M$,X,1): NEXT
X
90    PRINT  TAB( T);A$(1)
100   FOR X = 2 TO  LEN (M$)
110   FOR Y = 1 TO X
120   PRINT  TAB( T - (2 * (X - 1)));A$(Y);" ";
130   NEXT Y
140   FOR Z = (X - 1) TO 1 STEP  - 1
150   PRINT A$(Z);" ";
160   NEXT Z
170   PRINT
180   NEXT X
190   REM   --- BOTTOM ---
200   FOR X =  LEN (M$) TO 2 STEP  - 1
210   FOR Y = 1 TO X
220   PRINT  TAB( T - (2 * (X - 1)));A$(Y);" ";
230   NEXT Y
240   FOR Z = (X - 1) TO 1 STEP  - 1
250   PRINT A$(Z);" ";
260   NEXT Z
270   PRINT
280   NEXT X
290   PRINT  TAB( 20);A$(1)
299   END
```

ENTER A WORD COMPUTER

```
                      C
                    C O C
                  C O M O C
                C O M P M O C
              C O M P U P M O C
            C O M P U T U P M O C
          C O M P U T E T U P M O C
        C O M P U T E R E T U P M O C
        C O M P U T E R E T U P M O C
          C O M P U T E T U P M O C
            C O M P U T U P M O C
              C O M P U P M O C
                C O M P M O C
                  C O M O C
                    C O C
                      C
```

DESIGN 2

This program is similar to Design 1. However, it omits the space after each character and allows a message of 20 characters to be printed to the screen.

EXPLANATION

See the explanation for Design 1. The spaces on lines 120, 150, 220, and 250 have been omitted.

```
5    REM     === DIAMOND DESIGN 2 ===
10   DIM A$(20)
20   HOME
30   INPUT "ENTER A WORD ";M$
40   IF   LEN (M$) > 20 THEN 30
50   HOME
60 T = 20
70   REM   --- TOP ---
80   FOR X = 1 TO   LEN (M$):A$(X) =   MID$ (M$,X,1): NEXT
X
90   PRINT  TAB( T);A$(1)
100  FOR X = 2 TO   LEN (M$)
110  FOR Y = 1 TO X
120  PRINT  TAB( T - (X - 1));A$(Y);
130  NEXT Y
140  FOR Z = (X - 1) TO 1 STEP  - 1
150  PRINT A$(Z);
160  NEXT Z
170  PRINT
180  NEXT X
190  REM   --- BOTTOM ---
200  FOR X =  LEN (M$) TO 2 STEP  - 1
210  FOR Y = 1 TO X
220  PRINT  TAB( T - (X - 1));A$(Y);
230  NEXT Y
240  FOR Z = (X - 1) TO 1 STEP  - 1
250  PRINT A$(Z);
260  NEXT Z
270  PRINT
280  NEXT X
290  PRINT  TAB( 20);A$(1)
299  END
```

ENTER A WORD COMPUTER

```
                C
               COC
              COMOC
             COMPMOC
            COMPUPMOC
           COMPUTUPMOC
          COMPUTETUPMOC
         COMPUTERETUPMOC
         COMPUTERETUPMOC
          COMPUTETUPMOC
           COMPUTUPMOC
            COMPUPMOC
             COMPMOC
              COMOC
               COC
                C
```

This program draws a mirror image of an inputted name. But the characters are outside the diamond and the diamond is hollow. The name is limited to 20 characters.

EXPLANATION

Lines 50–70 form a new string R$, which holds the reverse name. The routine at lines 100–160 prints the right side of the name N$ and the left part of the reverse name R$. The routine at lines 170–220 is similar to lines 100–160 but prints the reverse.

```
5    REM    === MIRROR IMAGE ===
10   HOME
20   INPUT "ENTER YOUR NAME: ";N$
30   IF  LEN (N$) > 20 THEN  PRINT "PLEASE LIMIT YOUR NAM
E TO 20 LETTERS OR LESS": GOTO 20
40   HOME
45   REM   --- FORM REVERSE STRING ---
50   FOR X =  LEN (N$) TO 1 STEP  - 1
60 RN$ = RN$ +  MID$ (N$,X,1)
70   NEXT X
80 L =  LEN (N$)
90 H = 20 - L
95   REM   --- TOP ---
100   FOR N = L TO 1 STEP  - 1
110   HTAB H
120   PRINT  RIGHT$ (N$,N);
130   HTAB 20 + L - N
140   PRINT  LEFT$ (RN$,N)
150   HTAB H
160   NEXT N
165   REM   --- BOTTOM ---
170   FOR N = 1 TO L
180   HTAB H
190   PRINT  RIGHT$ (N$,N);
200   HTAB 20 + L - N
210   PRINT  LEFT$ (RN$,N)
220   NEXT N
299   END
```

ENTER YOUR NAME: SULLIVAN

```
SULLIVANNAVILLUS
ULLIVAN  NAVILLU
LLIVAN    NAVILL
LIVAN      NAVIL
IVAN        NAVI
VAN          NAV
AN            NA
N              N
N              N
AN            NA
VAN          NAV
IVAN        NAVI
LIVAN      NAVIL
LLIVAN    NAVILL
ULLIVAN  NAVILLU
SULLIVANNAVILLUS
```

or

ENTER YOUR NAME: APPLE II

```
APPLE IIII ELPPA
PPLE II  II ELPP
PLE II    II ELP
LE II      II EL
E II        II E
 II          II
II            II
I              I
I              I
II            II
 II          II
E II        II E
LE II      II EL
PLE II    II ELP
PPLE II  II ELPP
APPLE IIII ELPPA
```

CONTROL J USES

The following ideas show you how to print a message on the diagonal and how to add spaces to a REM statement.

EXPLANATION

CONTROL J is a line feed command with no carriage return. It is represented by the ASCII code 10. If you define a string or number and enter CONTROL J after each character, the result will be a word or number on the diagonal.

CONTROL J can be used in the assignment statement, DATA statements, or REM statements.

Enter the first character and press CONTROL J to move down a line without adding the carriage return (cr). Continue entering each character desired followed by CONTROL J until the message is complete.

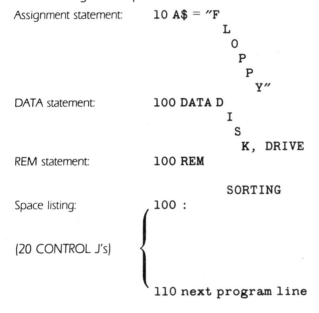

Assignment statement: 10 A$ = "F
                                       L
                                        O
                                         P
                                          P
                                           Y"

DATA statement: 100 DATA D
                                     I
                                      S
                                       K, DRIVE

REM statement: 100 REM

                                   SORTING

Space listing: 100 :

(20 CONTROL J's) {

                           110 next program line

z

ASCII CODE APPLICATIONS

Each character on the keyboard, along with the CONTROL commands, has a unique code number associated with it. This code is called the ASCII code (American Standard Code for Information Interchange).

These codes enable you to access such keys as ESC, space bar, RETURN, left, right, up, and down arrows, and the DELETE and TAB keys on the Apple IIe. The codes are useful for accessing the printer or disk from a BASIC program.

You can access the ASCII code of the character or keypress with the ASC(string variable) command. Conversely, each ASCII code from 0 to 255 has a character associated with it. You can access the character with the CHR$(ASCII code) command.

The INPUT command will not access all the keys, so use the GET command with ASCII or CHR$ commands.

To check on the ASCII code of any inputted character, use the following command.

General: **PRINT ASC(string variable)**
Specific ex.: **PRINT ASC("Z")**
           PRINT ASC(A$)

To check on the CHR$ of any number from 0 to 255, use the following command.

General: **PRINT CHR$(ASCII code)**
Specific ex.: **PRINT CHR$(91)**

See Appendix A for the ASCII code chart.

COMMONLY USED ASCII CODES

Some commonly used characters are given in Table 4-1.

TABLE 4-1. COMMONLY USED ASCII CODES

ASCII Code	Character
7	Bell
8	Left arrow
9*	TAB key
10*	Down arrow
11*	Up arrow
13	RETURN key
21	Right arrow
27	ESC key
32	Space bar
34	Quote
91	Left bracket
93	Right bracket
95	Underline
127*	DELETE key

*Available on Apple IIe/IIc only.

This statement allows you to display APPLE][on any Apple computer.

EXPLANATION

The characters associated with ASCII codes 93 and 91 are the right and left brackets, respectively. These characters can be concatenated to the string APPLE to print APPLE][wherever you desire.

```
10 A$ = "APPLE" + CHR$(93) + CHR$(91)
20 PRINT A$
```

MODIFICATION

You can call a subroutine in machine code to print the APPLE][message centered on the top of the screen by using CALL −1184 or CALL 64352.

QUOTES IN OUTPUT

The next two statements will let you print quotes to the screen.

EXPLANATION

Normally, you cannot use quotes within quotes to print a quoted message. However, you can use the CHR$ command to insert the quotes where needed. You can either use CHR$(34) or you can assign a string such as Q$ to be equal to CHR$(34) and use Q$ whenever needed.

```
10 Q$ = CHR$(34)
20 PRINT "HE SAID ";Q$;"NO COMMENT";Q$;" WHEN QUESTIONED."
RUN
HE SAID "NO COMMENT" WHEN QUESTIONED.
```

BACKING UP AND ERASING A CHARACTER

This program erases the characters when the user backs up while making an entry.

EXPLANATION

This program uses the CONTROL H with an ASCII code of 8 to allow the user to backspace while making an entry and have the computer erase as it backs up. PEEK(36) returns the current horizontal position of the cursor in the range 0–39. Since the GET command needs no carriage return, you remain on the same line, unless you are at the right edge of the screen. The carriage return is detected on line 60 as a signal that the message is complete and sends the computer to line 150.

Line 70 checks for the left arrow keypress. If the left arrow has not been pressed, the computer (line 110) concatenates the new character to M$, which represents the message being entered, and prints the character entered. If the left arrow has been pressed, the computer backs up one space, erases the most recent character of M$, and is then sent to line 50 to accept the next character. Line 90 checks for an empty entry and sends the computer to line 50.

```
5   REM   === ERASE CHARACTER ===
10   HOME
20  M$ = "": REM  NULL STRING
30   PRINT "ENTER YOUR MESSAGE ";
40  H =  PEEK (36)
50   GET A$
55  REM  --- CHECK FOR CARRIAGE RETURN ---
60   IF A$ =  CHR$ (13) THEN 150
65  REM  --- CHECK FOR BACKSPACE ---
70   IF A$ <  >  CHR$ (8) THEN 110
80   IF  PEEK (36) = H THEN  GOTO 50
85  REM  ---  BACKSPACE ---
90   PRINT  CHR$ (8) CHR$ (32) CHR$ (8);: IF  LEN (M$) =
1 THEN M$ = "": GOTO 50
100 M$ =  LEFT$ (M$, LEN (M$) - 1): GOTO 50
110 M$ = M$ + A$
120  PRINT A$;
130  GOTO 50
140  PRINT
150  PRINT : PRINT "YOUR WORD IS ";M$
199  END
```

STROBING THE KEYBOARD

The INPUT and GET commands stop the program while waiting for the response. Sometimes you want a routine to continue while waiting for the user to press a key. This can be accomplished by strobing the keyboard for a keypress while continuing the program. The strobe, like the GET command, only accepts one character and does not display that character on the screen. You can determine which key was pressed and act accordingly.

The keyboard strobe loads a character from the keyboard into memory location −16384 (or its equivalent 49152). That character stays there until the keyboard strobe is reset. You can tell whether or not a key has been pressed by printing PEEK (−16384). If the value of that location is greater than 127, then a key was pressed. If you subtract 128 from the value found, you will get the ASCII code for the key pressed.

The address −16384 or 49152 always contains the ASCII code of the last key pressed plus 128, unless the keyboard strobe is cleared. Clear the keyboard strobe at the beginning of the program. After a key has been pressed, clear the keyboard strobe again so it will be ready for the next strobing.

There are two ways to clear the keyboard strobe. You can either poke a 0 into the strobe address such as, POKE −16384,0 or its equivalent, POKE 49152,0. Or you can poke another address, which has the net result of clearing address −16384 by issuing the command POKE −16368,0 or its equivalent, POKE 49168,0.

The strobe command does not show a blinking cursor while waiting for the response as does GET A$. Once a key has been pressed, you can use GET A$ to capture the keypress and check the value of the string variable. Another method is to use K=PEEK(−16384) and then check the value of K − 128 for the ASCII value of the key pressed. Use the VAL and STR$ commands if needed to convert a string to a numeric or a numeric to a string. Any valid string or numeric variable name could be used in place of A$ or K.

STROBE DEMO

This program demonstrates how strobing the keyboard works. It prints PAGE 1 on the screen and waits either for a keypress (any keypress) or for the completion of a timing loop of 500 before it continues with printing PAGE 2 on the screen. It continues this for five pages.

EXPLANATION

Line 10 clears the keyboard strobe. The routine at lines 30–70 prints PAGE P on the screen, where P ranges from 1 to 5. The subroutine at lines 100–140 uses a delay loop that also strobes the keyboard for a keypress. If no key is pressed, it continues the timing loop from 1 to 500 and checks 500 times for a keypress. This is the reason that a timing loop of 500 takes so long. If a key is pressed, then line 110 recognizes the presence of the keypress and sets the ending value for the timing loop, so the subroutine will terminate and return to the main program at line 60.

```
5    REM   === STROBE DEMO ===
10   POKE   - 16368,0: REM   CLEAR STROBE
20   HOME
30   FOR P = 1 TO 5
40   PRINT "PAGE "P
50   GOSUB 100"DELAY LOOP WITH STROBE"
60   HOME
70   NEXT P
99   END
100  FOR T = 1 TO 500
105  REM   --- STROBE KEYBOARD ---
110  IF   PEEK ( - 16384) > 127 THEN T = 500
120  NEXT T
130  POKE   - 16368,0
140  RETURN
```

DICE ROLLER

This program simulates an automatic dice roller. It prints numbers 1–6 on the screen in random order and stops rolling the dice when any key is pressed.

EXPLANATION

This program selects a random number from 1 to N and prints the number on the screen in line 80. In this program, N equals 6, but the dice do not have to be limited to a six-sided die. You can select other values for N. The program selects and prints random numbers at column 19, row 12, until the user presses any key, and then it displays the last number selected.

If no key is pressed, the computer blanks out the random number printed by printing S$ at row 19, column 12. S$ holds X blank spaces, where X is the number of digits in N. S$ is necessary when the value of N is greater than 9. Change the value of N to a number greater than 9 and omit line 100 to see why it is needed.

```
5   REM   === DICE ROLLER ===
10 N = 6: REM   NUMBER OF SIDES OF DIE
20   FOR X = 1 TO  LEN ( STR$ (N)):S$ = S$ +  CHR$ (32):
NEXT X
30   POKE  - 16368,0: REM   CLEAR STROBE
40   HOME
50 X =  INT ( RND (1) * N) + 1
60   FOR D = 1 TO 5: NEXT D
70   VTAB 12: HTAB 19
80   PRINT X
85   REM   --- STROBE KEYBOARD ---
90   IF   PEEK (49152) > 127 THEN 120
100   VTAB 12: HTAB 19: PRINT S$
110   GOTO 50
120   GET A$
130   VTAB 20: PRINT "YOU HAVE ROLLED A ";X
199   END
```

RANDOMIZED RANDOM NUMBERS

This routine starts the series of random numbers at a quasi-random starting position. This is useful when you are dealing cards in a card game or generating the numbers for a math or logic game and want a different set of numbers each time you initially run the program or play the game.

EXPLANATION

When your computer generates a series of random numbers, the set of numbers is not truly random. You will get different numbers for each run of the program but the same sequence of numbers initially when you turn on the computer and run the program.

To randomize your number sequence, have the computer generate a series of numbers that will be discarded. This subroutine uses a strobe to continually generate random numbers, until you press a key to begin the program.

Try running the program without the subroutine. Run the program, record the numbers, turn off the computer, and run the program again. When you compare the series of numbers, they should be the same. Add the subroutine and it is very unlikely that you will obtain the same sequence of numbers twice in a row.

```
5   REM   === RANDOMIZED RANDOM NUMBERS ===
10   POKE  - 16368,0
20 N = 13: REM   HIGHEST RANDOM NUMBER
30   GOSUB 1000"RANDOMIZE NUMBERS"
40   HOME : PRINT "RANDOM NUMBERS": PRINT
50   FOR X = 1 TO 10
60 R =  INT ( RND (1) * N) + 1
70   PRINT R
80   NEXT X
899   END
995   REM   --- RANDOMIZER ---
1000   HOME
1010   PRINT "PRESS ANY KEY TO BEGIN ";
1020   IF   PEEK ( - 16384) < 128 THEN R =  INT ( RND (1)
* N) + 1: GOTO 1020
1030   GET K$: RETURN
```

PRESS ANY KEY

To impress on the user that any key can be pressed, you could put the word ANY in INVERSE or FLASH mode. There is another alternative. This program prints the word ANY and then blacks it out and continues this process until the user presses any key.

EXPLANATION

Line 60 prints the message with a blank space where the word ANY should be. It strobes the keyboard for a keypress. If a key has been pressed, it branches to line 120. If no keypress is made, it prints the message with the word ANY filled in and again waits for a keypress. If a key is pressed, it executes line 120. If, however, no key is pressed, it loops back to line 50 to start the process again.

```
5    REM   === PRESS ANY KEY ===
10  T = 25
20   POKE  - 16368,0
30   HOME
40  T = 25
50   VTAB 23: HTAB 8
60   PRINT "PRESS      KEY TO CONTINUE"
65   REM   --- STROBE KEYBOARD ---
70   FOR Z = 1 TO T:K =  PEEK ( - 16384): IF K < 128 THEN
   NEXT Z
80   IF K > 127 THEN 120
90   VTAB 23: HTAB 8
100   PRINT "PRESS ANY KEY TO CONTINUE"
105   REM   --- STROBE KEYBOARD ---
110   FOR Z = 1 TO T:K =  PEEK ( - 16384): IF K < 128 THE
N  NEXT Z: GOTO 50
120   POKE  - 16368,0
130   HOME
140   PRINT "NEXT PAGE"
199   END
```

TIME LIMIT

This program allows the user a certain amount of time to answer a question. The elapsed time is displayed in the upper right corner. The timing device stops when any key is pressed. This can be used for quizzes or adventure games.

EXPLANATION

Lines 60, 70, and 80 are used to calibrate the count down to clock seconds. If you want 30 seconds, change line 60 to:

```
60 T = 30
```

If you add more statements within the timing loop 70–170, then you will have to adjust the calibration in lines 70 and 80 and change 40 to a different number. Use a stopwatch or a watch with a second hand to make the proper adjustment.

```
5    REM  === STROBE TIME LIMIT ===
10   POKE  - 16368,0: REM  CLEAR STROBE
20   HOME
30   VTAB 10
40   PRINT "PLAY AGAIN (Y/N) ";
50   H =  PEEK (36):V =  PEEK (37)
60   T = 10: REM   NUMBER OF SECONDS
65   REM  --- TIMING LOOP ---
70   FOR X = T * 40 TO 1 STEP  - 1
75   REM  --- CALIBRATE WITH SECONDS ---
80   IF X / 40 =  INT (X / 40) THEN  VTAB 1: HTAB 35: PRI
NT X / 40; CHR$ (32)
85   REM   --- STROBE KEYBOARD ---
90   K =  PEEK ( - 16384)
100  IF K < 128 THEN 170
105  REM  --- CAPTURE AND CHECK KEYPRESS ---
110  POKE  - 16368,0
120  K = K - 128
130  A$ =  CHR$ (K)
140  VTAB V + 1: HTAB H + 1
150  IF A$ = "Y" THEN  PRINT A$: GOTO 200
160  IF A$ = "N" THEN  PRINT A$: GOTO 200
170  NEXT X
175  REM  --- RESPONSE TOO SLOW ---
180  POKE  - 16368,0
190  VTAB 23: HTAB 1: PRINT "TOO SLOW": GOTO 200
200  END
```

MODIFICATION

You can use a GET command to capture the keypress by deleting lines 110, 120, and 130 and adding the following line 110.

```
110 GET A$
```

CALL −756

This program will continue with the space bar and end with the ESC key. Any other key is ignored by the program.

EXPLANATION

This program strobes the keyboard and uses the CALL −756 command to wait for the keypress in line 70. CALL −756 can only be interrupted by the RESET key.

```
5    REM   === CALL-756 FOR KEYPRESS ===
10   POKE  - 16368,0
20   HOME
30   PRINT "PAGE 1"
40   VTAB 22
50   PRINT "PRESS <SPACE BAR> TO CONTINUE"
60   PRINT "PRESS <ESC> TO END ";
65   REM  --- STROBE KEYBOARD ---
70   CALL  - 756
80   IF  PEEK ( - 16384) = 27 THEN  HOME : GOTO 199
90   IF  PEEK ( - 16384) <  > 32 THEN 70
100   POKE  - 16368,0
110   HOME : PRINT "PAGE 2"
199   END
```

WAIT COMMAND

This program waits for any key to continue but will end when the Q key is pressed.

EXPLANATION

It strobes the keyboard and uses the WAIT command to wait for a keypress in line 50. The command WAIT checks memory location −16384 and continues when the eight bits represent the decimal number 128. The WAIT command can only be interrupted by the RESET key.

```
5    REM   === WAIT FOR KEYPRESS ===
10   HOME
20   PRINT "PAGE 1"
30   VTAB 22
40   PRINT : PRINT "HIT ANY KEY TO CONTINUE OR (Q) TO QUI
T"
45   REM   --- STROBE KEYBOARD ---
50   WAIT  - 16384,128
60   IF  PEEK ( - 16384) - 128 = 81 THEN  POKE  - 16368,0
: HOME : GOTO 99
70   POKE  - 16368,0
80   HOME
90   PRINT "PAGE 2"
99   END
```

MOVING MESSAGE

This program moves a message across the screen in a billboard fashion. The message is printed on one line, scrolls to the left, and wraps around to be printed again. Any keypress will terminate the printing.

EXPLANATION

A$ holds the message to be scrolled. Line 40 prints the first 39 characters of the message at row 24. Line 50 shifts the contents of A$ by putting the first character at the end of the string and moving all the other characters up one position in the string.

Lines 60 and 70 strobe the keyboard. Line 70 checks the strobe memory location. If it finds a value less than 128, then no key has been pressed and it continues with the scrolling and strobing. If a key was pressed, the value of K will be >128 and the scrolling stops.

```
5   REM === MOVING MESSAGE ===
10    HOME
20    VTAB 24
30 A$ = "THIS IS A MOVING MESSAGE FOR YOU TO READ AND DE
CIPHER..."
40    HTAB 1: PRINT  LEFT$ (A$,39);
45    REM  --- SHIFT CONTENTS OF A$ ---
50 A$ =  MID$ (A$,2) +  LEFT$ (A$,1)
55    REM  --- STROBE KEYBOARD ---
60 K =  PEEK ( - 16384)
70    IF K < 128 THEN  FOR K = 1 TO 150: NEXT K: GOTO 40
80    GET R$
90    PRINT
100   HOME
110   PRINT "PAGE 2"
199   END
```

MOVING MESSAGE WITH DUMMY CURSOR

This program prints a scrolling message while waiting for the user to enter a reply. It can be used as an interesting way to present a menu and wait for the user's response.

EXPLANATION

The strobe feature does not produce a cursor, so a dummy cursor is printed on line 170. Lines 200–210 store the scrolling message and pad it with spaces if necessary to obtain a message A$ with a length of 39 characters.

This program uses the strobe feature to wait for a keypress at lines 250–320 and scrolls a message at lines 220–240 while waiting. Line 230 prints the left 39 characters of A$.

Line 260 checks the strobe memory location. When a key is pressed the value of K will be >128. Line 270 captures the keypress before printing it to the screen. It does this so it can check that the keypress is a digit. Line 290 converts the string R$ to a numeric variable R. Lines 300–310 verify that R is within the range 1–5. Line 330 branches to desired subroutine.

Insert your subroutines at lines 1000, 2000, 3000, 4000, and 5000.

```
5    REM   === MOVING MESSAGE DUMMY CURSOR ===
10   N = 5: DIM A$(N)
15   REM   --- READ DATA INTO ARRAY ---
20   FOR X = 1 TO N: READ A$(X): NEXT X
30   DATA  HANGMAN, CONCENTRATION, NUMBER GUESS, SEVEN-EL
EVEN, FLIP
35   REM   --- DISPLAY SCREEN ---
40   H = 10
50   HOME
60   VTAB 2
70   INVERSE
80   HTAB 5: PRINT "<<< PROGRAMS AVAILABLE >>>"
90   NORMAL
100  PRINT
110  VTAB 6
120  FOR X = 1 TO N
130  HTAB H
140  PRINT X;") ";A$(X): PRINT
150  NEXT X
160  HTAB H - 7: PRINT "SELECT:";
165  REM   --- DUMMY CURSOR ---
170  FLASH : PRINT  CHR$ (32);
180  NORMAL
190  VTAB 24
195  REM   --- SCROLLING MESSAGE ---
200  A$ = "PRESS ANY NUMBER 1-5    0=QUIT"
205  REM   --- PAD SCROLLING MESSAGE ---
210  IF  LEN (A$) < 39 THEN A$ = A$ +  CHR$ (32): GOTO 2
10
220  VTAB 23
225  REM   --- PRINT SCROLLING MESSAGE ---
230  HTAB 1: PRINT  LEFT$ (A$,39);
235  REM   --- SHIFT CONTENTS OF A$ ---
240  A$ =  MID$ (A$,2) +  LEFT$ (A$,1)
245  REM   --- STROBE KEYBOARD ---
```

```
250 K =  PEEK ( - 16384)
260  IF K < 128 THEN  FOR Z = 1 TO 50: NEXT Z: GOTO 220
270  GET R$
275  REM  --- CHECK FOR DIGIT ---
280  IF  ASC (R$) < 48 OR  ASC (R$) > 57 THEN 220
290 R =  VAL (R$)
295  REM  --- CHECK THAT R IS WITHIN RANGE 1-5 ---
300  IF R = 0 THEN 340
310  IF R > 5 THEN 220
320  VTAB 18: HTAB H: PRINT R$
330  ON R GOTO 1000,2000,3000,4000,5000
340  TEXT : HOME : VTAB 12: HTAB 17: PRINT "THE END"
399  END
995  REM  --- SUBROUTINES ---
1000  HOME : PRINT A$(1): END
2000  HOME : PRINT A$(2): END
3000  HOME : PRINT A$(3): END
4000  HOME : PRINT A$(4): END
5000  HOME : PRINT A$(5): END
```

SAMPLE OUTPUT ═══

<<< PROGRAMS AVAILABLE >>>

1) HANGMAN

2) CONCENTRATION

3) NUMBER GUESS

4) SEVEN-ELEVEN

5) FLIP

SELECT:

PRESS ANY NUMBER 1-5   0=QUIT

MODIFICATION ═══

The program can be modified to run programs on your disk. Omit lines 1000–5000 and change line 330 to the following statement.

```
330 PRINT:HOME:VTAB 12:HTAB 10:PRINT"LOADING "A$(R):
    PRINT CHR$(4)"RUN "A$(R)
```

Be sure to add the names of your programs in the DATA statement on line 30.

TWIRLING CURSOR

The next two programs twirl the cursor until a key is pressed.

FOR APPLE II/II PLUS

This program will simulate a twirling cursor. The twirling will stop when any key is pressed. This is useful for a different cursor when waiting for a user reply. This program works on any Apple computer but was specially written for the Apple II and II Plus.

EXPLANATION ═══

The forward slash is not available on the Apple II Plus keyboard, so you need to use the character string to print special characters that are not available on the keyboard.

Lines 30 and 40 form a string variable C$ that contains four different positions of the cursor. Rapidly displaying these four characters in order simulates a twirling cursor. The variable C holds the position of the character of C$ that will be printed next.

Lines 80–90 check for a keypress. If a key was pressed, it continues with line 100. If there is no keypress, then it determines which character of the string C$ should be printed next.

```
5   REM  === TWIRLING CURSOR II+ ===
10  POKE  - 16368,0
20  TEXT : HOME
30  B$ =  CHR$ (92): REM  REVERSE OF BACKSLASH
35  REM  --- CHARACTERS OF CURSOR ---
40  C$ = "!/-" + B$
50  C = 1:L =  LEN (C$)
60  HOME : VTAB 12: PRINT  TAB( 8)"PRESS ANY KEY TO CONT
INUE."
65  REM  --- PRINT CHARACTER ---
70  VTAB 12: PRINT  TAB( 5) MID$ (C$,C,1)
75  REM  --- STROBE KEYBOARD ---
80 KEY =  PEEK ( - 16384)
90  IF KEY < 128 THEN C = C + 1 - L * (C = L): GOTO 70
100   GET A$
110   VTAB 23
120   HOME
130   PRINT "LET'S CONTINUE"
199   END
```

This program twirls the cursor until a key is pressed and works only on the Apple IIe or IIc.

EXPLANATION

The Apple IIe has more keyboard characters available than the Apple II Plus and they can be accessed directly in line 40.

See the explanation in the previous section for the Apple II Plus.

```
5   REM  === TWIRLING CURSOR IIE/C ===
10  POKE  - 16368,0
20  TEXT : HOME
35  REM  --- CHARACTERS OF CURSOR ---
40 C$ = "!/-\"
50 C = 1:L =  LEN (C$)
60  HOME : VTAB 12: PRINT  TAB( 8)"PRESS ANY KEY TO CONT
INUE."
65  REM  --- PRINT CHARACTER ---
70  VTAB 12: PRINT  TAB( 5) MID$ (C$,C,1)
75  REM  --- STROBE KEYBOARD ---
80 KEY =  PEEK ( - 16384)
90  IF KEY < 128 THEN C = C + 1 - L * (C = L): GOTO 70
100  GET A$
110  VTAB 23
120  HOME
130  PRINT "LET'S CONTINUE"
199  END
```

MODIFICATION

Experiment with different combinations of characters for the cursor. Other possibilities for C$ (without concatenating B$) are:

```
C$  =  "*<>*"
C$  =  "ZNZN"
C$  =  "X+X+"
C$  =  "HIHI"
```

SLIDING CHARACTERS ACROSS THE SCREEN

PRESENTING

This program prints a message in a small box in the center of the screen. Only 8 characters are present at any one time. The message is presented one character at a time moving from right to left.

EXPLANATION ══

Lines 20–60 print the box for the message. The string variable M$ holds the message to be printed. The routine at 90–130 prints 8 characters of the message at a time. The 6 blank spaces at the beginning and end of M$ are necessary to start and end within the box.

```
5    REM  === PRESENTING --> ===
10   HOME
15   REM  --- DRAW BOX ---
20   VTAB 8: HTAB 10: PRINT "------------------": REM    1
8 DASHES
30   FOR X = 8 TO 12
40   VTAB X: HTAB 10: PRINT "-";: HTAB 28: PRINT "-"
50   NEXT X
60   VTAB 12: HTAB 10: PRINT "------------------": REM
 18 DASHES
70   FOR Z = 1 TO 500: NEXT Z
80 M$ = "      PRESENTING THE GREATEST PROGRAM ON EARTH
YET      "
85   REM  --- PRINT MOVING MESSAGE ---
90   FOR X = 1 TO  LEN (M$)
100   VTAB 10: HTAB 15
110   PRINT  MID$ (M$,X,8)
120   FOR Z = 1 TO 150: NEXT Z
130   NEXT X
199   END
```

SAMPLE OUTPUT ══

```
            ------------------
            -                -
            -     PRESENTI    -
            -                -
            ------------------
```

MODIFICATIONS ══

1. The characters that form the text box can be changed to other symbols such as asterisks (*), equal signs (=), or the underline (__). The sides of the box can also be changed to exclamation marks (!) or vertical bars (|).
2. The vertical position can be changed on lines 20 and 100, and the length of the box can also be modified in routine 20–60.
3. You may wish to print more or less than 8 characters at a time. The size of the box should be changed along with the 8 in line 110.

SLIDING/CENTERING TWO-WORD MESSAGE BY CHARACTER

This program slides a two-word message from the left edge of the screen to the center of the screen one character at a time.

EXPLANATION

The first and second messages are entered and checked for a maximum of 20 characters. Lines 90–120 set the variables for the first message. Lines 140–170 set the second message variables. The subroutine at lines 1000–1070 prints the message one character at a time. The message is reprinted to the right of the original message, giving the effect of a sliding message. The previous message is erased. Line 1000 determines the starting and ending tab positions for each message so the message will start at the left edge and end when it is centered on the screen.

L and LL hold the length of the message for subroutine 1000–1070. L decreases by 1 in line 1050 while LL remains stable. N$ represents the string to be printed, and V stands for the vertical printing position. The value of V can be changed to print the messages at different rows.

```
5    REM  === SLIDE 2 WORDS BY CHARACTER ===
10   HOME
20   INPUT "ENTER FIRST WORD ";N1$
30 L1 =  LEN (N1$)
40   IF L1 > 20 THEN 20
50   INPUT "ENTER SECOND WORD ";N2$
60 L2 =  LEN (N2$)
70   IF L2 > 20 THEN 50
80   HOME
85   REM  --- SET VARIABLES FIRST MESSAGE ---
90 L = L1
100 LL = L1
110 N$ = N1$
120 V = 7
130  GOSUB 1000
135  REM  --- SET VARIABLES SECOND MESSAGE ---
140 L = L2
150 LL = L2
160 N$ = N2$
170 V = 9
180  GOSUB 1000
189  END
195  REM  --- PRINT CHARACTER BY CHARACTER ---
1000  FOR X = (20 + LL / 2) - 1 TO (20 - LL / 2) STEP  -
   1
1010  FOR Y = 1 TO X
1020  VTAB V
1030  PRINT  TAB( Y) MID$ (N$,L,1)
1040  NEXT Y
1050 L = L - 1
1060  NEXT X
1070  RETURN
```

SLIDING/CENTERING TWO MESSAGES FROM OPPOSITE DIRECTIONS

This program slides a word or message from the left edge of the screen to the center of the screen and then slides a word or message from the right edge of the screen and centers that message.

EXPLANATION

SS represents the space character and is used to erase the used portion of the message. M stands for the starting tab position to center the word AS. Lines 70-120 slide the message from left to right, whereas lines 140-190 slide the message from right to left.

```
5    REM  === SLIDE TO CENTER FROM EDGES ===
10   HOME
20   INPUT "ENTER FIRST WORD ";A$
30   INPUT "ENTER SECOND WORD ";Z$
40   HOME
50  S$ =  CHR$ (32): REM  SPACE
55   REM  --- DETERMINE TAB TO CENTER MESSAGE ---
60  M = 20 -  LEN (A$) / 2
65   REM  --- SLIDE RIGHT -> LEFT ---
70   FOR X = 41 -  LEN (A$) TO M STEP  - 1
80   VTAB 10
90   HTAB X
100   PRINT A$;S$
110   FOR Z = 1 TO 100: NEXT Z
120   NEXT X
125   REM  --- DETERMINE TAB TO CENTER MESSAGE ---
130  M =  INT (20 -  LEN (Z$) / 2)
135   REM  --- SLIDE LEFT -> RIGHT ---
140   FOR X = 1 TO M - 1
150   VTAB 14
160   HTAB X
170   PRINT S$;Z$
180   FOR Z = 1 TO 100: NEXT Z
190   NEXT X
199   END
```

LEFT TO RIGHT AND RIGHT TO LEFT

This program prints a message from left to right at the top of the screen and then erases it. It then prints a message at the bottom of the screen from right to left but leaves that message on the screen.

EXPLANATION ═══

Lines 50–80 print the first message A$ from left to right. Lines 120–150 erase the first message. Lines 180–210 print the second message Z$ from right to left.

You can omit line 160 for the second message to be printed immediately below the first message.

```
5    REM   === MESSAGE LR AND RL ===
10   HOME
20 A$ = "THIS IS THE FIRST MESSAGE"
30 B$ = "THIS IS THE LAST MESSAGE"
35   REM   --- PRINT FIRST MESSAGE L->R ---
40   VTAB 1
50   FOR X = 1 TO  LEN (A$)
60   SPEED= 150
70   PRINT  MID$ (A$,X,1);
80   NEXT X
90   PRINT
100   FOR Z = 1 TO 200: NEXT Z
105   REM   --- ERASE FIRST MESSAGE L->R ---
110   VTAB 1
120   FOR X = 1 TO  LEN (A$)
130   SPEED= 150
140   PRINT  SPC( 1);
150   NEXT X
155   REM   --- PRINT SECOND MESSAGE R-L ---
160   VTAB 23
170 H = 39
180   FOR X =  LEN (B$) TO 1 STEP  - 1
190   HTAB H: PRINT  MID$ (B$,X,1);
200 H = H - 1
210   NEXT X
220   SPEED= 255
999   END
```

MOVING CHARACTER

This program prints a message to the screen and a random character bounces through the word until a key is pressed.

EXPLANATION

S represents the number of screen spaces to the left of the first character of the message. A$ holds the message to be printed. H ranges from 1 to the length of the message A$ and represents the horizontal tab position. Line 80 adds S to the value of H so the HTAB position starts at the leftmost character of A$. Line 90 selects a random number from 26 to 90, and line 100 prints the character that corresponds to the ASCII code. (See Appendix A for the ASCII code chart.)

The strobe is used on lines 140–150 to check for a keypress. If no key was pressed, the computer continues printing the message with a random letter bouncing throughout the message A$. If, however, a key is pressed, then the computer goes to line 160 and prints the original message again. If the keypress was the ESC key, the program ends. If any other key was pressed, the program continues with line 190.

```
5   REM  === MOVING CHARACTER ===
10  A$ = "PRESS ANY KEY TO CONTINUE"
20  H = 1:S = 6:L =  LEN (A$)
30   POKE  - 16368,0
40   HOME
50   VTAB 23: HTAB S + 1
60   PRINT A$
65   REM  --- DETERMINE WHERE TO PRINT BOUNCING CHARACTER
     ---
70  H = H + 1 - L * (H = L)
80   VTAB 23: HTAB H + S
90  R =  INT ( RND (1) * 26) + 65: REM  RANDOM LETTER A-Z
95   REM  --- PRINT BOUNCING LETTER ---
100   PRINT  CHR$ (R);
110   HTAB H + S
115   REM  --- REPLACE CHARACTER OF STRING A$ ---
120   FOR Z = 1 TO 10: NEXT Z
130   PRINT  MID$ (A$,H,1)
135   REM  --- STROBE KEYBOARD ---
140  K =  PEEK ( - 16384)
150   IF K < 128 THEN 70
160   VTAB 23: HTAB 5: PRINT A$
170   POKE  - 16368,0
180   IF K - 128 = 27 THEN  END
190   HOME : PRINT "PAGE 2"
199   END
```

MODIFICATION

You can select a particular character to be bounced through the word. Omit line 90 and change line 100 to the following line if you want an asterisk to do the bouncing:

```
100 PRINT "*";
```

SORTING, SEARCHING, AND SCRAMBLING

The "Information Age" made possible by the computer has produced volumes of facts, names, and numbers. However, information is meaningful only when it is categorized or sorted.

Sorting means placing a set of data elements in order. There are various methods of sorting data. The method you use depends on the arrangement of your data and the number of data items to be sorted. Most of the time you will start with a list that is partially in order.

The sort routines presented provide an alphabetical sort of words, names, or items. In the following sort explanations, the phrase "largest value" refers to the alphabetical value. When comparing SMITHE and SMYTH, SMYTH has the largest value because it is closer to the end of the list when arranged alphabetically from A to Z.

Each sort routine can easily be modified to sort numbers. The routines sort in increasing order and can be modified to sort in decreasing order.

The Linear or Sequential search is a straightforward, but time-consuming search. The Binary search is a more time-efficient method but requires that the list be in order.

Since searching and sorting are among the most time-consuming operations of any program, display a message so the user will be patient and stand by for the result. A message such as PLEASE STAND BY, ONE MOMENT PLEASE, SORTING, or SEARCHING in the inverse or flashing mode can be printed when the program search or sort is being performed.

Sometimes, however, you may want to shuffle the data items instead of sorting them. This would be useful for a spelling test in which you want the data presented in a different order each time the program is run. The sort and shuffle routines can be modified to sort and scramble the letters of words. This can be used in a word guessing game. This chapter will help you sort, search, shuffle, and scramble your data.

SORTING

BUBBLE SORT

This program presents a subroutine to perform an alphabetical sort for a list of names, words, or items. It can easily be modified to sort in decreasing order or to sort numbers either in increasing or decreasing order.

BACKGROUND

The Bubble sort is the easiest to understand but is inefficient for large lists and performs noticeably slower as the list gets longer. It is adequate for a list of up to 100 items.

There are several versions of the Bubble sort. You can use either one or two loops. On an increasing sort, you can shift the largest value to the right with each pass or you can shift the smallest value to the left. The net result is the same: a sorted list.

EXPLANATION

The following Bubble sort uses two loops to sort a list of words in increasing order. It scans the list and compares the items two at a time starting with the first word and switches whenever the words are not in increasing or alphabetical order.

To sort a list of N elements, only N − 1 passes are needed on the outer loop at lines 1000–1070. On an increasing sort, the first pass places the largest item at the end of the list. After the second pass, the second largest item is in place. This continues until all the items are in place. The inner loop at lines 1020–1050 controls the interchange process between pairs of words, ensuring that the largest value is to the right. The switching is performed at line 1040.

The variable SW acts as a flag to signal that the list may be in order before the entire sort has been completed. This increases the efficiency of the sort when the original list is already partially in order.

```
5    REM  === BUBBLE SORT ===
10   READ N: REM  NUMBER OF ITEMS
20   DIM A$(N)
30   HOME
35   REM  --- READ ITEMS INTO ARRAY AND PRINT TO SCREEN -
--
40   FOR X = 1 TO N: READ A$(X): PRINT A$(X): NEXT X
50   GOSUB 1000"SORT ROUTINE"
55   REM  --- PRINT SORTED LIST ---
60   VTAB 1
70   FOR X = 1 TO N: HTAB 20: PRINT A$(X): NEXT X
99   END
995  REM  --- SORT ROUTINE ---
1000 FOR Y = 1 TO N - 1
1010 SW = 0: REM  FLAG
1020 FOR X = 1 TO N - Y
1025 REM  --- COMPARE ---
1030 IF A$(X) < = A$(X + 1) THEN 1050
1035 REM  --- SWITCH ---
1040 T$ = A$(X):A$(X) = A$(X + 1):A$(X + 1) = T$:SW = 1
1050 NEXT X
1060 IF SW = 0 THEN 1080
1070 NEXT Y
1080 RETURN
2000 DATA  20: REM  NUMBER OF ITEMS
2010 DATA  T,S,R,Q,P,O,N,M,L,K,J,I,H,G,F,E,D,C,B,A
```

The following shows how the Bubble sort routine sorts six elements. Each inner loop compares adjacent elements and switches if necessary to get the largest element to the end of the set of items.

Original list:	F E D C B A
1st outer loop:	F E D C B A
	E F D C B A
	E D F C B A
	E D C F B A
	E D C B F A
	E D C B A F
2nd outer loop:	E D C B A F
	D E C B A F
	D C E B A F
	D C B E A F
	D C B A E F
3rd outer loop:	D C B A E F
	C D B A E F
	C B D A E F
	C B A D E F
4th outer loop:	C B A D E F
	B C A D E F
	B A C D E F
5th outer loop:	B A C D E F
	A B C D E F
Sorted list:	A B C D E F

You can use any inputting routine of your choice. The words can be inputted by the user, read from DATA statements, or read in from Text files. The printing routine can also be modified according to your needs.

In a list of 20 items, the maximum number of passes of the outer loop is 19 (20 − 1), and the maximum number of switches is 19 + 18 + 17 + 16 + 15 +. . .+ 1 = 190.

The following list of letters indicates the arrangement of the letters after each pass of the outer loop. On each pass one more letter is shifted to its correct place in the list.

```
Original list:      T S R Q P O N M L K J I H G F E D C B A

After 1st pass:     S R Q P O N M L K J I H G F E D C B A T
After 2nd pass:     R Q P O N M L K J I H G F E D C B A S T
After 3rd pass:     Q P O N M L K J I H G F E D C B A R S T
After 4th pass:     P O N M L K J I H G F E D C B A Q R S T
After 5th pass:     O N M L K J I H G F E D C B A P Q R S T
After 6th pass:     N M L K J I H G F E D C B A O P Q R S T
After 7th pass:     M L K J I H G F E D C B A N O P Q R S T
After 8th pass:     L K J I H G F E D C B A M N O P Q R S T
After 9th pass:     K J I H G F E D C B A L M N O P Q R S T
After 10th pass:    J I H G F E D C B A K L M N O P Q R S T
After 11th pass:    I H G F E D C B A J K L M N O P Q R S T
After 12th pass:    H G F E D C B A I J K L M N O P Q R S T
After 13th pass:    G F E D C B A H I J K L M N O P Q R S T
After 14th pass:    F E D C B A G H I J K L M N O P Q R S T
After 15th pass:    E D C B A F G H I J K L M N O P Q R S T
After 16th pass:    D C B A E F G H I J K L M N O P Q R S T
After 17th pass:    C B A D E F G H I J K L M N O P Q R S T
After 18th pass:    B A C D E F G H I J K L M N O P Q R S T
After 19th pass:    A B C D E F G H I J K L M N O P Q R S T

Sorted list:        A B C D E F G H I J K L M N O P Q R S T
```

MODIFICATIONS

1. To sort in descending or decreasing order, change the inequality sign on line 1030. Line 1030 should then read:

```
1030 IF A$(X) > = A$(X+1) THEN 1050
```

2. To use the sort for numbers, simply change all the string array variables A$( ) to numeric variables A( ). Try entering numbers (with different numbers of digits) in a string array sort to see how the computer interprets them.

ANOTHER SORT (SHELL)

The Bubble sort is easy to understand but operates slowly on long lists that are out of order, since many time-consuming switches must be performed. The Shell sort is an alternate sort routine that minimizes the number of switches, although more comparisons may be made. However, comparisons can be performed faster than switches.

LOGARITHMS

In order to understand the Shell sort, you must know how the built-in function LOG works, since logarithms are used. A log of a number N base 10 is the power of 10 that produces a number equal to N. For example, $Log_{10} 1000 = 3$, since 10 to the third power equals 1000. In base 2, the $log_2 32 = 5$, since 2 to the fifth power is 32.

You may already be familiar with logs to the base 10 or base 2. These are called common logs. However, the computer works with natural logarithms rather than logs to base 10 or 2. A natural log is a log to the base e, where e is Euler's number and is approximately 2.71828. In mathematical notation, the natural log is represented by ln N. In BASIC, the natural log is written as LOG(N) and uses a base of e.

The following formula converts the natural log of N with base e to the common log of N where:

B is the base desired
LOG(N) represents the natural log of N base e
LOG(B) represents the natural log of B base e
L represents the common log of N base B

$$L = LOG(N) / LOG(B)$$

SHELL SORT

This subroutine demonstrates the Shell sort, which is faster than the Bubble sort when the list is in general disorder. However, if the list is generally in order, this sort takes more time than the Bubble sort.

EXPLANATION

There are several variations of the Shell sort. Each one essentially divides the list into a large number of small partitions and sorts the words within each partition by switching elements that are out of order.

The number of groups decreases while the number of items per group increases as the sort progresses.

Lines 1000–1010 determines the number of elements in each group. Line 1000 can be interpreted as:

$$1000 \; G = 2^{INT\left(\frac{\ln N}{\ln 2}\right)} - 1$$
$$G = 2^{INT(\log_2 N)} - 1$$
$$G = 2^{INT(\log_2 20)} - 1 \quad \text{where } N = 20$$
$$G = 2^{INT(4.3219281)} - 1$$
$$G = 2^4 - 1$$
$$G = 16 - 1$$
$$G = 15$$

Line 1010 then divides G by 2 and takes the integer portion.

$$1010 \; G = INT(G/2)$$
$$G = INT(15/2) \text{ where } G = 15$$
$$G = 7$$

The first time through this routine the number of elements per group is G. After these groups are sorted, the computer computes a new value for G by again executing line 1010. This is continued until $G < 1$, at which time the sort is complete. For a list of 20 elements the values of G start at 7 and are then computed as 3 and 1.

With a list of 100 elements, the value of G is evaluated at line 1000 to two to the sixth power minus one, or 63. Line 1010 computes G to the following values: 31, 15, 7, 3, and 1, successively. The 100 items would thus be divided into groups of 31 elements, then 15 elements per group, then 7, 3, and 1 elements per group.

```
5    REM   === SHELL SORT ===
10   HOME
20   READ N: DIM A$(N)
25   REM   --- READ DATA INTO ARRAY ---
30   FOR X = 1 TO N: READ A$(X): PRINT A$(X): NEXT X
40   GOSUB 995
45   REM   === PRINT OUT SORTED LIST ===
50   VTAB 1
60   FOR X = 1 TO N: HTAB 20: PRINT A$(X): NEXT X
99   END
995  REM   === SHELL SORT ===
997  REM   --- CALCULATE NUMBER OF GROUPS ---
1000 G = (2 ^ INT ( LOG (N) /  LOG (2))) - 1
1010 G =  INT (G / 2)
1020  IF G < 1 THEN 45
1025  REM   --- STEP THROUGH GROUPS ---
1030  FOR J = 1 TO G
1040  FOR K = J + G TO N STEP G
1050 M = K:T$ = A$(M)
1055  REM   --- COMPARE ELEMENTS ---
1060  IF A$(M - G) <  = T$ THEN 1090
1070 A$(M) = A$(M - G):M = M - G
1080  IF M > G THEN 1060
1085  REM   --- SWITCH ELEMENTS ---
1090 A$(M) = T$
1100  NEXT K,J
1110  GOTO 1010
1120  RETURN
2000  DATA  20 : REM  NUMBER OF ITEMS
2010  DATA  T,S,R,Q,P,O,N,M,L,K,J,I,H,G,F,E,D,C,B,A
```

The following list of items represents the arrangement after each completion of the outer loop. The elements of each group are sorted. At line 1010, G = 15, where N = 20.

Original list: T S R Q P O N M L K J I H G F E D C B A

The first pass of the outer loop divides the list of 20 elements into seven groups and sorts the elements in each group (G = 7).

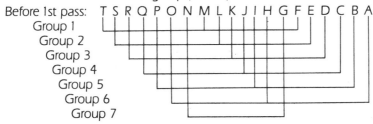

Before 1st pass: T S R Q P O N M L K J I H G F E D C B A
                  Group 1
                  Group 2
                  Group 3
                  Group 4
                  Group 5
                  Group 6
                  Group 7

Elements to be sorted: List during 1st pass of outer loop:

Group 1: T M F   F S R Q P O N M L K J I H G T E D C B A
Group 2: S L E   F E R Q P O N M L K J I H G T S D C B A
Group 3: R K D   F E D Q P O N M L K J I H G T S R C B A
Group 4: Q J C   F E D C P O N M L K J I H G T S R Q B A
Group 5: P I B   F E D C B O N M L K J I H G T S R Q P A
Group 6: O H A   F E D C B A N M L K J I H G T S R Q P O
Group 7: N G   F E D C B A G M L K J I H N T S R Q P O

After 1st pass: F E D C B A G M L K J I H N T S R Q P O

SORTING, SEARCHING, AND SCRAMBLING _____ 107

The second pass of the outer loop divides the partially sorted list into three groups and sorts the elements of each group (G = 3).

Before 2nd pass: F E D C B A G M L K J I H N T S R Q P O

Group 1
Group 2
Group 3

Elements to be sorted: List during 2nd pass of outer loop:

Group 1: F C G K H S P   C E D F B A G M L H J I K N T P R Q S O
Group 2: E B M J N R O   C B D F E A G J L H M I K N T P O Q S R
Group 3: D A L I T Q   C B A F E D G J I H M L K N Q P O T S R

After 2nd pass: C B A F E D G J I H M L K N Q P O T S R

The third and final pass of the outer loop takes all the elements as one group and sorts them (G = 1).

Before 3rd pass: C B A F E D G J I H M L K N Q P O T S R

Elements to be sorted: List during 3rd pass of outer loop:

Group 1   C B A F E D G J I H M L K N Q P O T S R
  (All the elements)
After 3rd pass: A B C D E F G H I J K L M N O P Q R S T

Sorted list: A B C D E F G H I J K L M N O P Q R S T

MODIFICATIONS

1. To sort in descending order, change the inequality sign in line 1060 so the statement reads:

   ```
   1060 IF A$(M - G) > = T$ THEN 1090
   ```

2. To change the string sort to a numeric sort, replace the string variables TS and array elements AS( ) with numeric variables T and numeric elements A( ).

SEARCHING

LINEAR OR SEQUENTIAL SEARCH

The following subroutine presents a Linear or Sequential search for a particular item in a set of elements.

EXPLANATION

The Linear or Sequential search searches through a list of items one at a time until the desired element is found or it reaches the end of the list. The items do not have to be in any order.

The items being searched could be anywhere from the 1st to the Nth element in a list of N elements. On the average, N/2 searches will be made to find the element.

The subroutine at lines 1000–1050 searches the items of the list one at a time. Line 1010 is not necessary for the search. It is used to demonstrate how the computer searches through the elements one at a time.

You can omit lines 65–90 and 1010 when you use the Linear search routine in your programs. They are used here solely for demonstration purposes.

```
5    REM  === LINEAR/SEQUENTIAL SEARCH ===
10   READ N: DIM A$(N)
15   REM  --- READ ELEMENTS INTO ARRAY ---
20   FOR X = 1 TO N: READ A$(X): NEXT X
30   HOME
40   PRINT  TAB( 8)"LINEAR/SEQUENTIAL SEARCH": PRINT
50   INPUT "ENTER ITEM FOR SEARCH ";S$
60   PRINT
65   REM  --- PRINT ELEMENTS TO SCREEN ---
70   FOR X = 1 TO N / 2
80   PRINT  TAB( 5);X; SPC( 1);A$(X); TAB( 20);X + 13; SP
C( 1);A$(X + 13)
90   NEXT X
100   GOSUB 1000"SEARCH ROUTINE"
199   END
995   REM  --- SEARCH ROUTINE ---
1000  FOR X = 1 TO N
1010  VTAB 20: HTAB 1: PRINT "TESTING ENTRY # ";X
1020  IF S$ = A$(X) THEN 1050
1030  NEXT X
1040  PRINT : PRINT "ITEM NOT FOUND": RETURN
1050  PRINT "ITEM FOUND AT ";X: RETURN
2000  DATA  26: REM  NUMBER OF ITEMS
2010  DATA  Q,W,E,R,T,Y,U,I,O,P,A,S,D,F,G,H,J,K,L,Z,X,C,
V,B,N,M
```

BINARY SEARCH

The following subroutine provides a Binary search for items in an ordered list.

BACKGROUND

If you have a short list, then you can do a Linear or Sequential search and search through the list one item at a time until the item is found. But if the list is lengthy or you will do many searches, then sort the list first and do a Binary search to save time.

EXPLANATION

A Binary search is a method of searching for an entry in an ordered list by dividing the list successively by half. Each pass of the outer loop eliminates half of the remaining list.

After 1st pass: 1/2 list eliminated and 1/2 list remains.
After 2nd pass: 3/4 list eliminated and 1/4 list remains.
After 3rd pass: 7/8 list eliminated and 1/8 list remains.

The middle element of an array is looked at and determined if it is the desired element. If not, then a determination is made as to whether the element being searched is before or after the middle one. Then the remaining half is searched by examining the middle element of that half. This method eliminates half of the remaining records. This process is continued until the item is found or you run out of elements.

H represents the high position, L represents the low position, and M the middle position.

Each pass will eliminate half of the remaining list. You will converge quickly to the desired record.

This diagram illustrates how the computer searches the list of letters A–T to locate the letter A.

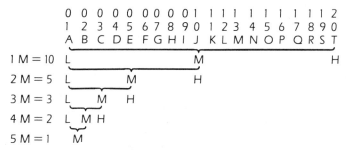

The elements to be sorted are entered into an array at lines 10–20. Line 50 requests the name of the item you are searching for. Lines 70–90 print the list in two columns so you can verify that the item is in the list, and if so at which position. These lines are used soley for verification and can be omitted from the program.

The routine at 1000–1060 performs the Binary search. L represents the position of the lowest value of the list, H represents the position of the highest value, and M indicates the middle value in the range L–H. If the item exists in the list, the value of M eventually equals the position of the item being searched and that position is printed at line 1040. If the item is not in the list, the value of H will be less than the value of L, and line 1020 will report that the item is not in the list.

```
5   REM  === BINARY SEARCH ===
7   REM  --- ENTER ELEMENTS INTO ARRAY ---
10  READ N: DIM A$(N)
20  FOR X = 1 TO N: READ A$(X): NEXT X
30  HOME
40  PRINT  TAB( 14)"BINARY SEARCH": PRINT : PRINT
50  INPUT "ENTER NAME YOU ARE SEARCHING: ";N$
60  PRINT
65  REM  --- PRINT OUT LIST ---
70  FOR X = 1 TO N / 2
80  PRINT  TAB( 5);X; SPC( 1);A$(X); TAB( 20);X + 13; SP
C( 1);A$(X + 13)
90  NEXT X
100  PRINT
110  GOSUB 1000"SEARCH ROUTINE"
199  END
995  REM  --- SEARCH ROUTINE ---
1000 L = 1: REM  LOW
1010 H = N: REM  HIGH
1020  IF H < L THEN  PRINT N$;" NOT IN LISTING": RETURN
1030 M =  INT ((L + H) / 2)
1040  IF N$ = A$(M) THEN  PRINT N$;" FOUND AT POSITION "
;M: RETURN
1050  IF N$ > A$(M) THEN L = M + 1: GOTO 1020
1060  IF N$ < A$(M) THEN H = M - 1: GOTO 1020
2000  DATA  26: REM  NUMBER OF ITEMS
2010  DATA  A,B,C,D,E,F,G,H, I,J,K,L,M
2020  DATA    N,O,P,Q,R,S,T,U,V,W,X,Y,Z
```

A Linear search will search each item sequentially until a match is made or the end of the list is reached. On the average, it will find a target item in a list after searching half the list. Thus, a search requires a maximum of N searches and averages N/2 attempts, where N is the number of items in the list.

The Binary search looks at the midpoint of the list and reduces the numbers of items to check by half on each such comparison. It thus requires only the number of attempts that it takes to reduce the number of items in the list to 1 by dividing it successively by 2.

Mathematically, the Binary search requires a maximum of INT(LOG(N)/LOG(2))+1 searches, where LOG(N)/LOG(2) returns the common log of N base 2 and N represents the number of items in the list. For large arrays, this is very efficient. The maximum number of comparisons is represented by the power of 2 that results in a number equal to the number of items in the list plus one.

List Size	Max. No. of Comparisons
10	4
100	7
1000	10
10000	14
S	INT(LOG(S)/LOG(2))+1

The formula INT(LOG(S)/LOG(2))+1 is useful in determining the maximum number of guesses allowed in a number guessing game where the user is guessing a number that the computer has randomly selected from 1 to S. Binary search should be used to continually guess the middle number of the range until the number is guessed.

SHUFFLING AND SCRAMBLING

SHUFFLING ITEMS IN A LIST

This program provides a routine to shuffle the items of a list. It produces a different arrangement of the list each time the program is run. In a game or educational program, you might want to scramble the items of a list so the words do not always appear in the same order.

EXPLANATION ══

Line 40 reads the items into the array. The routine at 1000–1050 does the shuffling and forms a new array SS( ) of the scrambled list.

Line 1000 sets the elements of a flag array to zero. The flag array F( ) is used to indicate if an item in the original list has been placed in the scrambled list. Then a loop of N executions is performed to select a random number from 1 to N, where N is the number of data items. If the flag array indicates a 1 in that position, the computer selects another random number from 1 to N. If, however, the flag element is zero, then the Rth item of the original list is selected to be the Xth element of the new shuffled list SS( ) and the flag is set to 1.

```
5    REM   === SHUFFLE LIST ===
10   CLEAR : HOME
20   READ N: REM   NUMBER OF ELEMENTS
30   DIM A$(N),F(N),S$(N)
40   FOR X = 1 TO N: READ A$(X): PRINT A$(X): NEXT X
50   GOSUB 1010"SHUFFLE"
60   VTAB 1
70   FOR X = 1 TO N: HTAB 20: PRINT S$(X): NEXT X
199  END
995  REM   --- SHUFFLE ROUTINE ---
997  REM   --- SET FLAG TO ZERO ---
1000  FOR X = 1 TO N:F(X) = 0: NEXT X
1010  FOR X = 1 TO N
1020 R =   INT ( RND (1) * N) + 1
1030  IF F(R) = 1 THEN 1020
1035  REM   --- SELECT ITEM / SET FLAG TO 1 ---
1040 S$(X) = A$(R):F(R) = 1
1050  NEXT X
1060  RETURN
2000  DATA   20: REM   NUMBER OF ITEMS
2010  DATA   A,B,C,D,E,F,G,H,I,J,K,L,M,N,O,P,Q,R,S,T
```

The Shuffle routine can be used to shuffle a deck of 52 cards and deal them out one at a time without duplicates. One way to arrange such data would be the following set of statements.

```
2000 DATA 52
2010 DATA AS,AD,AH,AC
2020 DATA 2S,2D,2H,2C
2030 DATA 3S,3D,3H,3C
2040 DATA 4S,4D,4H,4C
2050 DATA 5S,5D,5H,5C
2060 DATA 6S,6D,6H,6C
2070 DATA 7S,7D,7H,7C
2080 DATA 8S,8D,8H,8C
2090 DATA 9S,9D,9H,9C
2100 DATA 10S,10D,10H,10C
2110 DATA JS,JD,JH,JC
2120 DATA QS,QD,QH,QC
2130 DATA KS,KD,KH,KC
```

SCRAMBLING LETTERS OF A WORD

The following program scrambles the letters of the word inputted by the user. It produces L versions of the scrambled word, where L is the number of letters of the original word. This can be used in a word guessing game, spelling test, or special effect.

EXPLANATION

The scramble routine is similar to the shuffle routine in the previous program.

The scramble routine at lines 1000–1120 produces L arrangements of the letters of N$. The arrangements are not unique and duplicates may appear, especially on shorter words.

Line 1020 sets the flag array to zero. The flag array determines if the letter has been selected. The inner loop from 1030–1070 selects random numbers from 1 to L, where L is the number of letters in the word. It checks the flag array to see if the letter at the original position of R has been selected yet. If the flag element is 1, then another random number from 1 to N is generated. If the flag element is zero, however, the letter at that position in the original word is chosen for the Xth letter of the scrambled word and the flag is set to 1.

```
5    REM    === SCRAMBLE LETTERS ===
10   DIM F(239),L$(239)
20   TEXT : HOME
30   PRINT  TAB( 15)"THE SCRAMBLER": PRINT : PRINT
40   PRINT "TO QUIT TYPE " CHR$ (34)"END" CHR$ (34): PRIN
T : PRINT
50   POKE 34,5: HOME
60   INPUT "ENTER A WORD ";N$
70   PRINT
80   IF N$ = "END" THEN  TEXT : GOTO 199
90   GOSUB 1000"SCRAMBLE ROUTINE"
100   PRINT : GOTO 60
199   END
995   REM    --- SCRAMBLE LETTERS OF WORD ROUTINE ---
1000 L =  LEN (N$)
1010  FOR S = 1 TO L
1015  REM   --- SET FLAG TO ZERO ---
1020  FOR X = 1 TO L:F(X) = 0: NEXT X
1030  FOR X = 1 TO L
1040 R =  INT ( RND (1) * L) + 1
1045  REM   --- CHECK IF LETTER USED ---
1050  IF F(R) = 1 THEN 1040
1055  REM   --- SELECT LETTER, SET FLAG TO 1 ---
1060 L$(X) =  MID$ (N$,R,1):F(R) = 1
1070  NEXT X
1075  REM   --- CONCATENATE LETTERS ---
1080 S$ = "": REM   NULL STRING
1090  FOR X = 1 TO L:S$ = S$ + L$(X): NEXT X
1100  PRINT S". ";S$
1110  NEXT S
1120  RETURN
```

1. This program can be modified to produce only one scrambled word. If you run the routine often with short words such as NO, YES, or OK, you might get the original word back. To avoid this when outputting only one scrambled word, check the scrambled word so it does not equal the original word.

   Delete line 1010 so the scramble routine is performed only once. Change line 1110 to read:

   1110 PRINT S$

   and change line 1100 to verify a truly scrambled word:

   1100 IF S$ = N$ THEN 1000

2. The words can be read from DATA statements as well as be inputted by the user.

```
5    REM   === SCRAMBLE LETTERS ONCE ===
10   DIM F(239),L$(239)
20   TEXT : HOME
30   PRINT  TAB( 15)"THE SCRAMBLER": PRINT : PRINT
40   PRINT "TO QUIT TYPE " CHR$ (34)"END" CHR$ (34): PRIN
T : PRINT
50   POKE 34,5: HOME
60   INPUT "ENTER A WORD ";N$
70   PRINT
80   IF N$ = "END" THEN  TEXT : GOTO 199
90   GOSUB 1000"SCRAMBLE ROUTINE"
100   PRINT : GOTO 60
199   END
995   REM   --- SCRAMBLE LETTERS OF WORD ROUTINE ---
1000 L =  LEN (N$)
1015  REM   --- SET FLAG TO ZERO ---
1020  FOR X = 1 TO L:F(X) = 0: NEXT X
1030  FOR X = 1 TO L
1040 R =  INT ( RND (1) * L) + 1
1045  REM   --- CHECK IF LETTER USED ---
1050  IF F(R) = 1 THEN 1040
1055  REM   --- SELECT LETTER, SET FLAG TO 1 ---
1060 L$(X) =  MID$ (N$,R,1):F(R) = 1
1070  NEXT X
1075  REM   --- CONCATENATE LETTERS ---
1080 S$ = "": REM   NULL STRING
1090  FOR X = 1 TO L:S$ = S$ + L$(X): NEXT X
1100  IF S$ = N$ THEN 1000
1110  PRINT S$
1120  RETURN
```

ALPHABETIZING LETTERS OF A WORD

This program alphabetizes the letters of a word entered into the computer. This often makes it harder to guess a word in a spelling quiz or guessing game.

EXPLANATION

The subroutine at lines 1000–1090 uses the Bubble sort routine to sort the letters. Lines 1000–1010 take the letters of the word apart and store them as separate array elements in L$( ). The Bubble sort routine is at lines 1020–1090. Once the letters are alphabetized, the computer concatenates the letter to form a new string A$ that represents the alphabetized word.

```
5    REM    === ALPHABETIZE LETTERS OF WORD ===
10   DIM L$(239)
20   HOME
30   PRINT  TAB( 8): PRINT "<THE GREAT LETTER SORTER>": P
RINT
40   PRINT "ENTER <DONE> TO QUIT"
50   PRINT : PRINT
60   POKE 34,4
70   HOME
80   INPUT "ENTER A WORD ";W$
90   IF W$ = "DONE" THEN 199
100  PRINT : PRINT
110  GOSUB 1000"BUBBLE SORT"
120  PRINT W$,A$
130  PRINT : PRINT
140  GOTO 80
199  END
995  REM    --- SEPARATE WORD INTO LETTERS ---
1000 L =  LEN (W$)
1010  FOR X = 1 TO L:L$(X) =  MID$ (W$,X,1): NEXT X
1015  REM    --- BUBBLE SORT ---
1020  FOR J = 1 TO L - 1
1030 SW = 0
1040  FOR K = 1 TO L - J
1050  IF L$(K) <  = L$(K + 1) THEN 1070
1060 T$ = L$(K):L$(K) = L$(K + 1):L$(K + 1) = T$:SW = 1
1070  NEXT K
1080  IF SW = 0 THEN 1100
1090  NEXT J
1095  REM    --- CONCATENATE LETTERS ---
1100 A$ = "": REM    NULL STRING
1110  FOR X = 1 TO L:A$ = A$ + L$(X): NEXT X
1120  RETURN
```

MODIFICATION

The words can be read from DATA statements as well as be inputted by the user.

LOW RESOLUTION GRAPHICS

Low resolution graphics allows you to draw pictures and designs on a 40 × 40 grid. Full screen graphics can be used to obtain an additional eight rows in place of the text window.

The standard method of getting a background is to execute a loop 40 times to draw 40 vertical and/or horizontal lines. This is effective but slow. A background can be achieved more quickly by using a machine language routine to fill the screen, since assembly language programs can be executed much faster than programs in BASIC.

Interesting designs can be drawn with vertical and horizontal lines and symmetric dots. Warps and spirals can add to the graphics effect. Mosaic designs can be used to sparkle a program.

The lo-res screen can be erased immediately with the GR command. However, if you want to add variety to your programs, you can clear the screen with a program that erases from a corner or center of the screen.

There will be pictures or designs that you will want to use in other programs. You will be shown how to save and load graphics pictures so that they can be used in slide shows and adventure games or quizzes.

Machine language routines will be given to switch the colors of a graphics picture, flip a picture upside down or left to right, and scroll a picture left, right, up, or down.

The machine language routines in this book will be entered as numbers in DATA statements that get poked into unused memory locations. Save the program and you are ready to either BLOAD or BRUN the routine and call it when needed.

FULL SCREEN GRAPHICS

This program displays full screen graphics in the low resolution mode. The text window will hold graphics dots instead of text.

EXPLANATION ══

The screen grid is 40 X 40 with a four-line text window at the bottom. Full screen graphics displays a grid 40 dots across by 48 dots down and no text window. The screen is numbered 0–39 across and 0–47 down.

The command POKE −16302,0 instructs the computer to use full screen graphics. Line 30 fills in the top 40 rows with the desired color. Line 40 fills in the bottom 8 lines with the same color.

Some problems may occur, since the Applesoft text screen and the lo-res graphics screen use the same memory block. As soon as you enter some text, the bottom of the screen represents the text in graphics dots and ruins the effect of the picture. You will have no problem with full screen lo-res graphics provided you avoid using text at the same time.

The strobe command is used to avoid the presence of the cursor on the screen. After the keyboard strobe is cleared on line 60, line 70 strobes the keyboard. The computer waits for a keypress before continuing with the program. The variable A$ on line 80 holds the key pressed.

```
5   REM  === FULL SCREEN GRAPHICS ===
10  GR : HOME
20  COLOR= 6
30  FOR X = 0 TO 39: HLIN 0,39 AT X: VLIN 0,39 AT X: NEX
T X
40  POKE  - 16302,0
50  FOR Y = 40 TO 47: HLIN 0,39 AT Y: NEXT Y
60  POKE  - 16368,0
70  IF  PEEK ( - 16384) < 128 THEN 70
80  GET A$
90  TEXT : HOME : PRINT "NEXT PAGE"
99  END
```

FILLING IN BACKGROUND

FOR. . .NEXT LOOP FILL

You have probably been using a program similar to the following program to fill the screen with a solid color. It fills the screen with 40 horizontal and vertical lines.

```
5   REM  === BACKGROUND ===
10  GR : HOME
20  COLOR= 6
30  FOR X = 0 TO 39: HLIN 0,39 AT X: VLIN 0,39 AT X: NEX
T X
99  END
```

There is a faster way to fill the screen using a machine language program.

INSTANT BACKGROUND 1

This routine will fill the full screen background quickly with your selected color.

EXPLANATION

The following program uses a subroutine to load a machine language program into memory locations 768-812. The values in the DATA statements are codes for machine language instructions and must be copied exactly for this routine to work correctly. Once the machine code is set up, the routine can be accessed with a CALL command.

Line 10 executes the subroutine starting at line 1000. Line 20 sets the graphics mode and clears the text window. The POKE command on line 30 sets full screen graphics. Line 40 calls the machine code subroutine starting at address 768 and fills the screen with color number 12. Line 50 strobes the keyboard. This waits for a keypress and prevents the cursor from appearing on the screen.

The routine starting at line 1000 enters the values from the DATA statements into memory locations 768-812. Line 1010 contains values for machine instructions. Line 1020 returns to the main program. The machine language routine at 1000-1020 needs to be executed only once in the program to set up the machine program at memory location 768. Whenever you want a different color background, simply use CALL 768 followed by a comma and the color number.

The value for the color on line 40 can be any integer from 0 to 255 or any numeric variable or expression that represents a number from 0 to 255.

```
5    REM  === INSTANT BACKGROUND 1 ===
10   GOSUB 1000
20   GR : HOME
30   POKE  - 16302,0
40   CALL 768,12
50   IF  PEEK ( - 16384) < 127 THEN 50
60   TEXT : HOME : PRINT "NEXT PAGE"
99   END
995  REM  --- DATA FOR MACHINE LANGUAGE ROUTINE ---
1000 FOR X = 0 TO 36: READ V: POKE 768 + X,V: NEXT X
1010 DATA    32,76,231,138,41,15,133,254,10,10,10,10,5,
254,160,4,132,7,160,0,132,6,145,6,200,208,251,166,7,232,
134,7,224,8,144,242,96
1020 RETURN
```

INSTANT BACKGROUND 2

This subroutine fills the background quickly with the desired color and does not affect the text window. You may want to include text at the bottom of the screen rather than have full screen graphics or you may already have text in the text window and want the text to remain when the background is changed.

EXPLANATION

This program works in similar manner to Instant Background 1. (See the explanation for that routine.) The subroutine starting at line 1000 writes a slightly different machine language program so text can be included below the background.

The strobe is not needed, since you can write directly to the text window. Use the VTAB command to start the message at the top of the text window.

```
5    REM  === INSTANT BACKGROUND 2 ===
10   GOSUB 1000
20   GR : HOME
30   CALL 768,12
50   VTAB 22: HTAB 13: PRINT "FAST BACKGROUND"
99   END
995  REM  --- DATA FOR MACHINE LANGUAGE ROUTINE ---
1000  FOR X = 0 TO 63: READ V: POKE 768 + X,V: NEXT X
1010  DATA  165,38,141,63,3,165,39,141,64,3,32,76,231,13
8,41,15,133,254,10,10,10,10,5,254,133,254,160,0,152,170,
32,71
1020  DATA  248,165,254,145,38,200,192,40,144,249,160,0,
232,224,20,176,3,138,208,234,173,63,3,133,38,173,64,3,13
3,39,96,234
1030  RETURN
```

AMPERSAND VARIATION OF INSTANT BACKGROUND

The following statement allows you to use the ampersand symbol (&) to call the machine language subroutine.

EXPLANATION

If you want to use the ampersand command instead of CALL 768, then add the following three POKE commands at line 1015 for Instant Background 1 or line 1025 for Instant Background 2.

Instant Background 1:

```
1015 POKE 1013,76: POKE 1014,0: POKE 1015,3
```

Instant Background 2:

```
1025 POKE 1013,76: POKE 1014,0: POKE 1015,3
```

Now you can enter &,C instead of CALL 768,C, where C is the value of the color.

BSAVE

You probably do not want to include the subroutine in every program to obtain a fast-fill background. The following two programs will save the Instant Background routines as binary files.

EXPLANATION ═══

Instant Background 1: This program enters the first machine language routine in memory and saves it as a binary file called FULL BACKGROUND. You can replace the filename FULL BACKGROUND with any legal filename of your choice.

```
1000 FOR X  =  0 TO 36: READ V: POKE 768 + X,V: NEXT X
1010 DATA 32,76,231,138,41,15,133,254,10,10,10,10,5,254,
     160,4,132,7,160,0,132,6,145,6,200,208,251,166,7,232,
     134,7,224,8,144,242,96
1020 PRINT CHR$(4)"BSAVE FULL BACKGROUND,A768,L37"
```

Instant Background 2: This program enters the second machine language routine in memory and saves it as a binary file called PARTIAL BACKGROUND. You can also change this filename.

```
1000 FOR X  =  0 TO 63: READ V: POKE 768 + X,V: NEXT X
1010 DATA 165,38,141,63,3,165,39,141,64,3,32,76,231,
     138,41,15,133,254,10,10,10,10,5,254,133,254,160,0,152,
     170,32,71
1020 DATA 248,165,254,145,38,200,192,40,144,249,160,0,
     232,224,20,176,3,138,208,234,173,63,3,133,38,173,64,
     3,133,39,96,234
1030 PRINT CHR$(4)"BSAVE PARTIAL BACKGROUND,A768,L64"
```

BLOAD

When you want to use one of the background routines in a program, BLOAD it into memory and issue a CALL 768,C, where C is the value of the color desired. As long as the routine is in memory, you do not have to BLOAD it every time you use it.

Do not BRUN the routine, since the results can be disastrous and you may have to reboot the disk.

RELOCATABILITY OF INSTANT BACKGROUND

These two fast-fill background subroutines are relocatable. That is, they can be put at other memory locations and still run the same. This is not always true of machine language programs.

EXPLANATION

If you need to use the memory space at 768 for music or a shape table, then relocate the routine by BLOADing it to a different memory address. For example, you can use 24576 as the starting address of the routine as one option. Then lines 1020 and 1030 in the previous programs would read as follows:

```
1020 PRINT CHR$(4) "BLOAD FULL BACKGROUND,A24576,L37"
```

or

```
1030 PRINT CHR$(4) "BLOAD PARTIAL BACKGROUND,A24576,L63"
```

Remember to use CALL n (n is the address where you loaded it) or unpredictable things can occur. Check the memory map in Appendix B for available space.

WARP IN/OUT

The next two programs produce a three-color warp that moves inward and outward.

EXPLANATION

These programs draw two vertical and two horizontal lines moving in and out from the center to create a warp effect similar to opening and closing a shutter. The effect is not a perfect square, since each dot is wider than it is high.

Boolean logic is used to alternate the color value between a color 1 through 15 and black, which is the color 0. It does this by alternating the value of A between 0 and 1. When A = 0, then the random color at line 40 is 0 or black; and when A = 1, then the color is a random number that ranges from 1 to 15.

Line 20 sets the variables: N stands for 20 executions of the loop, S indicates a step size of 1, and A = 0 initializes variable A to have a starting value of 0.

Line 50 uses a value of A to determine the starting, ending, and step size of the FOR. . .NEXT loop. If A = 0, then (A=1) is evaluated as 0, which is false, and the expression (A=0) is evaluated as 1, which is equivalent to true. The converse holds for A = 1.

The horizontal and vertical lines are drawn at lines 70 and 80. The value of A is switched from 1 to 0 or from 0 to 1 in line 100. If A is 0, then (A=0) is true and is evaluated as 1. Since 1 X 1 = 1, the value of A has switched to 1. The converse holds true for A = 1 initially. If A is 1 at line 100, then (A=0) is false and is evaluated as 0. Since 1 X 0 = 0, then the value of A has been switched from 1 to 0.

Line 85 provides a delay statement. Change the amount of delay to suit your needs.

WARP IN/OUT 1

The variable A on line 40 determines if the color will be a random number 1 to 15 or 0, which is black. A loop is set up on lines 30–110 to loop six times. The first time through the loop a color is selected, while the next time through the loop the color is black to erase the screen.

```
5    REM   === WARP IN/OUT 1 ===
10   GR : HOME
20   N = 20:S = 1:A = 0
30   FOR T = 1 TO 6
40   COLOR= ( INT ( RND (1) * 15) + 1) * (A = 0)
50   FOR X = N * (A = 1) TO N * (A = 0) STEP S * (A = 0)
   - S * (A = 1)
60 Y = 39 - X
70   HLIN Y,X AT Y: VLIN Y,X AT X
80   HLIN Y,X AT X: VLIN Y,X AT Y
85   FOR Z = 1 TO 50: NEXT Z
90   NEXT X
100 A = 1 * (A = 0)
110   NEXT T
199   END
```

MODIFICATION

If you want only one color, then delete lines 30 and 110.

Warp In/Out 2

This program lets you select your own three colors rather than letting the computer randomly select the colors. It is a modification of Warp In/Out 1.

Load Warp In/Out 1 and modify by adding line 25 and changing line 40 to use your selection of colors. Line 25 selects red (1), white (15), and blue (6). On the even times through the loop (30–110), black is used. On the odd times, your selected colors are used.

```
5    REM    === WARP IN/OUT 2 ===
10   GR : HOME
20 N = 20:S = 1:A = 0
25 C(1) = 1:C(3) = 15:C(5) = 6
30    FOR T = 1 TO 6
40    COLOR= C(T) * (A = 0)
50    FOR X = N * (A = 1) TO N * (A = 0) STEP S * (A = 0)
 - S * (A = 1)
60 Y = 39 - X
70    HLIN Y,X AT Y: VLIN Y,X AT X
80    HLIN Y,X AT X: VLIN Y,X AT Y
85    FOR Z = 1 TO 50: NEXT Z
90    NEXT X
100 A = 1 * (A = 0)
110    NEXT T
199    END
```

RECTANGULAR SPIRAL IN/OUT

This program draws a set of concentric rectangles in six selected colors while creating the illusion that it is drawing a spiral in and out.

EXPLANATION

This program is a modification of the Warp In/Out programs. However, it draws the vertical and horizontal lines in the form of a spiral rather than a rectangle. Line 20 initializes the variables: HC represents horizontal center, VC stands for vertical center, N determines the number of times through the FOR. . .NEXT loop, and S indicates a step size of 2, since you want every other line drawn to create a spiral effect.

Line 30 fills a five-dimensioned array C( ) to hold the five selected colors for the spiral. The variable A determines if a color (2, 6, 7, 3, or 11) or black (0) will be used.

The variables H1, H2, V1, and V2 determine the row or column of the horizontal and vertical lines, respectively.

The subroutine at lines 1000–1020 selects the color and provides a delay loop. The color used depends on the value of T.

```
5   REM  === RECTANGULAR SPIRAL IN/OUT ===
10  GR : HOME
20  HC = 19:VC = 19:N = 18:S = 2
30  C(1) = 14:C(2) = 6:C(3) = 11:C(4) = 7:C(5) = 2:C(6) =
    1
40  FOR T = 1 TO 6
50  GOSUB 1000
60  FOR X = N * (A = 0) TO N * (A = 1) STEP S * (A = 1)
    - S * (A = 0)
70  H1 = HC - X:H2 = HC + X + 1
80  V1 = VC - X:V2 = VC + X + 1
90  HLIN H1,H2 AT V1: GOSUB 1000
100   VLIN V1 + 1,V2 AT H2: GOSUB 1000
110   HLIN H2 - 1,H1 AT V2: GOSUB 1000
120   VLIN V2 - 1,V1 + 1 AT H1: GOSUB 1000
130   NEXT X
140 A = 1 * (A = 0)
150   NEXT T
299 END
995 REM  --- SELECT COLOR & DELAY ---
1000  COLOR= C(T)
1010  FOR Z = 1 TO 10: NEXT Z
1020  RETURN
```

MODIFICATION

Vary the step size and the speed of the delay statement.

SPIRAL IN/COLOR OUT/BLACK

This program draws a colored spiral inward in a clockwise direction and then erases the spiral in the reverse direction.

EXPLANATION

The loop at lines 20–110 draws the spiral in a random color starting at the position 0,0. The spiral is drawn in a clockwise direction ending in the center of the screen.

Lines 120–210 draw the spiral in reverse direction in black, giving the effect of erasing the spiral. It starts at the center of the spiral and ends at position 0,0.

Lines 40–60 determine the beginning, ending, and row or column values of the vertical and horizontal lines for the colored spiral. Lines 140 and 180–190 determine these same values for the horizontal and vertical lines that erase the spiral.

The speed of the program can be adjusted by changing the constant 50 in the delay loop subroutine at line 1000.

```
5    REM   === SPIRAL IN/COLOR OUT/BLACK ===
10   GR : HOME
15   REM   --- SPIRAL IN/COLOR ---
20   COLOR=  INT ( RND (1) * 15) + 1
30   FOR B = 0 TO 18 STEP 2
40 E = 39 - B
50   IF B > 0 THEN BB = B
60   IF B = 0 THEN BB = 1
70   HLIN BB - 1,E AT B: GOSUB 1000
80   VLIN B,E AT E: GOSUB 1000
90   HLIN B,E AT E: GOSUB 1000
100   VLIN B + 2,E AT B: GOSUB 1000
110   NEXT B
115   REM   --- SPIRAL OUT/BLACK ---
120   COLOR= 0
130   FOR B = 18 TO 0 STEP  - 2
140 E = 39 - B
150   VLIN B + 2,E AT B: GOSUB 1000
160   HLIN B,E AT E: GOSUB 1000
170   VLIN B,E AT E: GOSUB 1000
180   IF B > 0 THEN BB = B
190   IF B = 0 THEN BB = 1
200   HLIN BB - 1,E AT B: GOSUB 1000
210   NEXT B
299   END
1000   FOR Z = 1 TO 50: NEXT Z: RETURN
```

MODIFICATION

For a continual spiral of varied colors, delete the reverse routine at lines 115–210 and add an outer loop, where N equals the number of times that the spiral should be drawn.

```
16 N = 5
18 FOR X = 1 TO N

120 NEXT X
```

MOSAIC DIAMOND DESIGN

This program draws a mosaic design in a diamond shape. There are many kaleidoscopic effects that you can get with low resolution graphics.

EXPLANATION

C is initialized to 1 and C$ holds the colors of the design expressed as two-digit numbers. The outer loop is executed five times for a variety of colors. The inner loops J and K determine the color and position of the dots to be drawn.

The subroutine at lines 1000–1050 selects a new color from C$. After a color number is used, the contents of C$ are shifted so the used value goes to the end of the list and the next value in line is now in the beginning. The actual plotting is done within this routine. The four plots are symmetric for a balanced effect.

The keyboard is strobed after each completion of the inner loop J. You can stop the design whenever you like and save it as a binary file. See the next example.

```
5    REM   === MOSAIC DIAMOND DESIGN ===
10 C = 1
20 C$ = "020406081012141618202224262830"
30   POKE  - 16368,0: REM     SET STROBE TO ZERO
35   REM   --- MAIN ROUTINE ---
40   GR : HOME
50   FOR T = 1 TO 5
60   FOR J = 0 TO 19
70   IF J / 2 =  INT (J / 2) THEN  GOSUB 1000
80   COLOR= C
90   FOR K = 0 TO J
100 X = K:Y = J - K: GOSUB 1000
110 X = 19 - K:Y = 19 - J + K: GOSUB 1000
120   NEXT K,J
130   IF  PEEK ( - 16384) > 127 THEN 199
140   NEXT T
199   END
995   REM   --- COLOR SELECTION & PLOT DOTS ---
1000 C$ =  MID$ (C$,3) +  LEFT$ (C$,2)
1010 K$ =  LEFT$ (C$,2)
1020 C =  VAL (K$)
1030   PLOT X,Y: PLOT 38 - X,Y
1040   PLOT X,38 - Y: PLOT 38 - X,38 - Y
1050   RETURN
```

MODIFICATION

Change the contents of C$ to color numbers of your choice. The first example runs through all the available colors, while the second example uses only red, white, and blue.

```
C$ = "000102030405060708091011121314l5"
```

or

```
C$ = "011506"
```

PADDLE ADJUSTMENTS

The following statements adjust the paddles from a range of 0 to 255 to any desired range.

BACKGROUND

If you want to use the paddles for a low resolution etch-a-sketch program, you have probably used the following statements to obtain a range of 0 to 39. The 6.5 was obtained by dividing 255 by 39.

```
X = PDL(0)/6.5
Y = PDL(1)/6.5
```

The following two examples demonstrate another technique in general format to easily obtain any range.

EXPLANATION

The standard range of the paddles is 0 to 255. Often, you need a different range such as 1 to 100, 13 to 19, 0 to 39, 0 to 279, 0 to 159, or 0 to 191 for number games or etch-a-sketch programs in low and high resolution graphics.

RANGE 0 TO N

If you want to change the range of the paddle readout from 0 to 255 to a new range 0 to N, where N is the highest number in the new range, use the following technique.

Divide the highest number available on the paddle (255) by 255. This produces the range 0 to 1. Multiply this value by the highest number in your new range (N). This produces a new range of 0 to N.

This program demonstrates this technique. The integer of the paddle readout is needed to return a whole number in the desired range.

```
5   REM  === PADDLE ADJUSTMENT 0-N ===
10   HOME
20  N = 39
30  P0 =   INT ( PDL (0) / 255 * N)
40  P1 =   INT ( PDL (1) / 255 * N)
50   PRINT P0,P1
60   GOTO 30
```

RANGE A TO N

If you want the new range to start at some number other than 0, use the following technique to obtain a range of A to N, where A is the starting value and N is the highest value in the new range.

Divide the paddle readout by 255 to produce a new range of 0 to 1. Multiply this number by N−A, where N is the highest number in the new range and A is the starting number. Add the starting value A to this number to produce the new range A to N.

The following program demonstrates this technique.

```
5   REM  === PADDLE ADJUSTMENT A-N ===
10    HOME
20 N = 19:A = 13
30 P0 =  INT ( PDL (0) / 255 * (N - A)) + A
40 P1 =  INT ( PDL (1) / 255 * (N - A)) + A
50    PRINT P0,P1
60    GOTO 30
```

ANIMATION

MOVING A DOT ACROSS THE SCREEN

The following program moves a dot across the screen without leaving a trail.

EXPLANATION

If you want to make a candle on a cake look as if its flame is flickering, you would draw the dot orange, pause with a delay loop, draw the dot black, red, or yellow, and then replot the original orange dot.

In order to move a dot on the screen, you would perform a similar set of commands. Draw the dot at the desired location, execute a delay loop or ring a bell to stall for time, quickly erase the dot by drawing it in the background color, and redraw it at the new location.

In this program, B represents the starting (beginning) horizontal position, E is the ending horizontal position, and R is the row or vertical position.

```
5   REM  === MOVE LORES DOT 1 ===
10    GR : HOME
20 B = 0:E = 39:R = 10
30    FOR X = B TO E
40    COLOR= 1
50    PLOT X,R
60    FOR Z = 1 TO 50: NEXT Z
70    COLOR= 0
80    PLOT X,R
90    NEXT X
99    END
```

MODIFICATION

In order to move the dot from right to left, change line 30 to read to the following, where S has been defined in line 20 as the step value:

```
20 B = 30: E = 5: R = 10: S = -2
30 FOR X = B TO E STEP S
```

MOVING A DOT UP AND DOWN THE SCREEN

This program moves a dot down the screen.

EXPLANATION

This program is a modification of the previous program. The dot can move down the screen by switching the order of the X and Y coordinates on lines 50 and 80 and changing the R to a C, where C represents the column or horizontal position.

```
5   REM  === MOVE LORES DOT 2 ===
10   GR : HOME
20  B = 5:E = 30:C = 20
30   FOR X = B TO E
40   COLOR= 1
50   PLOT C,X
60   FOR Z = 1 TO 50: NEXT Z
70   COLOR= 0
80   PLOT C,X
90   NEXT X
99   END
```

MODIFICATION

The dot can move up the screen by changing the values of B, E, and S in line 20.

```
20 B = 35:  E = 5:  C = 20:  S = -2
30 FOR X = B TO E STEP S
```

MOVING AN OBJECT WITH FOR . . . NEXT LOOP

The following three programs demonstrate how to move an object on the screen using either a FOR. . .NEXT loop or the keyboard.

BACKGROUND

The object for the following three programs is a simple plus sign, although you can design any object of your choice. The larger the object, however, the slower it will move.

Draw the object to be moved. Select a central point and label it X,Y. Then identify the end points of the dots, horizontal lines, and vertical lines with respect to X and Y. The starting point of X and Y could also be located in a corner such as upper left.

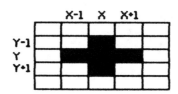

The following statements illustrate how to label the horizontal and vertical lines using X and Y.

```
HLIN X-1,X+1 AT Y
VLIN Y-1,Y+1 AT X
```

To move the object left and right, set the Y as a fixed value and change the value of X. Conversely, to move the object up and down, set X as a fixed value and change the value of Y.

You must check for screen boundaries to avoid an illegal quantity error message. The boundary limits vary depending on your design and which point you identify as the starting point X,Y.

ACROSS THE SCREEN

This program moves a plus sign from left to right without leaving a trail.

EXPLANATION

The subroutine 1000-1020 is used to plot the dots or lines. The advantage of the subroutine is that it saves you from retyping the same PLOT, HLIN, and VLIN commands. Simply change the color and execute the subroutine for animation.

The program could easily be modified to move the dot from right to left. See Moving a Dot Across the Screen for an example of switching the starting and ending points of the FOR. . .NEXT loop and adding a STEP command.

```
5    REM   === MOVE LORES OBJECT/LOOP 1 ===
10   GR : HOME
20 B = 1:E = 38:Y = 5
30   FOR X = B TO E
40   COLOR= 1: GOSUB 1000
50   FOR Z = 1 TO 50: NEXT Z
60   COLOR= 0: GOSUB 1000
70   NEXT X
199   HOME : END
995   REM   --- DRAW ---
1000   HLIN X - 1,X + 1 AT Y
1010   VLIN Y - 1,Y + 1 AT X
1020   RETURN
```

UP AND DOWN THE SCREEN

This program is a variation of the previous program. It moves the plus sign up and down the screen.

EXPLANATION

The subroutine at lines 1000–1020 draws the horizontal and vertical lines. The program could easily be changed to move the object from right to left.

```
5    REM    === MOVE LORES OBJECT/LOOP 2 ===
10   GR : HOME
20   B = 10:E = 30:X = 20
30   FOR Y = B TO E
40   COLOR= 1: GOSUB 1000
50   FOR Z = 1 TO 50: NEXT Z
60   COLOR= 0: GOSUB 1000
70   NEXT Y
199  HOME : END
995  REM   --- DRAW ---
1000  HLIN X - 1,X + 1 AT Y
1010  VLIN Y - 1,Y + 1 AT X
1020  RETURN
```

MOVING AN OBJECT WITH THE KEYBOARD

This program uses the keyboard to move the plus sign up, down, left, and right.

EXPLANATION

The keys A and Z move the plus sign up and down, respectively, while the arrow keys move the object left and right. Line 60 checks illegal keypress.

If you have an Apple IIe/IIc, then you can use the up and down arrow keys in place of A and Z. Change lines 60, 80, and 90.

```
60 IF A$ <> CHR$(11) AND A$ <> CHR$(10) AND A$ <> CHR$(21)
   AND A$ <> CHR$(8) THEN 40
80 IF A$ = CHR$(11) THEN Y = Y - 1
90 IF A$ = CHR$(10) THEN Y = Y + 1
```

The subroutine at lines 1000–1060 checks the end points of the plus sign to avoid an illegal quantity error. When the object reaches the edge of the screen it is drawn on the other side creating a wraparound effect. The commands to draw the plus sign are at 1040–1050.

```
5   REM   === MOVE LORES OBJECT/KEYBOARD ===
10  GR : HOME
20  X = 20:Y = 20
30  COLOR= 1: GOSUB 1000
35  REM  --- GET AND VERIFY KEYPRESS ---
40  VTAB 22: PRINT "ENTER COMMAND: ";: GET A$: PRINT
50  IF A$ =  CHR$ (27) THEN 199
60  IF A$ <  >  CHR$ (65) AND A$ <  >  CHR$ (90) AND A$
<  >  CHR$ (21) AND A$ <  >  CHR$ (8) THEN 40
70  COLOR= 0: GOSUB 1000
80  IF A$ =  CHR$ (65) THEN Y = Y - 1
90  IF A$ =  CHR$ (90) THEN Y = Y + 1
100  IF A$ =  CHR$ (21) THEN X = X + 1
110  IF A$ =  CHR$ (8) THEN X = X - 1
120  GOTO 30
199  HOME : END
995  REM  --- CHECK BOUNDARIES & DRAW ---
1000  IF X < 1 THEN X = 38
1010  IF X > 38 THEN X = 1
1020  IF Y < 1 THEN Y = 38
1030  IF Y > 38 THEN Y = 1
1040  HLIN X - 1,X + 1 AT Y
1050  VLIN Y - 1,Y + 1 AT X
1060  RETURN
```

POKING THE GRAPHICS COLOR

This program demonstrates how memory location 48 can be used to poke in color values. (See Appendix C for color chart.)

EXPLANATION

The program pokes in values from 0 to 255 into location 48. Different combinations of colors appear as alternating horizontal lines. The standard low resolution colors are represented as their value, which ranges from 0 to 15 times 17. Line 30 is used to print the value of the number poked divided by 17. When the standard colors appear, the value is an integer.

```
5   REM   === POKE ALL GR COLORS ===
10  GR : HOME
20  FOR C = 0 TO 255
30  VTAB 22: PRINT C,C / 17;"              "
40  POKE 48,C
50  FOR X = 0 TO 39: HLIN 0,X AT X: VLIN 0,X AT X: NEXT
X
60  VTAB 22: PRINT C,C / 17;"              "
70  GET A$
80  NEXT C
99  END
```

SCRN Command

SCRN Demonstration

This program demonstrates the SCRN command.

EXPLANATION

The SCRN(X,Y) command returns the color number of the dot plotted at coordinates X,Y. The general form is the following statement, where X and Y represent the X and Y coordinates of the point plotted. The variable C can be replaced by any legal numeric variable name. C will return a number from 0 to 15.

```
C = SCRN(X,Y)
```

This command can be used to locate enemy ships, targets, stars, et cetera. If there are several target objects, each of which is composed of various colors, you can test for the background color instead of the target colors.

The color of the target should differ from the object doing the shooting or moving.

The program draws 40 horizontal lines of random colors at lines 20–50 and asks for a row number at lines 60–80. It then uses the SCRN command to return the number of the color of that row at lines 90–110.

The subroutine at lines 1000–1040 clears the indicated row to black and replots the row one dot at a time while ringing a bell.

```
5   REM   === SCRN DEMO ===
10   GR : HOME
20   FOR Y = 0 TO 39
30   COLOR=  INT ( RND (1) * 16)
40   HLIN 0,39 AT Y
50   NEXT Y
55   REM   --- DETERMINE COLOR ---
60   VTAB 23
70   INPUT "ENTER ROW (0-39) ";R
80   IF R > 39 THEN 199
90 C =  SCRN( R,R)
100   VTAB 23: HTAB 22
110   PRINT "COLOR NUMBER IS ";C
120   GOSUB 1000
130   GOTO 70
199   HOME : END
995   REM   --- PLOT DOTS ALONG ROW ---
1000   COLOR= 0: IF C = 0 THEN   COLOR= 15
1010   FOR X = 0 TO 39: PLOT X,R: FOR Z = 1 TO 50: NEXT Z
: NEXT X
1020   COLOR= C
1030   FOR X = 0 TO 39: PLOT X,R: CALL  - 198: NEXT X
1040   RETURN
```

TEST FOR COLLISION

This program draws 10 random dots along the right edge of the screen and you try to hit the targets using the zero paddle.

EXPLANATION

As lines 50–110 loop from 0 to 299, 10 dots are randomly drawn along the right edge of the screen. The routine at 2000–2040 draws the 10 targets and rings a bell.

Line 100 checks if the button on paddle 0 is pressed. When the button is pressed, the routine at 1000–1070 is executed. This routine checks if there is a dot lit at the end of the laser and shoots the laser. If the dot is not lit, then the loop continues at 110. If the dot is lit, then a sound is made at routine 3000–3020.

The program ends when all 10 target dots are plotted and the loop at 50–110 terminates. The final score is printed.

```
5    REM   === LASER SHOOT ===
10   GR : HOME
20   NT = 0:H = 0:F = 0
30   PRINT  TAB( 16)"USE PADDLE 0"
40   HOME
45   REM   --- MAIN ROUTINE ---
50   FOR T = 0 TO 299
60   IF T / 30 =  INT (T / 30) THEN   GOSUB 2000"DRAW TARG
ET"
70   X = 0: COLOR= 0: PLOT X,Y
80   Y =  PDL (0) / 6.5
90   COLOR= 10: PLOT X,Y
100   IF  PEEK ( - 16287) > 127 THEN   GOSUB 1000"DRAW LAS
ER"
110   NEXT T
120   HOME : PRINT "YOU HIT "H" TARGETS OUT OF A POSSIBLE
 "NT
199   END
995   REM   --- CHECK SCREEN POSITION & SHOOT LASER ---
1000   IF  SCRN( 39,Y) = 6 THEN H = H + 1:F = 1
1010   FOR L = 1 TO 39: COLOR= 9: PLOT L,Y: NEXT L
1020   FOR L = 1 TO 39: COLOR= 0: PLOT L,Y: NEXT L
1050   IF F = 1 THEN   GOSUB 3000
1070   RETURN
1995   REM   --- DRAW TARGET ---
2000  TY =  INT ( RND (1) * 40)
2010   COLOR= 6: PLOT 39,TY
2020  NT = NT + 1
2030   PRINT  CHR$ (7)
2040   RETURN
2995   REM   --- SOUND ---
3000   FOR B = 1 TO 10:S =  PEEK ( - 16336):SOUND = S + S
 + S + S: NEXT B
3010  F = 0
3020   RETURN
```

ERASING THE GRAPHICS SCREEN

The next four subroutines demonstrate different methods of erasing the low resolution graphics picture. These routines can be used at the end of a graphics picture that is to be erased or they can be used as subroutines to be reused throughout the program. In each program, the screen is filled with a solid color for demonstration purposes.

FROM UPPER LEFT CORNER

This program is similar to the program of the same name in Chapter 3. The subroutine at 1000–1040 sets up a loop that will draw 40 black vertical and horizontal lines starting at the upper left corner.

```
5    REM   === ERASE GR UPPER LEFT CORNER ===
7    REM   --- GRAPHIC PROGRAM ---
10   GR : HOME : COLOR=  INT ( RND (1) * 15) + 1
20   FOR X = 0 TO 39: HLIN 0,39 AT X: VLIN 0,39 AT X: NEX
T X
30   GET A$
40   GOSUB 1000
499  END
995  REM   --- ERASE ROUTINE ---
1000  COLOR= C
1010  FOR X = 0 TO 39
1020  VLIN 0,39 AT X: HLIN 0,39 AT X
1030  NEXT X
1040  RETURN
```

FROM LOWER RIGHT CORNER

This program resembles the program of the same name in Chapter 3. Forty black vertical and horizontal lines are drawn starting at the lower right corner.

```
5    REM   === ERASE GR LOWER RIGHT CORNER ===
7    REM   --- GRAPHIC PROGRAM ---
10   GR : HOME : COLOR=  INT ( RND (1) * 15) + 1
20   FOR X = 0 TO 39: HLIN 0,39 AT X: VLIN 0,39 AT X: NEX
T X
30   GET A$
40   GOSUB 1000
499  END
995  REM   --- ERASE ROUTINE ---
1000  COLOR= 0
1010  FOR X = 39 TO 0 STEP  - 1
1020  VLIN 0,39 AT X: HLIN 0,39 AT X
1030  NEXT X
1040  RETURN
```

With Warp In

This routine is a modification of the program Warp Erase in Chapter 3. The subroutine at 1000–1050 draws rectangles from the edges toward the center creating a warp effect.

```
5   REM   === ERASE GR WARP IN ===
7   REM   --- GRAPHIC PROGRAM ---
10  GR : HOME : COLOR= INT ( RND (1) * 15) + 1
20  FOR X = 0 TO 39: HLIN 0,39 AT X: VLIN 0,39 AT X: NEX
T X
30  GET A$
40  GOSUB 1000
499 END
995 REM   --- ERASE ROUTINE ---
1000  COLOR= 0
1010  FOR X = 0 TO 19
1020  HLIN 0,39 AT X: HLIN 0,39 AT 39 - X
1030  VLIN 0,39 AT X: VLIN 0,39 AT 39 - X
1040  NEXT X
1050  RETURN
```

With Warp Out

This program is also a modification of Warp Erase in Chapter 3. The subroutine at lines 1000–1050 draws the warp starting in the center, extending it to the screen edges.

```
5   REM   === ERASE GR WARP OUT ===
7   REM   --- GRAPHIC PROGRAM ---
10  GR : HOME : COLOR= INT ( RND (1) * 15) + 1
20  FOR X = 0 TO 39: HLIN 0,39 AT X: VLIN 0,39 AT X: NEX
T X
30  GET A$
40  GOSUB 1000
499 END
995 REM   --- ERASE ROUTINE ---
1000  COLOR= 0
1010  FOR X = 19 TO 0 STEP  - 1
1020  HLIN X,39 - X AT X: HLIN X,39 - X AT 39 - X
1030  VLIN X,39 - X AT X: VLIN X,39 - X AT 39 - X
1040  NEXT X
1050  RETURN
```

SAVING A GRAPHICS PICTURE
IN THE PROGRAM MODE

This shows you how to save a low resolution graphics picture to disk using the command BSAVE. You may have a design or picture that you would like to keep and use in other programs. Perhaps you only want the design and do not care to see the design being created. You can save the picture as a binary file and load that picture whenever needed.

This can be used in a quiz, adventure game, simulation, demonstration, slide show presentation of your artwork, or as the first display when your disk is booted.

BACKGROUND

Saving a binary picture involves saving that portion of memory that holds the picture.

The command BSAVE saves the binary image. You must specify the picture name, starting address, and length. The length specifies the number of bytes in the image. You can express the address and length in either decimal or hexadecimal notation.

With low resolution graphics, the memory locations and addresses are always the same, unless you have changed some memory locations at the start of the program or are using page 2 of graphics. The standard starting address is $400 in hexadecimal notation or 1024 in decimal notation. The length is $400 in hexadecimal or 1024 in decimal. Hexadecimal notation is base 16, and the dollar sign is the signal to the computer that the number is a hexadecimal number.

The disk drive will save the picture as a B file. A binary file is not a program itself. It is the binary image of the low resolution graphics screen. A binary file can be locked, unlocked, renamed, and deleted just as an Applesoft, Integer, or Text file.

Binary files allow you to use graphics pictures without having to watch them being drawn and they permit the same pictures to be easily used in different programs.

EXPLANATION

Draw the picture on the screen. Type in one of the following statements, where picturename is the name of your picture. Follow the same rules for selecting a name for your binary file as you would when you save any other file or program.

If you try to BSAVE a picture in the immediate mode, the statement used to BSAVE the picture will be saved along with the picture in the text window. Therefore, use a short program to clear the text screen and save the file.

WITH BLANK TEXT WINDOW

Either of the two sets of the following statements can be used alone in the immediate mode or added to the program as the last line. If you are saving the picture from within a BASIC program, the BSAVE command must be preceded by a CONTROL D command, which is represented by CHR$(4).

The HOME command clears the screen so only the picture is saved and the text window is blank. These pictures can then be used in an adventure game, where you will add text to the picture after it is loaded.

```
890 HOME
900 PRINT CHR$(4) "BSAVE picturename,A$400,L$400"
```

or

```
890 HOME
900 PRINT CHR$(4) "BSAVE picturename,A1024,L1024"
```

After GET with Blank Text Window

If a GET command has been used before you BSAVE the picture, then concatenate a carriage return before the CHR$(4) command, since all disk drive commands must be preceded by a carriage return.

```
890 HOME
900 PRINT CHR$(13)+CHR$(4)"BSAVE picturename,A$400,L$400"
```

With Title

If you want a title or some writing at the bottom of the screen to identify the picture when it is loaded back, then place the title or message on the screen before you save the picture. This way the picture and title or message are saved together. This can be used to identify pictures, scenes, or the person who drew the picture for a slide show.

This can also be done in the immediate mode by using the following commands without line numbers. Either the hexadecimal or decimal notation can be used.

```
890 HOME
895 VTAB 22: HTAB 13: PRINT"THE BEST YET"
900 PRINT CHR$(4);"BSAVE picturename,A$400,L$400"
```

WITH VARIABLE NAME

You can write a program that lets the user draw interesting designs with an etch-a-sketch type of format. The user can use the keyboard, paddles, or a combination of keyboard and paddles to draw the picture. You can use the CONTROL S command to indicate that the user wants to save the picture. Ask the user for the name of the picture, center the title, and save the picture. The player can continue drawing on the picture or can erase the picture.

The following statements can be added to the program to indicate that the picture is to be saved as a binary file. The line numbers may differ in your program.

Line 300 gets your command to move the dot or draw a line. If a CONTROL S, which is equivalent to CHR$(19), is pressed, then branch to the subroutine at 1000. The subroutine at 1000–1040 asks for the filename and verifies that a filename has been entered, saves the program, and returns to the main program.

The quotes are used on line 1060 to enclose the command. The string variable F$ represents a string variable that holds the name of the picture and is not the name of the picture itself. So F$ must not be included in quotes or the computer will interpet it literally.

You can add a title to the picture or leave the text window blank. If a title is added, then line 1050 centers the title automatically.

```
290 PRINT "ENTER COMMAND:";
300 GET A$
310 IF A$=CHR$(19) THEN GOSUB 1000
320 rest of program
   .
   .
   .
995 REM === SAVE BINARY FILE ===
1000 HOME: VTAB 22: INPUT "ENTER FILENAME >>> ";F$
1010 IF A$="" THEN 1000
1020 INPUT "ENTER TITLE (RETURN IF NONE) ";T$
1030 HOME
1040 IF T$="" THEN 1060
1050 VTAB 22: HTAB 20-LEN(T$)/2: PRINT T$
1060 PRINT CHR$(13)+CHR$(4);"BSAVE";F$;",A1024,L1024"
1070 RETURN
```

You might want to add a check that the filename begins with a letter of the alphabet, has no commas within the name, and has 30 characters or less. You can also check that the title is 39 characters or less.

1. Add this line to check the length of the filename.

```
1002 IF LEN(F$) > 30 THEN 1000
```

2. Add this statement to check that the first character is a letter of the alphabet.

```
1004 IF ASC(LEFT(F$,1,1) < 64 OR ASC(LEFT$(F$,1,1) > 90
     THEN 1000
```

3. The following loop will check for a colon or quote.

```
1005 FOR X = 1 to LEN(F$)
1006 M$ = MID$(F$,X,1)
1007 IF M$ = ":" or M$ = CHR$(34) THEN X = LEN(F$):GOTO 1000
1008 NEXT X
```

RETRIEVING A GRAPHICS PICTURE

This demonstrates how to retrieve a saved graphics picture to be used in another program such as an adventure game, a quiz, a slide show, or as the title page of a program.

BACKGROUND

To retrieve a picture that has been saved with a BSAVE command for use later, simply load it back into memory with a BLOAD command. The computer will load it at the same address that you originally saved it unless you specify a different location.

Unlike the LOAD command, the BLOAD command will not erase the program or data values unless they reside in the same memory location where the image is stored. Only the locations within the BLOAD range are changed. No other memory location is affected.

Do not BRUN a binary graphics image or you will get unpredictable results.

EXPLANATION

You can retrieve a binary file in the immediate or the program mode. Enter the command GR to enter the graphics mode before loading the file. If you omit the GR command, the binary file will load in as text rather than graphics. Picturename refers to the name of the binary file that will store your picture. Substitute any legal filename for the word picturename.

```
GR
BLOAD picturename
```

or

```
40 GR
50 PRINT CHR$(4)"BLOAD picturename"
```

When you BLOAD the picture, it will load it onto the screen exactly as it looked at the time it was saved, including text in the text window.

SPECIAL EFFECTS WITH MACHINE LANGUAGE ROUTINES

The following routines provide special effects that can be executed fast enough only in machine language. The same effects can be obtained with BASIC commands, but it would take so long that the effect would be lost.

You do not have to know anything about machine language to enter or access these routines, since the coding for the machine language routines has been entered into DATA statements for your convenience. Copy the DATA statements exactly because each number corresponds to a specific command.

Once all the data items have been poked into memory, you can access the special effects routine with a CALL command, which directs the computer to the starting address of the machine language routine.

The address locations have been selected so that all seven special effects routines can be in memory at the same time. The routines load above one another. This enables you to access multiple routines without having to BLOAD each one when needed.

You can use the keyboard or paddles/joystick to access more than one routine in your BASIC program.

The five Applesoft programs poke the actual special effects routine into memory. Thus, once the routine is poked in, it is ready for use.

All but the Switch Color routines leave the text window intact.

The routines remain in memory until you turn off the computer or load another routine or program into their locations.

To view the full effect of the following special effects routines, BSAVE a low resolution picture that uses all the lo-res colors. Use that picture in the programs or write a simple etch-a-sketch program to draw a design.

In order to use the next five special effects routines, you must first follow certain steps. Step A need only be followed the very first time. Thereafter, start with Step 1.

STEP A: ENTERING ROUTINES FOR THE FIRST TIME ONLY

Type in each of the following programs: LORES SCREEN EOR.A, GV SCREEN FLIP.A, GH SCREEN FLIP.A, LORES UPSCROLL.A, and LORES DOWNSCROLL.A. Save each program to disk and run each to set up the machine language routine in memory. The program will ask if you want to save the routine. If the routine has not already been saved, then answer Y. The special effects routine is now ready for use. Type NEW after each program has been run.

After you follow this step for all five Applesoft programs, you will have five binary files that contain the machine language code for the special effects routines.

After you run and answer Y to this Applesoft program:	You will obtain this binary file:
LORES SCREEN EOR.A	LORES SCREEN EOR
GV SCREEN FLIP.A	GV SCREEN FLIP
GH SCREEN FLIP.A	GH SCREEN FLIP
LORES UPSCROLL.A	LORES UPSCROLL
LORES DOWNSCROLL.A	LORES DOWNSCROLL

Step 1: BLOADing a Special Effects Routine

If you have followed the directions in Step A, then the routines are in memory and ready to use. However, if the routines have previously been BSAVEd and the computer has been turned off, or if a program has been loaded in its memory location, then a routine must be loaded into memory for you to access it. There are two ways to do this.

The first method is to run the Applesoft program again and answer N. The second technique is to BLOAD the routine with the following command, where filename is the name of the binary file saved when the Applesoft program was run and you answered Y.

    BLOAD filename

Step 2: Loading a Lo-Res Graphics Picture

Run a program to draw a low resolution graphics picture, or type GR and BLOAD a picture to get the image on the screen.

Step 3: Calling a Special Effects Routine

You are now ready to call the specific machine language routine by issuing a CALL A command, where A is the starting address of the special effects routine desired. The value for A will be provided for each routine.

REVERSING COLORS OF THE GRAPHICS SCREEN

This routine will change the colors of a graphics picture according to the number entered.

EXPLANATION ════════════════════════════════════

This program pokes the values contained in the DATA statements into memory starting at address 768.

Load this routine in memory with the following command:

    BLOAD LORES SCREEN EOR

After you get the graphics image on the screen, issue the command CALL 768,C (where C is a number 1–15). C can be a constant or a numeric expression that evaluates to a value of 1–15. For example, you could use CALL command

```
10  CALL 768,15
20  HOME
```

or

```
10  C = 5
20  CALL 768,C
30  HOME
```

or

```
10  X = 2
20  CALL 768, (X = 2) * 13
30  HOME
```

If you enter a number such that C < 1 or C > 15, then this routine will not function properly.

To get the original colors back after calling this routine with a specific number, call it again with the exact same number.

Since this routine affects the text window, issue a HOME command after you call the routine.

```
5   REM  === LORES SCREEN EOR.A ===
10   HOME
20   FOR X = 0 TO 51: READ V: POKE 768 + X,V: NEXT
30   PRINT "SAVE TO DISK (Y/N): ";: GET A$: IF A$ = "N" T
HEN  END
40   IF A$ < > "Y" THEN 30
50   PRINT  CHR$ (13); CHR$ (4);"BSAVE LORES SCREEN EOR,A
$300,L$34"
99   END
100   DATA 32,76,231,189,36,3,141,35,3,169
110   DATA 0,133,6,168,169,4,133,7,170,177
120   DATA 6,77,35,3,145,6,200,208,246,230
130   DATA 7,202,208,241,96,0,0,17,34,51
140   DATA 68,85,102,119,136,153,170,187,204,221
150   DATA 238,255
```

FLIPPING THE SCREEN UPSIDE DOWN

This routine flips the screen upside down.

EXPLANATION

Load this routine into memory with the command:

`BLOAD GV SCREEN FLIP`

This routine loads into memory starting at address 24576. After your graphics image is on the screen, access this routine with a CALL 24576 command. To return the screen to its original position, reissue the CALL command.

```
5    REM  === GV SCREEN FLIP.A ===
10   HOME
20   FOR X = 0 TO 79: READ V: POKE 24576 + X,V: NEXT
30   PRINT "SAVE TO DISK (Y/N): ";: GET A$: IF A$ = "N" T
HEN  END
40   IF A$ < > "Y" THEN 30
50   PRINT  CHR$ (13); CHR$ (4);"BSAVE GV SCREEN FLIP,A$6
000,L$50"
99   END
100  DATA 169,0,141,81,96,169,19,141,82,96
110  DATA 32,71,248,165,38,133,6,165,39,133
120  DATA 7,173,81,96,32,71,248,160,39,177
130  DATA 6,32,62,96,72,177,38,32,62,96
140  DATA 145,6,104,145,38,136,16,237,238,81
150  DATA 96,206,82,96,173,82,96,201,9,208
160  DATA 205,96,170,74,74,74,74,141,80,96
170  DATA 138,10,10,10,10,24,109,80,96,96
```

FLIPPING THE SCREEN LEFT TO RIGHT

This routine gives the mirror image of the original picture by flipping the screen (left becomes right and right becomes left).

EXPLANATION

Load this routine into memory with the following command:

`BLOAD GH SCREEN FLIP`

After you have your graphics picture on the screen, use the CALL 24659 to flip the picture. This routine has been loaded in memory starting at address 24659. To return the image to its starting position, issue the same CALL command.

```
5   REM  === GH SCREEN FLIP.A ===
10    HOME
20    FOR X = 0 TO 60: READ V: POKE 24659 + X,V: NEXT X
30    PRINT "SAVE TO DISK (Y/N): ";: GET A$: IF A$ = "N" T
HEN  END
40    IF A$ < > "Y" THEN 30
50    PRINT  CHR$ (13); CHR$ (4);"BSAVE GH SCREEN FLIP,A$6
053,L$3D"
99    END
100   DATA 169,0,141,144,96,141,145,96,168,32
110   DATA 71,248,172,145,96,177,38,72,169,39
120   DATA 56,237,145,96,168,177,38,170,104,145
130   DATA 38,172,145,96,138,145,38,200,140,145
140   DATA 96,192,20,208,226,160,0,140,145,96
150   DATA 238,144,96,173,144,96,201,20,208,205,96
```

SCROLLING THE SCREEN UP

This routine scrolls the graphics image up the screen.

EXPLANATION

Load this routine into memory with the following command:

BLOAD LORES UPSCROLL

This routine is loaded into memory at location 24722. Each time the routine is called, it scrolls the screen up two horizontal lines. The top two horizontal lines reappear at the bottom to provide a wraparound effect. To access this routine, use CALL 24722.

```
5   REM  === LORES UPSCROLL.A ===
10    HOME
20    FOR X = 0 TO 136: READ V: POKE X + 24722,V: NEXT
30    PRINT "SAVE TO DISK (Y/N): ";: GET A$: IF A$ = "N" T
HEN  END
40    IF A$ < > "Y" THEN 30
50    PRINT  CHR$ (13); CHR$ (4);"BSAVE LORES UPSCROLL,A$6
092,L$89"
99    END
100   DATA 160,0,185,0,4,141,255,63,185,128
110   DATA 4,153,0,4,185,0,5,153,128,4
120   DATA 185,128,5,153,0,5,185,0,6,153
130   DATA 128,5,185,128,6,153,0,6,185,0
140   DATA 7,153,128,6,185,128,7,153,0,7
150   DATA 185,40,4,153,128,7,185,168,4,153
160   DATA 40,4,185,40,5,153,168,4,185,168
170   DATA 5,153,40,5,185,40,6,153,168,5
180   DATA 185,168,6,153,40,6,185,40,7,153
190   DATA 168,6,185,168,7,153,40,7,185,80
200   DATA 4,153,168,7,185,208,4,153,80,4
210   DATA 185,80,5,153,208,4,185,208,5,153
220   DATA 80,5,173,255,63,153,208,5,200,192
230   DATA 40,240,3,76,148,96,96
```

SCROLLING THE SCREEN DOWN

This routine scrolls the graphics image down the screen.

EXPLANATION ══

Load this routine with the following command:

BLOAD LORES DOWNSCROLL

This routine is stored starting at memory location 24859. Each time this routine is accessed, it scrolls the screen down two horizontal lines. Use a CALL 24859 to use this routine. This routine also wraps the picture around.

```
5    REM  === LORES DOWNSCROLL.A ===
10   HOME
20   FOR X = 0 TO 136: READ V: POKE 24859 + X,V: NEXT
30   PRINT "SAVE TO DISK (Y/N): ";: GET A$: IF A$ = "N" T
HEN  END
40   IF A$ < > "Y" THEN 30
50   PRINT  CHR$ (13); CHR$ (4);"BSAVE LORES DOWNSCROLL,A
$611B,L$89"
99   END
100  DATA 160,0,185,208,5,141,255,63,185,80
110  DATA 5,153,208,5,185,208,4,153,80,5
120  DATA 185,80,4,153,208,4,185,168,7,153
130  DATA 80,4,185,40,7,153,168,7,185,168
140  DATA 6,153,40,7,185,40,6,153,168,6
150  DATA 185,168,5,153,40,6,185,40,5,153
160  DATA 168,5,185,168,4,153,40,5,185,40
170  DATA 4,153,168,4,185,128,7,153,40,4
180  DATA 185,0,7,153,128,7,185,128,6,153
190  DATA 0,7,185,0,6,153,128,6,185,128
200  DATA 5,153,0,6,185,0,5,153,128,5
210  DATA 185,128,4,153,0,5,185,0,4,153
220  DATA 128,4,173,255,63,153,0,4,200,192
230  DATA 40,240,3,76,29,97,96
```

SETTING UP AND ACCESSING LEFT AND RIGHT SCROLLING ROUTINES

The following two special effects routines are entered in a manner different from the previous five. As mentioned earlier, each program creates a machine language generator routine that then creates the special effects routine.

This double creation method was designed with you in mind. It saves you from entering 100 additional data items.

In order to use the next two special effects routines, you must first follow these steps. Step A need only be followed the very first time. Thereafter, start with Step 1.

STEP A: ENTERING THE GENERATOR ROUTINES FOR THE FIRST TIME ONLY

Type in each of the following two programs: LORES LEFTSCROLL.A and LORES RIGHTSCROLL.A. Save each program to disk and run each to set up the machine language generator routine in memory. The program will ask if you want to save the routine. If the routine has not already been saved, then answer Y. Type NEW before typing in the next program.

After you follow this step for both Applesoft programs, you will have two binary files that contain the machine language code for the generator routines.

After you run and answer Y to this Applesoft program:

You will obtain this binary file:

```
LORES LEFTSCROLL.A    LORES LEFTSCROLL
LORES RIGHTSCROLL.A   LORES RIGHTSCROLL
```

STEP 1: CREATING A SPECIAL EFFECTS ROUTINE

If you have followed the directions in Step A, then each generator routine has been saved to disk. The special effects routine is not yet ready for use. You must issue a BRUN filename command, where filename is either LORES LEFTSCROLL or LORES RIGHTSCROLL, depending on the routine you want loaded into memory. The BRUN command instructs the computer to execute the generator routine that creates the actual scrolling routine. The special effects routine is now ready for use.

STEP 2: LOADING A LO-RES GRAPHICS PICTURES

Run a program to draw a low resolution graphics picture, or type GR and BLOAD a picture to get the image on the screen.

STEP 3: CALLING A SPECIAL EFFECTS ROUTINE

After you have your graphics image on the screen, issue the command CALL A to activate the desired routine, where A is the starting address of the special effects routine. The value of A will be provided for each routine.

SCROLLING THE SCREEN LEFT

This routine scrolls the graphics screen left one line at a time.

EXPLANATION

Load the routine into memory with the following command:

BRUN LORES LEFTSCROLL

The machine language routine starts at address 24996. The command CALL 24996 scrolls the screen one line to the left with a wraparound effect.

```
5    REM  === LORES LEFTSCROLL.A ===
10   HOME
20   FOR X = 0 TO 230: READ V: POKE 28672 + X,V: NEXT
30   PRINT "SAVE TO DISK (Y/N): ";: GET A$: IF A$ = "N" T
HEN   END
40   IF A$ < > "Y" THEN 30
50   PRINT  CHR$ (13); CHR$ (4);"BSAVE LORES LEFTSCROLL,A
$7000,L$E7"
100   DATA 169,164,133,6,160,0,169,97,133,7
110   DATA 140,231,112,152,162,23,32,71,248,169
120   DATA 173,145,6,200,165,38,145,6,200,165
130   DATA 39,145,6,200,169,141,145,6,200,138
140   DATA 232,145,6,200,169,99,145,6,32,207
150   DATA 112,238,231,112,173,231,112,201,20,208
160   DATA 211,169,160,145,6,200,169,0,145,6
170   DATA 32,207,112,140,231,112,162,1,142,232
180   DATA 112,169,185,32,181,112,206,232,112,169
190   DATA 153,32,181,112,238,232,112,238,231,112
200   DATA 173,231,112,201,20,208,230,160,7,185
210   DATA 223,112,145,6,136,16,248,160,7,32
220   DATA 207,112,140,231,112,152,162,23,32,71
230   DATA 248,169,173,145,6,200,138,145,6,200
240   DATA 169,99,145,6,200,169,141,145,6,200
250   DATA 165,38,24,105,39,145,6,200,165,39
260   DATA 145,6,32,207,112,232,238,231,112,173
270   DATA 231,112,201,20,208,208,169,96,145,6
280   DATA 96,72,173,231,112,32,71,248,160,0
290   DATA 104,145,6,200,165,38,24,109,232,112
300   DATA 145,6,200,165,39,145,6,200,24,152
310   DATA 101,6,133,6,165,7,105,0,133,7
320   DATA 160,0,96,200,192,39,240,3,76,30
330   DATA 98
```

This routine scrolls the graphics screen to the right.

EXPLANATION

Load this routine into memory with this command:

BRUN LORES RIGHTSCROLL

This routine starts at location 25387 and scrolls the screen right one vertical line with a wraparound effect each time it is called. To access this routine, use the command CALL 25387.

```
5    REM  === LORES RIGHTSCROLL.A ===
10   HOME
20   FOR X = 0 TO 228: READ V: POKE 28672 + X,V: NEXT
30   PRINT "SAVE TO DISK (Y/N): ";: GET A$: IF A$ = "N" T
HEN  END
40   IF A$ < > "Y" THEN 30
50   PRINT  CHR$ (13); CHR$ (4);"BSAVE LORES RIGHTSCROLL,
A$7000,L$E5"
99   END
100  DATA 169,43,133,6,160,0,169,99,133,7
110  DATA 140,229,112,152,162,156,32,71,248,169
120  DATA 173,145,6,200,165,38,24,105,39,145
130  DATA 6,200,165,39,145,6,200,169,141,145
140  DATA 6,200,138,232,145,6,200,169,100,145
150  DATA 6,32,207,112,238,229,112,173,229,112
160  DATA 201,20,208,208,169,160,145,6,200,169
170  DATA 38,145,6,32,207,112,140,229,112,162
180  DATA 0,142,230,112,169,185,32,181,112,238
190  DATA 230,112,169,153,32,181,112,206,230,112
200  DATA 238,229,112,173,229,112,201,20,208,230
210  DATA 160,5,185,223,112,145,6,136,16,248
220  DATA 160,5,32,207,112,140,229,112,152,162
230  DATA 156,32,71,248,169,173,145,6,200,138
240  DATA 145,6,200,169,100,145,6,200,169,141
250  DATA 145,6,200,165,38,145,6,200,165,39
260  DATA 145,6,32,207,112,232,238,229,112,173
270  DATA 229,112,201,20,208,211,169,96,145,6
280  DATA 96,72,173,229,112,32,71,248,160,0
290  DATA 104,145,6,200,165,38,24,109,230,112
300  DATA 145,6,200,165,39,145,6,200,24,152
310  DATA 101,6,133,6,165,7,105,0,133,7
320  DATA 160,0,96,136,48,3,76,165,99
```

PADDLE DEMONSTRATION OF SPECIAL EFFECTS ROUTINES

The following program demonstrates the use of the special effects routines with paddle control.

This program assumes that you have run all the special effects routines and answered Y to save the binary files for the routines. It also assumes that they are all on the same disk, and that disk is inserted in the logged disk drive.

Lines 20-70 present a simple etch-a-sketch program to plot a design on the low resolution graphics screen. The button on paddle 0 changes the colors of the dots, while the button on paddle 1 ends the sketching routine and executes line 80. This design can then be flipped upside down, scrolled in the four directions, and have its colors switched.

Line 80 BLOADs the five special effects routines that are listed in the DATA statement on line 1000, while line 90 BRUNs the left and right scrolling routines.

The routine at lines 100-180 allows you to access the machine language routines with paddle and button controls. The ESC key ends the program. Depending on the button you press or the reading of your paddle, the program calls the appropriate routine.

Table 6-1 indicates how to access the special effects routines.

TABLE 6-1. ACCESSING SPECIAL EFFECTS ROUTINES WITH PADDLE

Special Effects Routine	How to Access It
Switching colors	C and number 0-15 (RETURN)
Flipping upside down	Button on paddle 0
Flipping sideways	Button on paddle 1
Scrolling up	Paddle 1 when it reads <87
Scrolling down	Paddle 1 when it reads >167
Scrolling left	Paddle 0 when it reads <87
Scrolling right	Paddle 0 when it reads >167

```
5   REM   === LORES PADDLE DEMO ===
10  D$ =  CHR$ (13) +  CHR$ (4)
15   REM   --- DRAW LORES PICTURE ---
20   GR :C = 2: COLOR= C: HOME : VTAB 21: PRINT "COLOR="C
30  X =  PDL (0) * .153:Y =  PDL (1) * .153: PLOT X,Y: IF
    PEEK ( - 16286) > 127 THEN  HOME : GOTO 80
40   IF  PEEK ( - 16287) < 128 THEN CH = 0: GOTO 30
50   IF CH THEN 30
60  CH = 1:C = C + 1: IF C = 16 THEN C = 0
70   COLOR= C: VTAB 21: PRINT "COLOR="C" ": GOTO 30
75   REM   --- BLOAD ROUTINES ---
80   FOR X = 1 TO 5: READ N$: PRINT D$"BLOAD"N$: NEXT X
90   PRINT D$"BRUN LORES LEFTSCROLL": PRINT D$"BRUN LORES
    RIGHTSCROLL": POKE  - 16368,0
95   REM   --- EXECUTE ROUTINES ---
100  IF  PEEK ( - 16384) = 155 THEN 199
110  IF  PDL (0) > 167 THEN  CALL 25387
120  IF  PDL (0) < 87 THEN  CALL 24996
130  IF  PDL (1) > 167 THEN  CALL 24859
140  IF  PDL (1) < 87 THEN  CALL 24722
150  IF  PEEK ( - 16287) > 127 THEN  CALL 24576
160  IF  PEEK ( - 16286) > 127 THEN  CALL 24659
170  IF  PEEK ( - 16384) <  > 195 THEN 100
180  POKE  - 16368,0: VTAB 21: INPUT "EOR FACTOR: ";N$:N
  =  VAL (N$): CALL 768,N: HOME : GOTO 110
199  HOME : END
995  REM   --- NAMES OF FIRST FIVE ROUTINES ---
1000  DATA LORES SCREEN EQR,GV SCREEN FLIP,GH SCREEN FLI
P,LORES UPSCROLL,LORES DOWNSCROLL
```

KEYBOARD DEMONSTRATION OF SPECIAL EFFECTS ROUTINES

This program demonstrates the use of the special effects routines with keyboard control.

EXPLANATION _____

The program assumes that you have run all the special effects routines and answered Y to save the binary files for the routines. It also assumes that they are all on the disk that is inserted in the drive that you are logged onto.

Lines 20–90 draw a simple etch-a-sketch. The keys I, J, K, and M move the dot up, left, right, and down, respectively. Line 30 gets the keypress and adjusts the X and Y values accordingly. Line 40 prevents an illegal quantity error by keeping the dot on the graphics screen. The space bar at lines 50 and 80–90 changes the color, which can range from 0 to 15.

The ESC key executes line 100, which BLOADs the programs in DATA statement 100. Then line 100 BRUNs the left and right scrolling routines.

The routine at lines 120–210 allows you to access the machine language routines with keyboard control. The ESC key ends the program. Depending on the key you press, the program calls the appropriate routine.

Table 6-2 indicates how to access the special effects routines. The space bar stops the scrolling or flipping.

TABLE 6-2. ACCESSING SPECIAL EFFECTS ROUTINES WITH KEYBOARD

Special Effects Routine	How to Access It
Switching colors	C and number 0–15
Flipping upside down	Q
Flipping sideways	W
Scrolling up	I
Scrolling down	M
Scrolling left	J
Scrolling right	K

```
5   REM  === LORES KEYBOARD DEMO ===
10  D$ =  CHR$ (13) +  CHR$ (4)
15   REM  --- DRAW LORES PICTURE ---
20   GR :C = 2: COLOR= C:X = 20:Y = 20: HOME : VTAB 21: P
RINT "COLOR="C
30   GET A$:X = X + (A$ = "K") - (A$ = "J"):X = X + (X <
0) - (X > 39)
40 Y = Y + (A$ = "M") - (A$ = "I"):Y = Y + (Y < 0) - (Y
> 39)
50   IF A$ = " " THEN 80
60   IF  ASC (A$) = 27 THEN  HOME : GOTO 100
70   PLOT X,Y: GOTO 30
80 C = C + 1: IF C = 16 THEN C = 0
90   COLOR= C: VTAB 21: PRINT "COLOR="C" ": GOTO 30
95   REM  --- BLOAD ROUTINES ---
100   FOR X = 1 TO 5: READ N$: PRINT D$"BLOAD"N$: NEXT X
110   PRINT D$"BRUN LORES LEFTSCROLL": PRINT D$"BRUN LORE
S RIGHTSCROLL": POKE  - 16368,0
115   REM  --- EXECUTE ROUTINES ---
120   IF  PEEK ( - 16384) = 155 THEN 299
130   IF  PEEK ( - 16384) = 203 THEN  CALL 25387
140   IF  PEEK ( - 16384) = 202 THEN  CALL 24996
150   IF  PEEK ( - 16384) = 205 THEN  CALL 24859
160   IF  PEEK ( - 16384) = 201 THEN  CALL 24722
170   IF  PEEK ( - 16384) = 209 THEN  CALL 24576: GOTO 12
0
180   IF  PEEK ( - 16384) = 215 THEN  CALL 24659: GOTO 12
0
190   IF  PEEK ( - 16384) = 160 THEN 120
200   IF  PEEK ( - 16384) <  > 195 THEN 120
210   POKE  - 16368,0: VTAB 21: INPUT "EOR FACTOR: ";N$:N
 =  VAL (N$): CALL 768,N: HOME : GOTO 120
299   HOME : END
995   REM  --- NAMES OF FIRST FIVE ROUTINES ---
1000   DATA LORES SCREEN EOR,GV SCREEN FLIP,GH SCREEN FLI
P,LORES UPSCROLL,LORES DOWNSCROLL
```

HIGH RESOLUTION GRAPHICS

High resolution graphics offers finer detail in your pictures than low resolution graphics, but fewer colors.

A machine language already built into Applesoft BASIC that gives you an instant background in the color of your choice is discussed, and a routine to erase the screen in a novel way is presented.

There are two pages of high resolution graphics—page 1 and page 2. The command HGR sets page 1, while the command HGR2 sets page 2 of graphics. You can draw full screen graphics on page 1 or page 2 of graphics.

This chapter introduces the set of soft switches that you can either POKE or PEEK to switch between low and high resolution graphics, between page 1 and page 2 of memory, between mixed screen and full screen graphics, or between the graphics and the text page.

You will be shown how to save and load hi-res graphics pictures for use in other programs or a slide show. The slide show will be explained in Chapter 9.

Shape tables will be used to change the colors of your picture to their complementary colors for an interesting effect. The complementary sets of colors are: black and white, blue and orange/red, and violet and green.

High resolution graphics offers eight colors, including two blacks and two whites. More colors can be obtained by alternating the colors of horizontal lines or poking in a value and calling a built-in routine to fill the screen with a variety of colored vertical lines.

Bit-mapped graphics is introduced to enable you to add alphanumeric characters to the high resolution graphics screen. You can also design any other character that fits on a grid 7 dots across by 8 dots down.

The addressing of the screen does not correlate exactly with the memory addresses. A formula is provided to convert any row and column to the correct memory address for that block on the graphics screen.

Several machine language programs are presented that allow you to take a high resolution graphics picture and reverse the colors to their complementary color, flip the picture from left to right, and turn it upside down. Routines to scroll the picture left or right in either the original color or the complementary color and to scroll the picture up and down the screen are also provided.

BACKGROUND

The following program draws a solid background, but it does so slowly.

```
10 HGR:HCOLOR=7
20 FOR X = 0 TO 279:HPLOT X,0 TO X,159: NEXT X
```

There is another way of getting a solid background by using a built-in machine language routine that you can call when needed.

There are two methods. They are demonstrated in HGR on page 1, but you could also use HGR2.

INSTANT BACKGROUND METHOD 1

The following program provides an instant background.

EXPLANATION

Both methods use a built-in machine language routine at address −3082. Memory location −3082 is the same as memory location 62454.

With this method, you must plot a dot (anywhere) on the screen in the color that you want for the background. This program plotted a point at the origin 0,0 where it is least noticeable. Then, when you call the routine, it fills in the background in the last color plotted.

```
10 HGR: HCOLOR=6: HPLOT 0,0: CALL −3082
```

or

```
10 HGR: HCOLOR=6: HPLOT 0,0: CALL 62454
```

INSTANT BACKGROUND METHOD 2

This program fills the screen instantly with a solid color.

EXPLANATION

With this method you poke in the value for the color. There is a different set of numbers to get the high resolution colors than the standard 0–7. Table 7-1 indicates the standard colors.

TABLE 7-1. COLOR CHART

Number	Color
0	Black
42	Green
85	Violet
127	White
128	Black
170	Orange/red
213	Blue
255	White

```
10 HGR: X = 213: POKE 28,X: CALL −3082
```

or

```
10 HGR: X = 213: POKE 28,X: CALL 62454
```

SCREEN ERASER

This subroutine erases a screen in high resolution graphics and provides a different effect than the standard HGR or HGR2 command to erase the screen.

EXPLANATION

Black is the color selected, and vertical lines are drawn from each edge of the screen to the opposite edge.

Use this subroutine whenever you want to erase the screen in a different manner.

```
5    REM    === HIRES SCREEN ERASER ===
7    REM    --- YOUR HIRES PROGRAM ---
10   HGR2
20   FOR T = 1 TO 50
30 C =   INT ( RND (1) * 7) + 1
40   IF C = 4 THEN 30
50   HCOLOR= C
60 X1 =   INT ( RND (1) * 280)
70 Y1 =   INT ( RND (1) * 192)
80 X2 =   INT ( RND (1) * 280)
90 Y2 =   INT ( RND (1) * 192)
100   HPLOT X1,Y1 TO X2,Y2
110   NEXT T
120   GET A$
130   GOSUB 1000
199   END
1000   HCOLOR= 0
1020   FOR X = 0 TO 279 STEP 2
1030   HPLOT X,0 TO X,191
1040   HPLOT 279 - X,0 TO 279 - X,191
1050   NEXT
1060   TEXT : HOME
1070   RETURN
```

SOFT SWITCHES

The video display is controlled by sets of soft switches that are located in the read only memory (ROM). These switches can be set in two different positions. They are located at eight reserved memory locations that are addressed by −16304 to −16297 or their positive equivalents, 49232 to 49239 (Table 7-2).

The addresses can be expressed as a positive number such as 49232 or its negative equivalent −16304. The negative number is obtained by taking the positive number and subtracting 65536 (or 2 raised to the 16th power) from it: 49232 − 65536 = − 16304.

TABLE 7-2.
SOFT SWITCHES

SET	FUNCTION	ADDRESS
1a	Graphics mode	−16304 or 49232
1b	Text mode	−16303 or 49233
2a	Full screen	−16302 or 49234
2b	Mixed screen	−16301 or 49235
3a	Page 1	−16300 or 49236
3b	Page 2	−16299 or 49237
4a	Text/lo-res	−16298 or 49238
4b	Hi-res	−16297 or 49239

You can access these locations by poking a 0 into their location or they can be toggled by peeking them.

When you issue the command HGR, the computer sets the switches to 1a, 2b, 3a, and 4b. When you issue the command HGR2, the computer automatically sets the switches to 1a, 2a, 3b, and 4b. The command TEXT sets the switches to 1b, 2a, 3a, and 4a.

SOFT SWITCHES

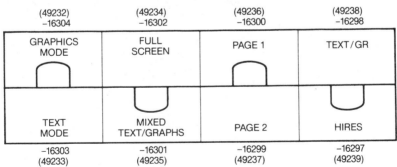

Switches in up or down position

POKING MEMORY LOCATIONS

PAGE 1 WITH FULL SCREEN GRAPHICS

This statement uses the command HGR and a particular POKE command to get full screen graphics on page 1.

BACKGROUND

HGR uses page 1 of graphics, while HGR2 uses page 2. HGR also gives a mixed text/graphics screen, while HGR2 gives a full graphics screen with no text window.

The page refers to a specific area of memory and not whether it is mixed or full screen. See the memory map in Appendix B. It is possible to obtain full screen graphics on page 1 by adding a particular POKE command.

EXPLANATION

You can get full screen graphics on page 1 using the HGR command along with the POKE command POKE −16302,0, which sets full screen graphics.

```
HGR: POKE -16302,0
```

Full screen graphics extends the number of horizontal rows by adding on 32 additional lines of graphics. Mixed mode graphics ranges from 0 to 159 and full screen ranges from 0 to 191 lines.

However, if you try to access page 2 in the mixed text/graphics mode, you get garbage (a random mixture of characters) in the text window that cannot be erased with the HOME command. The text window normally holds the last four lines of page 1 of text. In this case, the last four lines of page 2 of text are being displayed.

You cannot easily write in the text window of page 2 in the mixed text/graphics unless you have a specific routine. Thus, page 2 is primarily for full screen graphics, whereas page 1 can be used for either full screen or mixed text and graphics.

POKE COMMANDS EQUIVALENT TO HGR OR HGR2

Instead of the commands HGR or HGR2, you can use the equivalent POKE commands. The commands HGR and HGR2 erase the graphics screen, whereas the POKE commands do not affect the screen.

EXPLANATION

The commands HGR and HGR2 erase the high resolution page selected. You may want to use the graphics mode without erasing the display screen. This can be done by accessing the graphics mode with either POKE −16304,0 or K = PEEK(−16304) and then using additional POKE or PEEK commands to determine the full or mixed screen mode, page 1 or page 2, and low or high-resolution graphics.

Replace HGR with:

```
POKE −16304,0:POKE −16301,0:POKE −16300,0:POKE −16297,0
```

Replace HGR2 with:

```
POKE −16304,0:POKE −16302,0:POKE −16299,0:POKE −16297,0
```

If you switch pages with the POKE commands and want to go back to the original page and continue plotting on it, then you must enter an additional POKE command that tells the computer on which page the HPLOTs or HPLOT TOs will be drawn.

To plot on page 1 enter:

```
POKE 230,32
```

To plot on page 2 enter:

```
POKE 230,64
```

Switching Between Text and Graphics Page

This program allows you to switch between the text page and graphics screen. This can be used for an adventure program to switch between viewing the text description of the location and the high resolution graphics picture of the location without erasing either screen.

EXPLANATION

The following commands switch between the text screen and the graphics screen.

```
POKE -16303,0        (graphics to text page)
POKE -16304,0        (text to graphics page)
```

This can also be used for printing a message on the text page while waiting for a graphics design to be drawn on the graphics page. Once the design is drawn, it can then be viewed.

The next chapter introduces designs that are drawn using the sine and cosine functions. Some of these designs take a while to be HPLOTed. The text screen can give a description of the program or concept, and when the design is complete it can switch to the graphics screen.

```
5    REM   === TEXT-GRAPHICS FLIP ===
7    REM   --- GRAPHIC SCREEN ---
10   TEXT : HGR
20   HCOLOR= 3
30   HPLOT 0,0 TO 279,159
40   HPLOT 279,0 TO 0,159
45   REM   --- STROBE KEYBOARD ---
50   POKE  - 16368,0
60   HOME
70   VTAB 22: PRINT "PRESS ANY KEY FOR TEXT SCREEN ";
80   WAIT  - 16384,128
90 K =  PEEK ( - 16384): IF K - 128 = 27 THEN 199
100   POKE  - 16368,0: REM   RESET STROBE
105   REM   --- TEXT SCREEN ---
110   TEXT : HOME : VTAB 12: HTAB 10
120   INVERSE : PRINT "THIS IS THE TEXT SCREEN": NORMAL
125   REM   --- STROBE KEYBOARD ---
130   VTAB 22: PRINT "PRESS ANY KEY TO RETURN TO PICTURE
";
140   WAIT  - 16384,128
150 K =  PEEK ( - 16384): IF K - 128 = 27 THEN 199
160   POKE  - 16368,0
165   REM   --- DISPLAY HIRES PAGE 1 MIXED MODE ---
170   POKE  - 16304,0: POKE  - 16301,0: POKE  - 16300,0:
POKE  - 16297,0
180   GOTO 60
199   TEXT : HOME : END
```

SAVING A PICTURE WITH BSAVE

The following statements show you how to save a high resolution graphics picture from either page 1 or page 2, in the immediate mode or from a program.

EXPLANATION

Chapter 6 explained how to save a low resolution graphics picture. Refer to that section for an explanation of how to BSAVE a picture.

The hi-res picture can be saved from either page 1 or page 2 of graphics. This can be done in the immediate mode or from within a program.

Since the hi-res graphics page 1 and page 2 are separate from the text window, you cannot save a picture with the text window displaying a title or message. The full hi-res picture gets saved whether you are viewing it as a full screen or mixed text/graphics screen. If you want a title or message, then you will have to add it after the picture is loaded.

FROM PAGE 1

To save a hi-res picture from page 1 in the immediate mode, enter the following line, where picturename is the name of your hi-res picture. You can use either decimal or hexadecimal notation. The dollar sign ($) indicates hexadecimal notation. The number after the letter A represents the starting address of memory, while the number following L represents the length of the binary file.

```
BSAVE picturename,A8192,L8192
```

or

```
BSAVE picturename,A$2000,L$2000
```

The numbering of line 990 may have to be adjusted for your program. If the command to BSAVE a picture is preceded by a GET command, be sure to concatenate a carriage return to the beginning of line 990.

```
990 PRINT CHR$(4)"BSAVE picturename,A8192,L8192"
```

or

```
990 PRINT CHR$(4)"BSAVE picturename,A$2000,L$2000"
```

FROM PAGE 2

To save a hi-res picture from page 2 in the immediate mode, enter the following line, where picturename is the name of your hi-res picture. Either the decimal or hexadecimal notation can be used. The number after the letter A represents the starting address of memory, while the number following L represents the length of the binary file.

```
BSAVE picturename,A16384,L8192
```

or

```
BSAVE picturename,A$4000,L$2000
```

The numbering of line 990 may have to be adjusted for your program. If the command to BSAVE a picture is preceded by a GET command, be sure to concatenate a carriage return to the beginning of line 990.

```
990 PRINT CHR$(4)"BSAVE picturename,A16384,L8192"
```

or

```
990 PRINT CHR$(4)"BSAVE picturename,A$4000,L$2000"
```

SAVING AN EXTRA SECTOR ON THE DISK

Normally, the high resolution graphics image takes 34 sectors on a disk. If you enter a length of 8184 (L8184) instead of 8192, the image will take 33 sectors. By dropping the last eight bytes of the binary image, you save a sector on the disk without affecting the graphics picture. You can use the decimal length 8192 or the hexadecimal equivalent $1FF8.

From Page 1:

```
BSAVE picturename,A8192,L8184
```

or

```
BSAVE picturename,A$2000,L$1FF8
```

From Page 2:

```
BSAVE picturename,A16384,A8184
```

or

```
BSAVE picturename,A$4000,L$1FF8
```

LOADING A PICTURE WITH BLOAD

This presents the statement that retrieves a high resolution picture from disk and loads it into memory. A picture can be loaded to either page 1 or page 2 of memory regardless of the page on which it was originally saved. This is useful for page flipping, which is demonstrated in Chapter 9.

LOADING TO SAME PAGE

The following statements load a hi-res picture to the page on which it was originally drawn and from which it was saved. Use the commands HGR or HGR2 or the equivalent POKE commands, depending on which page the picture was originally drawn and saved from. These sets of statements can be issued in either the immediate or program mode.

```
HGR or HGR2
BLOAD picturename
```

or

```
980 HGR or HGR2
990 PRINT CHR$(4) "BLOAD picturename"
```

LOADING TO DIFFERENT PAGE

The following statements allow you to load a high resolution graphics picture to page 2 if it was saved on page 1, and to page 1 if it was saved on page 2. Enter the necessary POKE commands to get full screen graphics or mixed text and graphics.

LOADING TO PAGE 1 FROM PAGE 2

These statements load a picture originally saved from page 2 onto page 1 and can be issued in either the immediate or program mode.

```
HGR: POKE -16302,0
BLOAD picturename,A8192
```

or

```
980 HGR: POKE -16302,0
990 PRINT CHR$(4)"BLOAD picturename,A8192"
```

LOADING TO PAGE 2 FROM PAGE 1

These statements load a picture originally saved from page 1 onto page 2 and can be issued in either the immediate or program mode.

```
HGR2
BLOAD picturename,A16384
```

or

```
980 HGR2
990 PRINT CHR$(4)"BLOAD picturename,A16384"
```

SHOWING FULL GRAPHICS

This statement allows you to view the full graphics screen.

EXPLANATION

If you load a picture onto page 1 after issuing the HGR command, you may only see part of the picture. This occurs if the picture was originally drawn on page 2 with full screen graphics using either HGR2 or HGR:POKE −16302,0.

If you type the following POKE command, the text window will close and allow the rest of the graphics picture to be displayed.

```
POKE −16302,0
```

or

```
POKE 49234,0
```

PICTURE INVERSER

The following two subroutines can be added to the end of your program to change the colors of a graphics picture to their complementary colors: black to white, blue to orange/red, and violet to green, and vice versa.

Shape tables and the XDRAW command are used to produce the color flip.

VERTICAL INVERSER

This subroutine draws the graphics picture in its complementary colors starting at the left edge of the screen.

EXPLANATION

This program uses a shape table to draw one shape. The shape moves and plots up one space. It is scaled to 192 so the line will fill the entire screen from top to bottom. When a shape is XDRAWn, it draws in the complement of the background color.

This program draws a random design at lines 10–100 in order to demonstrate the inverser subroutine. When you want to use your own graphics image, delete lines 10–110 and BLOAD the high resolution graphics picture to page 1 with full screen graphics or to page 2 using the following commands, where picturename is the name of the picture:

Loading to page 1:

```
HGR:POKE −16302,0
BLOAD picturename,A$2000
```

Loading to page 2:

```
HGR2
BLOAD picturename,A$4000
```

Lines 1000–1040 set up the shape table at memory location 24576 with a zero rotation and scale size of 192. The loop at lines 1050–1070 XDRAWs the shape to create the complementary color effect.

```
5    REM === VERTICAL INVERSER ===
7    REM  --- BLOAD OR DRAW HIRES PICTURE ---
10   HGR2
20   FOR N = 1 TO 25
30 C =  INT ( RND (1) * 7) + 1: IF C = 4 THEN 30
40   HCOLOR= C
50 X1 =  INT ( RND (1) * 280)
60 Y1 =  INT ( RND (1) * 192)
70 X2 =  INT ( RND (1) * 280)
80 Y2 =  INT ( RND (1) * 192)
90   HPLOT X1,Y1 TO X2,Y2
100   NEXT N
110   GET A$
120   GOSUB 1000
199   END
995   REM  --- INVERSE COLORS ---
1000 L = 24576
1010  FOR X = L TO L + 5: READ V: POKE X,V: NEXT X
1020  DATA  1,0,4,0,4,0
1030  POKE 232,0: POKE 233,96
1040  ROT= 0: SCALE= 192
1050  FOR X = 0 TO 279
1060  XDRAW 1 AT X,0
1070  NEXT X
1080  RETURN
```

HORIZONTAL INVERSER

This subroutine draws the graphics picture in its complementary colors starting at the top edge of the screen.

EXPLANATION

This program uses a shape table to draw one shape. The shape moves right and plots two spaces. It is scaled to 140 so the line will fill the entire screen from left to right. Two vectors are used, since the maximum value for the SCALE command is 255 and the screen is 280 dots across. With two vectors (move right and plot two times) the scale can be set at 140 for a full line across the screen.

This program draws a random design at lines 10-100 in order to demonstrate the inverser subroutine. When you want to use your own graphics image, delete lines 10-110 and BLOAD the high resolution graphics picture to page 1 with full screen graphics or to page 2 using the following commands, where picturename is the name of the picture:

Loading to page 1:

```
HGR:POKE -16302,0
BLOAD picturename,A$2000
```

Loading to page 2:

```
HGR2
BLOAD picturename,A$4000
```

Lines 1000-1040 set up the shape table at memory location 24576 with a zero rotation and scale size of 140. The loop at lines 1050-1070 XDRAWS the shape to create the complementary color effect.

```
5    REM   === HORIZONTAL INVERSER ===
7    REM   --- BLOAD OR DRAW HIRES PICTURE ---
10   HGR2
20   FOR N = 1 TO 25
30 C =  INT ( RND (1) * 7) + 1: IF C = 4 THEN 30
40   HCOLOR= C
50 X1 =  INT ( RND (1) * 280)
60 Y1 =  INT ( RND (1) * 192)
70 X2 =  INT ( RND (1) * 280)
80 Y2 =  INT ( RND (1) * 192)
90   HPLOT X1,Y1 TO X2,Y2
100   NEXT N
110   GET A$
120   GOSUB 1000
199   END
995   REM   --- INVERSE COLORS ---
1000 L = 24576
1010  FOR X = L TO L + 6: READ V: POKE X,V: NEXT X
1020  DATA  1,0,4,0,5,5,0
1030  POKE 232,0: POKE 233,96
1040  ROT= 0: SCALE= 140
1050  FOR Y = 0 TO 191
```

```
1060    XDRAW 1 AT 0,Y
1070    NEXT Y
1080    RETURN
```

COLOR

PIXEL

The resolution of the graphics screen is expressed in terms of pixels. Pixel is short for picture element, which represents the smallest unit that can be turned on or off on the video display screen. The Apple offers a resolution of 280 × 192, which means 280 pixels or dots horizontally by 192 vertically.

The screen does not show every color in every location. Only black and white pixels can be plotted at every position. The remaining four colors appear in alternate columns. When you HPLOT a vertical line, you can plot the even colors 2 and 6 only at even-numbered columns, and the odd colors green and orange only at the odd-numbered columns.

Both page 1 and page 2 contain 8192 bytes of memory. Each of these bytes contains eight bits. Seven of these eight bits determine which pixels will be lit. Each pixel on the hi-res graphics screen has a bit in memory assigned to it. If the bit is a 1, then the corresponding pixel on the screen is lit. If the bit is a 0, then the pixel is not lit. The eighth bit, or high bit, determines the color.

The color of a dot depends on its position on the screen and the value of the leftmost bit. The leftmost bit, often called the high bit or most significant bit, controls the color of the other seven bits by determining which color group will be displayed. Bits in even columns are either violet or blue, while bits in odd columns are either green or orange. If the leftmost bit (high bit) is off, the colors are violet and green. If the leftmost bit is on, the colors are blue and orange.

There is no white color per se. When blue and orange are next to each other they appear white, and when green and violet are next to each other they also appear white. Therefore, there are two different whites possible. There are also two different blacks. When the seven rightmost bits are 0, the high bit can be on or off.

Any dot on an even X-coordinate will appear as white, black, violet, or blue, whereas any dot on an odd X-coordinate will appear as white, black, orange, or green. When the high bit is on you get blue, orange, white, or black. When the high bit is off you get violet, green, white, or black.

Table 7-3 indicates the color of the pixel (or dot) on the screen when it is in an even or odd column with its high bit on or off.

TABLE 7-3.
PIXEL COLORS

| High | X-coordinate | |
bit	Even	Odd
On	Blue	Orange
Off	Violet	Green

The command HGR turns all the dots off on page 1, whereas HGR2 turns all the dots off on page 2. This is accomplished by changing every byte to 0, thereby changing every bit to 0 and thus clearing the screen.

PREVENTING THE LOSS OF VERTICAL LINES

These methods prevent the loss of vertical lines.

FIXED COLOR

If you have set the color at a fixed color number, then use even columns to plot the even colors (colors 2 and 6) and odd columns to plot the odd colors (colors 1 and 5).

RANDOM COLORS

If you use random colors and want to avoid losing the vertical lines, then double plot the vertical lines. Double plotting means plotting a line at location X and another at location X+1. When the color number is even (colors 2 and 6), the line at the even column will be plotted, and when the color number is odd (colors 1 and 5), the line at the odd columns will be plotted.

Line 40 draws a border at the screen limits; line 50 double plots the border. Omit line 50 to see why it is needed.

```
5   REM  === RANDOM COLOR HIRES BORDER ===
10  HGR : HOME
20 C =  INT ( RND (1) * 7) + 1: IF C = 4 THEN 20
30  HCOLOR= C
40  HPLOT 0,0 TO 279,0 TO 279,159 TO 0,159 TO 0,0
50  HPLOT 1,0 TO 278,0 TO 278,159 TO 1,159 TO 1,0
60  FOR Z = 1 TO 500: NEXT Z
70  GOTO 20
```

GETTING 36 HGR COLORS

The following program alternates between two different colors for the horizontal lines creating a pattern of colors.

EXPLANATION

The nested loops at 40–90 draw 36 sets of vertical lines. Each set is composed of combinations of the six colors available (green, blue, white, black, orange, and violet).

The outermost loop counts from 20 to 140 in steps of 2 to set the row number. The middle loop (40–90) counts from 1 to 6 and places 36 horizontal lines five dots wide of that color plotting one row at a time. The innermost loop (50–90) counts from 1 to 6 and places 36 horizontal lines five dots wide of that color.

The following diagram indicates the combinations of the colors.

```
20      111111 222222 333333 444444 555555 666666
21      123456 123456 123456 123456 123456 123456
22      111111 222222 333333 444444 555555 666666
23      123456 123456 123456 123456 123456 123456

..       ...    ...    ...    ...    ...    ...

140     123456 123456 123456 123456 123456 123456
```

```
5   REM  === HGR 36 COLORS ===
10   HGR : HOME
20   FOR Y = 20 TO 140 STEP 2
30 XP = 13
40   FOR A = 1 TO 6
50   FOR B = 1 TO 6
60   HCOLOR= A: HPLOT XP,Y TO XP + 4,Y
70   HCOLOR= B: HPLOT XP,Y + 1 TO XP + 4,Y + 1
80 XP = XP + 7
90   NEXT B,A,Y
99   END
```

MIXING COLORS

This program demonstrates two ways to fill the background with a mix of two colors.

EXPLANATION

This program draws the full background in a variety of combinations of colors similar to the previous program. It shows two methods to fill in the background. The subroutine at lines 1000–1050 fills the background instantly with the command CALL —3082 (explained earlier in this chapter) and then fills in every other line with a different color.

The subroutine at lines 2000–2060 fills in one line with the first color and the next line with the second color, alternating until the screen is completely filled.

```
5    REM  === MIX HGR COLORS ===
10   HGR
20   HOME : VTAB 22
30   INPUT "ENTER TWO COLORS (0-7) ";C1,C2
40   INPUT "ENTER 1 OR 2  (3 TO QUIT) ";A
50   HGR
60   ON A GOSUB 1000,2000,99
70   GOTO 20
99   HOME : END
995  REM  --- INSTANT SCREEN AND FILL EVERY OTHER LINE -
--
1000  HCOLOR= C1: HPLOT 0,0: CALL  - 3082
1010  HCOLOR= C2
1020  FOR Y = 0 TO 159 STEP 2
1030  HPLOT 0,Y TO 279,Y
1040  NEXT Y
1050  RETURN
1995  REM  --- FILL EVERY OTHER LINE ---
2000  FOR Y = 0 TO 159 STEP 2
2010  HCOLOR= C1
2020  HPLOT 0,Y TO 279,Y
2030  HCOLOR= C2
2040  HPLOT 0,Y + 1 TO 279,Y + 1
2050  NEXT Y
2060  RETURN
```

MODIFICATION

Subroutine 2000–2060 can be easily modified to draw any rectangular shape of a variety of colors.

POKE HGR COLORS

This program demonstrates how you can use memory location 28 to poke in a value from 0 to 255 to obtain a variety of colored vertical lines.

EXPLANATION ───

Memory location 28 holds the high resolution color. Table 7-4 indicates the values that return the eight standard hi-res colors.

	Standard	No. in
TABLE 7-4. HI-RES COLOR VALUES IN LOCATION 28		
Color	Color No.	Location 28
Black 1	0	0
Green	1	42
Violet	2	85
White 1	3	127
Black 2	4	128
Orange	5	170
Blue	6	213
White 2	7	255

The loop at 30–80 loops through the numbers from 0 to 255 and pokes them into memory location 28. It then calls the routine to instantly fill in the background.

Eight of the numbers produce a solid screen, while the remaining 248 numbers produce a variety of colored vertical lines.

```
5    REM   === POKE ALL HGR COLORS ===
10   HGR : HOME
20   HPLOT 0,0
30   FOR X = 0 TO 255
40   VTAB 22: PRINT X
50   POKE 28,X
60   CALL  - 3082
70   GET A$
80   NEXT X
99   END
```

PEEK HCOLOR AND POSITION OF
LAST DOT PLOTTED

This program demonstrates four POKE commands that return the color (coded) and the horizontal and vertical positions of the last dot plotted on the screen.

EXPLANATION

This program draws a line from the origin 0,0 to a random location on the screen in a random color (0–8). Lines 80 and 90 print the value of the random color and the values of X and Y that determine the horizontal and vertical positions of the last dot HPLOTted.

Memory location 228 holds the value of the last HCOLOR command in the code format given in Table 7-5.

TABLE 7-5. HCOLOR VALUES IN MEMORY LOCATION 228

Color	Standard Color No.	No. in Location 228
Black 1	0	0
Green	1	42
Violet	2	85
White 1	3	127
Black 2	4	128
Orange	5	170
Blue	6	213
White 2	7	255

Line 100 prints the value of the HCOLOR command by peeking location 228.

Lines 110–120 print the horizontal and vertical values of the last dot HPLOTted. These values are obtained by peeking locations 225 (high byte of X), 224 (low byte of X), and 226 (Y).

The Apple has 65536 (2^{16}) possible memory locations. Two bytes are needed to store a number in the range 0–65535. If the number of the address is in the range 0–255, the low or least significant byte holds the address, and the high or most significant byte holds 0. When the number is in the range 256–65535, then two bytes are needed to express that number.

Memory location 225 returns the high byte of the X-coordinate, while 224 returns the low byte. To convert this to a number in the range 0–279, multiply the high byte by 256 and add the low byte.

Memory location 226 returns the low byte of the Y-coordinate. Since Y ranges from 0 to 191, only a low byte is needed.

```
5   REM   === PEEK HCOLOR & POSITION ===
10   HGR : HOME
20 X =   INT ( RND (1) * 280)
30 Y =   INT ( RND (1) * 160)
40 C =   INT ( RND (1) * 8)
50   HCOLOR= C
60   HPLOT 0,0 TO X,Y
70   VTAB 22
80   PRINT "RND: COLOR="C,
90   PRINT "X = "X,"Y = "Y
100   PRINT "PEEK:COLOR=" PEEK (228),
110   PRINT "X = " PEEK (225) * 256 +  PEEK (224),
120   PRINT "Y = " PEEK (226)
130   GET A$
140   GOTO 10
```

BIT MAPPING

A correspondence between the dots of light on the high resolution graphics screen and the value of the bit is called a map. This technique for generating video displays is called bit mapping. Each dot on the graphics screen is "mapped" into a certain bit in memory. If you set a certain bit in memory to 1, then the corresponding pixel on the screen will light up.

CORRELATION OF MEMORY ADDRESSING

Adjacent screen columns on the hi-res graphics screen are consecutively numbered, but the rows are not.

Table 7-6 displays the screen numbering as it correlates with memory addressing.

The memory locations assigned to the hi-res graphics screen are displayed on the screen as 40 columns and 24 rows of blocks. Each block represents 1 byte across and 8 bytes down. Each byte contains 8 bits. Seven of these bits control 7 pixels on the graphics screen and the 8th bit (high bit or most significant bit) controls the color group.

The 7 rightmost bits of each of these 40 bytes plot a dot for a total of 280 dots or pixels across the screen. Each of the 24 rows contains 8 bytes for a total of 192 (24 × 8 = 192) dots or pixels down the screen.

Pages 1 and 2 of hi-res graphics use only 7680 bytes (24 rows × 40 blocks × 8 bytes/block) of the possible 8192 bytes allocated for those pages. There are 512 memory addresses that do not plot to the hi-res graphics screen.

TABLE 7-6. MEMORY MAP OF HI-RES GRAPHICS SCREEN PAGE 1

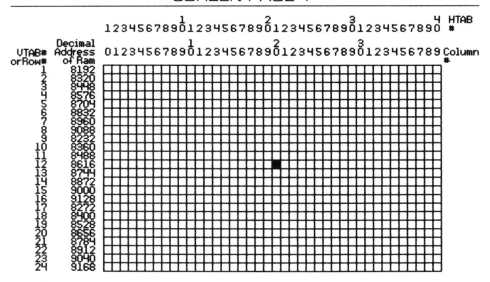

SHADED BLOCK

To obtain the starting address of any block, take the decimal number from the row address plus the column number (0–39). The addresses of the next bytes in the block are obtained by adding 1024 to the previous address and continuing until you have the addresses of all 8 bytes of the block (see Table 7-7).

TABLE 7-7. DECIMAL ADDRESSES OF THE 8 BYTES

7x8 BLOCK	BYTE	ADDRESS	COMPUTATION
	1st byte*	8636	= 8616 + 20
	2nd byte	9660	= 8636 + 1024
	3rd byte	10684	= 9660 + 1024
	4th byte	11708	= 10684 + 1024
	5th byte	12737	= 11708 + 1024
	6th byte	13756	= 12737 + 1024
	7th byte	14780	= 13756 + 1024
	8th byte	15804	= 14780 + 1024

* Starting Address of block

SUBSEQUENT ADDRESSES

The starting address of subsequent blocks down the screen is obtained by adding 128 to the previous address within rows 1–8, 9–16, and 17–24. The starting address of the block at the 9th row is equal to the starting address of the 1st row plus 40, whereas the starting address of the block at the 17th row is equal to the starting address of the 1st row plus 80.

You can think of the screen as divided into three major sets called triads. The first triad holds rows 1–8, the second holds rows 9–16, and the third holds rows 17–24.

The following rules indicate how to get from one address in memory to another:

1. Add 1 to get from one column to the next.
2. Add 40 to go from one triad to the next.
3. Add 128 to get from one row within the triad to the next.
4. Add 1024 to get from one horizontal line of the block to the next line of the block.

SCREEN ADDRESSING

This program demonstrates how the memory addressing correlates with the screen addressing.

EXPLANATION ═══

The value of N, which can range from 0 to 255, is poked into each memory location from 8192 to 16383.

The screen is not filled in from left to right and then down the screen as you might expect. One row of each triad is filled in at a time until the screen is completely filled in.

```
5    REM   === SCREEN ADDRESSING DEMO ===
10   HGR : POKE   - 16301,0: HOME
20 N = 255
30   FOR A = 8192 TO 16383
40   POKE A,N
50   NEXT A
99   END
```

SPECIFIC BIT-MAPPED CHARACTER

This program places the letter S at any position on the high resolution graphics screen that you specify.

EXPLANATION ═══

The program demonstrates the correlation of the pixels or dots on the hi-res screen with the bits in memory.

Bit pattern mapping is used to create the letter S. If you want to display the alphanumeric characters that appear on the text screen, use a block for each character. Leave a border of unused bits on two edges so the characters can be spaced on the graphics screen.

Lines 20 and 30 let you enter the starting address of the block. Use addresses in Table 7-6. If you use addresses outside the range of page 1, unpredictable results may occur, and you may have to reboot or enter FP and reload your program. This program is designed to end when an address of zero is entered.

Line 40 calculates the addresses of the 8 bytes in a block. The values for the bytes are read in and poked into the appropriate memory address.

You can place more than one S on the screen. The RESTORE command is needed to set the DATA statement pointer to the first data item again.

The image on the graphics screen is not exactly a bit-by-bit correlation of the pixels on the graphics screen and the bits in memory. The leftmost bit or most significant bit in memory controls the color leaving the remaining 7 bits to control 7 pixels on the graphics screen. However, the mapping of these 7 bits is not straightforward. The rightmost or least significant bit in memory controls the leftmost pixel in that set of 7 dots. The leftmost or most significant bit, which controls the color, is not displayed on the graphics screen.

No color command is needed, since you are poking in the information in the high bit for the color group. The color depends on the value of the high bit and the column on the screen.

```
5    REM  === BIT MAPPED S ===
10   HGR : POKE  - 16301,0: HOME
20   VTAB 22: INPUT "ENTER STARTING ADDRESS OF BLOCK ";AD
30   IF AD = 0 THEN 99
40   FOR A = AD TO AD + (7 * 1024) STEP 1024
50   READ B: POKE A,B
60   NEXT A
70   RESTORE : GOTO 20
99   HOME : END
1000  DATA  0,28,34,2,28,32,34,28
```

DESIGN OF A CHARACTER

You can design your own characters. If you look closely at the characters of text on a green or amber monitor, you can see the individual pixels or dots that make up that character. The dots appear fuzzy on a television set.

To display a specific pattern of 7 bits across by 8 bits down, shade in the appropriate squares to form a design of your choice. Interpret each shaded square as a 1 and each blank square as a 0, where a value of 1 represents the lit pixel and 0 the unlit pixel. Label the bits in reverse order using the binary place value, convert to their decimal equivalents, and poke the set of 8 numbers into the addresses of the block desired.

You are labeling the bits in reverse order, since the screen interprets the bits in memory in reverse order when plotting. The high bit is the color bit. In the following examples, the high bit equals 0 and is therefore off. If you want the other set of colors with the high bit on, set the high bit on and add 128 to every decimal number computed. Table 7-8 shows the bit pattern needed to create the letter S.

TABLE 7-8. CREATING THE LETTER S

Hi-Res Screen Bit Pattern								Decimal
1	2	4	8	16	32	64	128*	No.
0	0	0	0	0	0	0	0	0
0	0	1	1	1	0	0	0	28
0	1	0	0	0	1	0	0	34
0	1	0	0	0	0	0	0	2
0	0	1	1	1	0	0	0	28
0	0	0	0	0	1	0	0	32
0	1	0	0	0	1	0	0	34
0	0	1	1	1	0	0	0	28

*High bit = color

Table 7-9 represents the 8 bytes needed to poke into memory for the corresponding characters. These characters vary slightly from the characters on the text screen. You can easily redefine your own set of characters. Enter the set of 8 bytes into a DATA statement.

TABLE 7-9. BYTES HOLDING BIT PATTERN FOR EACH CHARACTER

Character	Bytes for DATA Statement							
	8*	7	6	5	4	3	2	1
space	0	0	0	0	0	0	0	0
!	0	4	4	4	4	4	0	4
"	0	20	20	0	0	0	0	0
#	0	20	20	62	20	62	20	20
$	0	8	28	42	12	24	42	28
%	0	6	38	16	8	4	50	48
&	0	8	20	8	84	36	88	0
'	0	8	8	4	0	0	0	0
(	0	16	8	4	4	4	8	16
)	0	4	8	16	16	16	8	4
*	0	8	42	28	62	28	42	8
+	0	0	8	8	62	8	8	0
,	0	0	0	0	0	8	8	4
—	0	0	0	0	62	0	0	0
.	0	0	0	0	0	0	0	4
/	0	0	32	16	8	4	2	0
0	0	28	34	50	42	38	34	28
1	0	2	8	8	8	8	8	28
2	0	28	34	32	24	4	2	62
3	0	28	34	32	24	32	34	28
4	0	18	18	18	62	16	16	16
5	0	62	2	2	28	32	32	30
6	0	60	2	2	30	34	34	28
7	0	62	32	16	8	8	8	8
8	0	28	34	34	28	34	34	28
9	0	28	34	34	60	32	34	28
:	0	0	0	8	0	8	0	0
;	0	0	0	8	0	8	8	4
<	0	16	8	4	2	4	8	16
=	0	0	0	62	0	62	0	0
>	0	4	8	16	32	16	8	4
?	0	28	34	34	16	8	0	8
@	0	56	68	84	116	52	4	120

*Color bit.

TABLE 7-9. (CONT.)

Character	Bytes for DATA Statement						
	8*	7	6	5	4	3	2	1
A	0	28	34	34	62	34	34	34
B	0	30	34	34	30	34	34	30
C	0	60	2	2	2	2	2	60
D	0	30	34	34	34	34	34	30
E	0	62	2	2	14	2	2	62
F	0	62	2	2	14	2	2	2
G	0	60	2	2	2	50	34	28
H	0	34	34	34	62	34	34	34
I	0	62	8	8	8	8	8	62
J	0	32	32	32	32	34	34	28
K	0	34	18	10	6	10	18	34
L	0	2	2	2	2	2	2	62
M	0	34	54	42	34	34	34	34
N	0	34	38	42	50	34	34	34
O	0	28	34	34	34	34	34	28
P	0	30	34	34	30	2	2	2
Q	0	28	34	34	34	42	18	44
R	0	30	34	34	30	10	18	34
S	0	28	34	2	28	32	34	28
T	0	62	8	8	8	8	8	8
U	0	34	34	34	34	34	34	28
V	0	34	34	34	34	34	20	8
W	0	34	34	42	42	42	54	34
X	0	34	34	20	8	20	34	34
Y	0	34	34	20	8	8	8	8
Z	0	62	32	18	8	4	2	62

*Color bit.

The following are bit-mapped representations of all the characters.

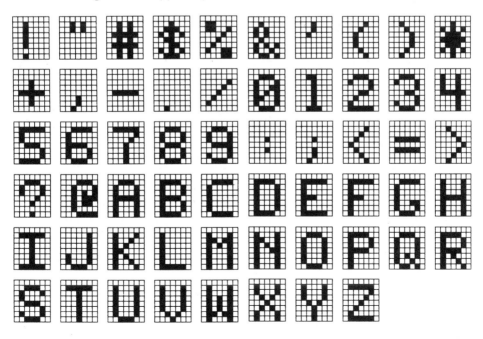

ADDRESS FINDER

This program returns the value on page 1 or 2 of memory that represents the starting address of a block at column C, row R on the high resolution graphics screen. A formula is used to obtain the starting address of any block.

EXPLANATION ══

The following formula calculates the starting address for a block on the hi-res graphics screen. You must provide the column and row number represented by C and R, respectively. The value of the column is in the range 1–40 and is represented on the map of the graphics screen as the HTAB number. The range of the row is 1–24 and is represented on the graphics screen map as the VTAB or row number. The expression INT((R−1)/8) holds a 0, 1, or 2 depending on the triad.

$$A = 8063 - 984 * INT((R-1)/8) + 128 * R + C$$

Use Table 7-6 to correlate the row and column numbers with the starting address of a block.

```
5   REM  === ADDRESS FINDER ===
10    HOME
20    PRINT  TAB( 15)"ADDRESS FINDER": PRINT : PRINT
30    INPUT "ENTER PAGE 1 OR 2: ";P
40    IF P > < 1 AND P > < 2 THEN 199
50    IF P = 1 THEN AD = 8063
60    IF P = 2 THEN AD = 16255
70    INPUT "ENTER ROW & COLUMNS NUMBERS R,C: ";R,C
80    IF (R < 1) OR (R > 24) OR (C < 1) OR (C > 40) THEN 7
0
90 A = AD - 984 *  INT ((R - 1) / 8) + 128 * R + C
100   PRINT "THE ADDRESS IS: ";A
110   PRINT : PRINT : GOTO 30
199   END
```

If you want an address on hi-res graphics page 2, replace 8063 with 16255.

DERIVATION OF FORMULA

The following mathematical calculations indicate how this formula was obtained.

Depending on the triad (rows 1–8, rows 9–16, or rows 17–24), the following mathematical statement indicates the value of the starting address in memory of the block at row R, column C on the graphics screen.

In this formula, row R represents the row or VTAB number (1–24), while column C represents the HTAB number (1–40). The VTAB and HTAB numbers were used to correlate the numbering of the graphics screen with the numbering of text screen, which uses the VTAB and HTAB commands.

Rows 1–8: $8063 + 0 + 128 \times (Row-0) + Column$
Rows 9–16: $8063 + 40 + 128 \times (Row-8) + Column$
Rows 17–24: $8063 + 80 + 128 \times (Row-16) + Column$

These formulas can be further represented as:

Rows 1–8: $8063 + 40 \times 0 + 128 \times (Row-(0 \times 0)) + Column$
Rows 9–16: $8063 + 40 \times 1 + 128 \times (Row-(8 \times 1)) + Column$
Rows 17–24: $8063 + 40 \times 2 + 128 \times (Row-(8 \times 2)) + Column$

If you let $F = INT((R-1)/8)$, then F can be used to multiply by 0, 40, or 80 to obtain the address. Whether you multiply by 0, 40, or 80 depends on which triad the block is located in.

Using formula $F = INT((R-1)/8)$

If R = number in range 1–8, then F = 0
If R = number in range 9–16, then F = 1
If R = number in range 17–24, then F = 2

The following is a general mathematical statement of the above formulas. It can be reduced to the formula presented that calculates the starting address for any block.

$$A = 8063 + 40 \times F + 128 \times (R-(8 \times F)) + C$$
$$A = 8063 + 40 \times F + 128 \times R - 1024 \times F + C$$
$$A = 8063 - 984 \times F + 128 \times R + C$$

In BASIC, this would translate to:

```
A = 8063 - 984 * INT((R-1)/8) + 128*R + C
```

USING ARRAYS TO HOLD DATA FOR
BIT-MAPPED CHARACTERS

The following program lets you enter four bit-mapped characters anywhere on the screen. This is useful when you want to draw a few characters on the graphics screen, such as identifying the X and Y axis, or adding your initials or a short message.

EXPLANATION

The high resolution graphics screen on page 1 is used, since you need the text window for directions for this program. The starting address of page 1 is set at line 20.

The number of characters is entered in line 1000. The bytes for the desired characters are stored in DATA statements. Lines 30–60 read in the data in a two-dimensional array. The row corresponds to the set of 8 bytes for each character. The column corresponds to the individual 8 bytes.

A(R,C)	1	2	3	4	5	6	7	8
1	0	34	34	30	8	20	34	34
2	0	34	34	20	8	8	8	8
3	0	0	8	8	62	8	8	0
4	0	0	0	0	62	0	0	0

Array element A(3,2) holds 0, while array element A(2,3) holds 34. The general form of a two-dimensional array element is A(R,C), where R represents the row and C the column.

Lines 70–80 draw a border to show how graphics and bit-mapped text characters can be mixed on the hi-res graphics screen.

Lines 90–140 ask for the character to be displayed, as well as the row and column. Lines 110 and 140 check for an invalid keypress. The rows are limited to 1–20, since the text window covers the bottom four rows of the graphics screen.

Line 120 calculates the value of CH to determine which character is to be displayed on the screen. If a Y was entered on line 100, then line 120 calculates CH as:

```
CH = 0 + (1) * 2 + 0 + 0 = 2
```

Since the second characters were selected, array element A(2,X) will be poked into memory, where X ranges from 1 to 8 (8 bytes in a block).

The routine at lines 150–190 determines the memory address and pokes in the 8 bytes for the character selected.

```
5   REM   === BIT MAPPED XY+- ===
10   HGR : HOME
20 AD = 8063: REM   PAGE 1
25   REM   --- READ BYTES INTO ARRAYS ---
30   READ N: DIM A(N,8)
40   FOR X = 1 TO N: FOR B = 1 TO 8
50   READ A(X,B)
60   NEXT B,X
65   REM   --- DRAW BORDER ---
70   HCOLOR= 3
80   HPLOT 0,0 TO 279,0 TO 279,159 TO 0,159 TO 0,0
85   REM   --- GET & CHECK ENTRIES ---
90   VTAB 22: CALL  - 958
100   INPUT "ENTER X Y + - ";A$
110   IF (A$ >  < "X") AND (A$ >  < "Y") AND (A$ >  < "+"
) AND (A$ >  < "-") THEN 299
120 CH = (A$ = "X") + (A$ = "Y") * 2 + (A$ = "+") * 3 +
(A$ = "-") * 4
130   INPUT "ENTER ROW AND COLUMNS  R,C ";R,C
140   IF (R < 1) OR (R > 20) OR (C < 1) OR (C > 40) THEN
130
145   REM   --- POKE CHARACTER INTO MEMORY ---
150   FOR X = 1 TO N
160 A = AD - 984 *  INT ((R - 1) / 8) + 128 * R + C
170   FOR B = 1 TO 8
180   POKE A + (B - 1) * 1024,A(CH,B)
190   NEXT B,X
200   GOTO 100
299   HOME : END
1000   DATA  4: REM   # OF CHARACTERS
1010   DATA  0,34,34,20,8,20,34,34: REM   X
1020   DATA  0,34,34,20,8,8,8,8: REM   Y
1030   DATA  0,0,8,8,62,8,8,0: REM   +
1040   DATA  0,0,0,0,62,0,0,0: REM   -
```

MODIFICATION ═══

Enter any of the 59 characters defined or create some characters of your own design. Line 1000 holds the number of characters.. Change lines 100, 110, 120, and 1000 if you change or add characters to the program.

CHARACTER GENERATOR

This program demonstrates the character set shown on page 187. It prints any message in a vertical and a horizontal manner and also centers the message on the screen.

EXPLANATION

Lines 10–70 set up the graphics screen and load the 8 bytes for each of the 59 characters into a two-dimensional array A(N,8). The memory is set for page 1 of graphics on line 80.

Lines 100–120 accept your message and check that it is 24 characters or less. Your message can be made up of any of the 59 characters listed in the DATA statements, including the space. To use a colon or comma, enter your message with leading and ending quotes. The order of the DATA statements is important in this program. The ordering is in the same order as the ASCII code chart (Appendix A).

The routine at lines 130–160 takes the message apart, finds the ASCII code of each character, and converts that ASCII code to a number from 1 to 59, where 1 represents the first character, 2 represents the second character, and X represents the Xth character. This number is stored in array A(X). See Appendix A.

The graphics screen is cleared on line 170. The routine at 180–250 prints the message across the screen starting at row 1, column 1. R and C represent the row and column. The formula for finding addresses is used to determine the starting address of each byte.

The routine at lines 260–320 prints the message down the screen starting at row 1, column 1. R and C represent the row and column. The formula computes the memory addresses.

The last routine at lines 330–410 uses the length of the message to calculate the center of the screen. The message is printed across the screen at row 12.

The program continues at line 90 and waits for you to enter a new message. If you enter QUIT as your message, the program ends.

If your message is printed at rows 21–24, it will not show up because of the text window. Exit from the program with a CONTROL C RETURN and enter POKE −16302,0 for full screen graphics. If you wish to continue with the program, add the text window with the command POKE −16301,0 and issue the GOTO 90 command.

```
5    REM  === CHARACTER GENERATOR ARRAYS ===
10   HGR : POKE  - 16301,0: HOME
20   VTAB 22: HTAB 5: PRINT "LOADING IN CHARACTER GENERAT
OR"
30   READ N: DIM A(N,8),A$(24),N(24)
40   FOR C = 1 TO N
50   FOR B = 1 TO 8
60   READ A(C,B)
70   NEXT B,C
80 AD = 8063: REM  PAGE 1
90   HOME
100  VTAB 22: INPUT "ENTER YOUR MESSAGE OR <QUIT> ";N$
110  IF N$ = "QUIT" THEN 499
120 L =  LEN (N$): IF L > 24 THEN 90
130  FOR X = 1 TO L
140 A$(X) =  MID$ (N$,X,1)
150 N(X) =  ASC (A$(X)) - 31
160  NEXT X
```

```
170   HGR
175   REM  --- ACROSS ---
180   FOR X = 1 TO L
190 R = 1:C = X
200 A = AD - 984 *  INT ((R - 1) / 8) + 128 * R + C
210   FOR B = 1 TO 8
220   POKE A + (B - 1) * 1024,A(N(X),B)
230   NEXT B
240 A = AD + X
250   NEXT X
255   REM  --- DOWN ---
260   FOR Y = 1 TO L
270 R = Y:C = 1
280 A = AD - 984 *  INT ((R - 1) / 8) + 128 * R + C
290   FOR B = 1 TO 8
300   POKE A + (B - 1) * 1024,A(N(Y),B)
310   NEXT B
320   NEXT Y
325   REM  --- CENTER ---
330 C =  INT (20 - (L / 2))
340 R = 12
350   FOR X = 1 TO L
360 A = AD - 984 *  INT ((R - 1) / 8) + 128 * R + C
370   FOR B = 1 TO 8
380   POKE A + (B - 1) * 1024,A(N(X),B)
390   NEXT B
400 C = C + 1
410   NEXT X
420   GOTO 90
499   END
1000   DATA  59: REM    NUMBER OF CHARACTERS
1010   DATA  0,0,0,0,0,0,0,0: REM   SPACE
1020   DATA  0,4,4,4,4,4,0,4: REM  !
1030   DATA  0,20,20,0,0,0,0,0: REM   "
1040   DATA  0,20,20,62,20,62,20,20: REM  #
1050   DATA  0,8,28,42,12,24,42,28: REM  $
1060   DATA  0,6,38,16,8,4,50,48: REM  %
1070   DATA  0,4,10,10,4,42,18,44: REM  &
1080   DATA  0,8,8,4,0,0,0,0: REM  '
1090   DATA  0,16,8,4,4,4,8,16: REM  (
1100   DATA  0,4,8,16,16,16,8,4: REM  )
1110   DATA  0,8,42,28,62,28,42,8: REM  *
1120   DATA  0,0,8,8,62,8,8,0: REM  +
1130   DATA  0,0,0,0,0,8,8,4: REM  ,
1140   DATA  0,0,0,0,62,0,0,0: REM  -
1150   DATA  0,0,0,0,0,0,0,4: REM  .
1160   DATA  0,0,32,16,8,4,2,0: REM  /
1170   DATA  0,28,34,50,42,38,34,28: REM  0
1180   DATA  0,12,8,8,8,8,8,28: REM  1
1190   DATA  0,28,34,32,24,4,2,62: REM  2
1200   DATA  0,28,34,32,24,32,34,28: REM  3
1210   DATA  0,18,18,18,62,16,16,16: REM  4
1220   DATA  0,62,2,2,28,32,32,30: REM  5
1230   DATA  0,60,2,2,30,34,34,28: REM  6
1240   DATA  0,62,32,16,8,8,8,8: REM  7
```

(continued on next page)

```
1250    DATA    0,28,34,34,28,34,34,28: REM    8
1260    DATA    0,28,34,34,60,32,34,28: REM    9
1270    DATA    0,0,0,8,0,8,0,0: REM    :
1280    DATA    0,0,0,8,0,8,8,4: REM    ;
1290    DATA    0,16,8,4,2,4,8,16: REM    <
1300    DATA    0,0,0,62,0,62,0,0: REM    =
1310    DATA    0,4,8,16,32,16,8,4: REM    >
1320    DATA    0,28,34,34,16,8,0,8: REM    ?
1330    DATA    0,56,68,84,116,52,4,120: REM    @
1340    DATA    0,28,34,34,62,34,34,34: REM    A
1350    DATA    0,30,34,34,30,34,34,30: REM    B
1360    DATA    0,60,2,2,2,2,2,60: REM    C
1370    DATA    0,30,34,34,34,34,34,30: REM    D
1380    DATA    0,62,2,2,14,2,2,62: REM    E
1390    DATA    0,62,2,2,14,2,2,2: REM    F
1400    DATA    0,60,2,2,2,50,34,28: REM    G
1410    DATA    0,34,34,34,62,34,34,34: REM    H
1420    DATA    0,62,8,8,8,8,8,62: REM    I
1430    DATA    0,32,32,32,32,34,34,28: REM    J
1440    DATA    0,34,18,10,6,10,18,34: REM    K
1450    DATA    0,2,2,2,2,2,2,62: REM    L
1460    DATA    0,34,54,42,34,34,34,34: REM    M
1470    DATA    0,34,38,42,50,34,34,34: REM    N
1480    DATA    0,28,34,34,34,34,34,28: REM    O
1490    DATA    0,30,34,34,30,2,2,2: REM    P
1500    DATA    0,28,34,34,34,42,18,44: REM    Q
1510    DATA    0,30,34,34,30,10,18,34: REM    R
1520    DATA    0,28,34,2,28,32,34,28: REM    S
1530    DATA    0,62,8,8,8,8,8,8: REM    T
1540    DATA    0,34,34,34,34,34,34,28: REM    U
1550    DATA    0,34,34,34,34,34,20,8: REM    V
1560    DATA    0,34,34,42,42,42,54,34: REM    W
1570    DATA    0,34,34,20,8,20,34,34: REM    X
1580    DATA    0,34,34,20,8,8,8,8: REM    Y
1590    DATA    0,62,32,16,8,4,2,62: REM    Z
```

USING A BINARY FILE TO STORE
CHARACTER GENERATOR

This program stores the 8 bytes for the bit-mapped characters as a binary file. This is convenient, since you do not have to enter the 60 DATA statements each time you want to use the character set.

A binary file is used to store the 8 bytes per character of the 59 available characters.

Enter and save the program entitled Character Generator Arrays. Run the program several times testing each of the characters. If you wish to change the design of a character, then change the 8 items in the appropriate DATA statement.

Delete lines 5–499 (DEL 5,499) and insert the following lines 5–199 to use the same DATA statements without having to retype them.

The routine at lines 30–40 reads in the data items as a one-dimensional array or list instead of a two-dimensional array. N holds the number of data lines, and NB holds the number of data elements.

The routine at lines 70–90 pokes the list into free memory starting at location 24576. Line 100 saves the contents of memory starting at 24576 and ending NB addresses later. You can substitute any legal filename for the name CHARACTERS. Be sure that the name is not a duplicate of any other name on your disk.

Make certain you have a disk in the drive when you run this program because the program writes a binary file to the disk. The disk will spin for a while while it stores the data. Wait until the disk stops spinning or you may lose your data.

Appropriate messages are printed at lines 20, 60, and 120 to let you know what is happening, since the screen would otherwise go blank during this program.

```
5    REM  === CREATE CHARACTERS ===
10   HOME : VTAB 5: HTAB 5
20   PRINT "LOADING IN CHARACTER GENERATOR"
30   READ N:NB = 8 * N: DIM A(NB)
40   FOR X = 1 TO NB: READ A(X): NEXT X
50   HOME : VTAB 5: HTAB 5
60   PRINT "SAVING CHARACTERS AS BINARY 4FILE"
70   FOR X = 1 TO NB
80   POKE 24575 + X,A(X)
90   NEXT X
100   PRINT  CHR$ (4)"BSAVE CHARACTERS,A24576,L"NB
110   HOME
120   VTAB 5: HTAB 15: PRINT "FINISHED"
199   END
```

LOADING A BINARY FILE OF BIT-MAPPED CHARACTERS

This program loads the binary file that stored the bytes for the bit-mapped characters. It can be used to add bit-mapped characters to any image that you have saved as a binary file.

EXPLANATION

The following program is one example of many programs that you can write to retrieve and use the data for the characters stored in the binary file called CHARACTERS.

This binary file contains the bytes that represent the bit-mapped characters. Line 50 instructs the computer to BLOAD this binary file into memory. It is loaded into the same memory locations that it was saved from. The routine at 60–90 peeks these addresses starting at location 24576 and stores the values in a two-dimensional array that is 59 rows by 8 columns.

Line 100 sets page 1 of hi-res graphics with a text window. The address for page 1 is 8063.

Lines 120–180 let you exit the program, clear the graphics screen, or continue with the program. Lines 190–220 accept your message. Lines 230–260 take the message apart, determine the ASCII code, and assign a number to the character depending on its position in the list of characters. The number ranges from 1 to 59.

Lines 270 to 330 request either vertical or horizontal printing and the row and column number of the first character of the message. Row values range from 1 to 24 and column values range from 1 to 40.

The subroutine at lines 1000–1070 prints the message vertically, while the subroutine at lines 2000–2070 prints the message horizontally.

LOADING A BINARY IMAGE OR CREATING A HI-RES PICTURE

You can BLOAD a binary image to the screen, run this program to add text characters to the image, and then BSAVE the image with the same or a different name. You can draw your own hi-res graphics picture by changing line 100 to:

```
100 HGR: HOME: GOSUB 3000 "DRAW HIRES PICTURE"
```

Then line 3000 should start your graphics picture.

MISSING FOUR LINES

The last four rows of the graphics screen are covered by the text window. The program will write to them, but they will not be visible unless you exit the program with a CONTROL C RETURN command and enter POKE −16302,0 to obtain full screen graphics. Return to the program with a GOTO 100 command.

ERASING A CHARACTER

If you print a character or characters and want to erase them, enter the appropriate number of spaces preceded by a leading quotation mark. Draw the blanks at the location to be blanked out.

```
5    REM   === RETRIEVE CHARACTERS ===
7    REM   --- LOAD IN TEXT FILE ---
10   HOME : VTAB 5: HTAB 5
20   PRINT "LOADING IN CHARACTER GENERATOR"
30 N = 59
40   DIM A(N,8),A$(24),N(24)
50   PRINT  CHR$ (4)"BLOAD CHARACTERS"
60   FOR X = 1 TO N
70   FOR B = 1 TO 8
80 A(X,B) =  PEEK (24567 + X * 8 + B)
90   NEXT B,X
95   REM   --- SET HGR SCREEN PAGE 1 - DO NOT ERASE IMAGE
100   POKE  - 16304,0: POKE  - 16301,0: POKE  - 16300,0:
POKE  - 16297,0
110 AD = 8063: REM   PAGE 1
115   REM   --- GET & CHECK ENTRIES ---
120   HOME
130   VTAB 21: PRINT "ENTER <ESC> TO QUIT"
140   PRINT "ENTER <C> TO CLEAR HGR SCREEN"
150   PRINT "ENTER <SPACE> TO CONTINUE ";
160   GET A$: IF A$ < > CHR$ (32) AND A$ < > CHR$ (27
) AND A$ < > "C" THEN 160
170   IF A$ = CHR$ (27) THEN 399
180   IF A$ = "C" THEN  HGR
190   PRINT : HOME
200   VTAB 22: INPUT "ENTER YOUR MESSAGE ";N$
205   REM   --- CALCULATE POSITION OF CHARACTER IN LIST --
210 L = LEN (N$)
220   IF L > 20 THEN 120
230   FOR X = 1 TO L
240 A$(X) = MID$ (N$,X,1)
250 N(X) = ASC (A$(X)) - 31
260   NEXT X
265   REM   --- SELECT DIRECTION ---
270   INPUT "V)ERTICAL OR H)ORIZONTAL ";HV$
280   IF HV$ < > "H" AND HV$ < > "V" THEN 270
290   INPUT "ENTER ROW & COLUMN  R,C ";R,C
300   IF R < 1 AND R > 40 AND C < 1 AND C > 20 THEN 290
310   IF  LEFT$ (HV$,1) = "V" THEN  GOSUB 1000"VERTICAL R
OUTINE"
320   IF  LEFT$ (HV$,1) = "H" THEN  GOSUB 2000"HORIZONTAL
 ROUTINE"
330   GOTO 120
399   HOME : END
995   REM   --- VERTICAL ROUTINE ---
1000   FOR X = 1 TO L
1010 A = AD - 984 *  INT ((R - 1) / 8) + 128 * R + C
1020   FOR B = 1 TO 8
1030   POKE A + (B - 1) * 1024,A(N(X),B)
1040   NEXT B
1050 R = R + 1
1060   NEXT X
1070   RETURN
1995   REM   --- HORIZONTAL ROUTINE ---
2000 A = AD - 984 *  INT ((R - 1) / 8) + 128 * R + C
```

(continued on next page)

```
2010   FOR X = 1 TO L
2020   FOR B = 1 TO 8
2030   POKE A + (B - 1) * 1024,A(N(X),B)
2040   NEXT B
2050 A = A + 1
2060   NEXT X
2070   RETURN
```

MODIFICATION

If you wish to draw to page 2, then change the address at line 110 to read:

```
110 AD = 16255:   REM PAGE 2
```

You will no longer have a text window. Change the input statements to assignment statements or poke the screen to get a text window and use the program as is. When you BSAVE the picture, you will get the full screen saved.

SPECIAL EFFECTS WITH MACHINE LANGUAGE ROUTINES

The following routines provide high resolution effects that can only be achieved by using machine language routines, since Applesoft BASIC is too slow to accomplish the same effect.

You do not have to be familiar with machine language to enter or access these routines because the machine language coding has been transferred to DATA statements for your convenience. Since the values in the DATA statements correspond to specific commands in machine language, be sure to enter the values in the DATA statements exactly or the routine will produce unpredictable results.

To view the full effect of the following special routines, BSAVE a high resolution picture either from page 1 or page 2 that uses all the hi-res graphics colors. Use that picture in the programs or write a simple etch-a-sketch program to draw a design.

The first four routines flip the screen and change its colors. The last six routines scroll the screen up, down, left, and right.

The memory locations have been arranged so that you can load three of the first four routines one above the other in memory. This enables you to use either the set of routines SCREEN EOR, HV SCREEN FLIP, HH SCREEN FLIP or the set composed of SCREEN EOR, HV SCREEN FLIP, HH SCREEN FLIP2 simultaneously.

In addition to this set of flipping routines, one of the six scrolling routines can also be used simultaneously. These scrolling routines are too lengthy for more than one to be in memory at a time.

Two demonstration programs show how these special effects routines can be used in your programs. One program uses keyboard control, whereas the other uses paddle/button/keyboard control.

The last program of this chapter lets you display a hi-res graphics picture in a spiral fashion. This routine cannot be used with any of the preceding routines, since they all occupy the same memory locations.

In order to use the special effects routines, you must first follow certain steps. Step A need only be followed the very first time. Thereafter start with Step 1.

Step A: Entering Routines for the First Time Only

First type in one of the programs, SCREEN EOR.A, HH SCREEN FLIP.A, HH SCREEN FLIP2.A, or HV SCREEN FLIP.A. SAVE and run the program. The program will ask whether it should save the routine to disk. Answer Y if it has not already been saved. Now the routine is in memory and ready for use.

When you run and answer Y to this Applesoft program: You will obtain this binary file:

```
SCREEN EOR.A          SCREEN EOR
HV SCREEN FLIP.A      HV SCREEN FLIP
HH SCREEN FLIP.A      HH SCREEN FLIP
HH SCREEN FLIP2.A     HH SCREEN FLIP2
```

Step 1: BLOADing a Special Effects Routine

If you have already saved the routine and it is not currently in memory, you can load it to memory with two different techniques.

The first method is to run the Applesoft program that corresponds to the routine and answer N to save it, since it is already on disk.

The second technique is to BLOAD the binary file from disk using the following command, where <u>filename</u> is the name of the special effects routine you want to use:

```
BLOAD filename
```

Step 2: Loading a Hi-Res Graphics Picture

To use the routine, enter either HGR or HGR2 or the equivalent POKE commands to set the proper page. Load your high resolution graphics picture with a BLOAD command or use your etch-a-sketch program.

POKE Option for Setting Up Page 1 or Page 2

In some situations you may already have a hi-res graphics picture on the screen and may want to use one of the following special effects routines. If you type TEXT in order to run one of the routines, your graphics picture is temporarily erased from the screen. However, the picture is still in memory and can be displayed with the POKE commands that are equivalent to HGR or HGR2.

The following POKE commands set page 1 or 2 without erasing the graphics screen. You must also poke values into location 230 to inform the special effects routines which page of hi-res graphics will be modified.

The equivalent of HGR is:

```
POKE -16304,0:POKE -16301,0:POKE -16300,0:POKE
-16297,0:POKE 230,32
```

The equivalent of HGR2 is:

```
POKE -16304,0:POKE -16302,0:POKE -16299,0:POKE
-16297,0:POKE 230,64
```

STEP 3: CALLING A SPECIAL EFFECTS ROUTINE

If you omit the HGR or HGR2 command (or equivalent POKE commands), before you CALL the routines, the computer will not function properly and you will have to turn the computer off and reboot.

Issue a CALL A command, where A represents the starting address of the special effects routine. The value of A will be given for each routine.

INSTANT INVERSER

This routine instantly switches the colors of a high resolution picture.

EXPLANATION

When you run the program SCREEN EOR.A, it will save a binary file called SCREEN EOR.

Load in this binary file with the following command:

BLOAD SCREEN EOR

To execute this routine, use the command CALL 768,C, where C represents a number from 0 to 6 and each number causes a different color switch. C can be a constant, variable, or any legal expression.

To reinstate the previous colors, issue the same CALL command.

Table 7-10 shows the color changes.

TABLE 7-10. COLOR CHANGES

Value of C	Original Colors							
	0	1	2	3	4	5	6	7
0	7	6	5	4	3	2	1	0
1	3	2	1	0	7	6	5	4
2	4	5	6	7	0	1	2	3
3	2	3	0	1	6	7	4	5
4	1	0	3	2	5	4	7	6
5	6	7	4	5	2	3	0	1
6	5	4	7	6	1	0	3	2

0 = Black1; 1 = green; 2 = violet; 3 = white1; 4 = black2; 5 = orange/red; 6 = blue; and 7 = white2.

```
5    REM   === SCREEN EOR.A ===
10   HOME
20   FOR X = 0 TO 84: READ V: POKE 768 + X,V: NEXT
30   PRINT "SAVE TO DISK (Y/N): ";: GET A$: IF A$ = "N" T
HEN  END
40   IF A$ < > "Y" THEN 30
50   PRINT  CHR$ (13); CHR$ (4);"BSAVE SCREEN EOR,A$300,L
$55"
100   DATA 32,76,231,189,71,3,141,85,3,141
110   DATA 87,3,189,78,3,141,86,3,165,230
120   DATA 133,7,169,0,133,6,168,162,32,177
130   DATA 6,77,87,3,145,6,200,240,20,152
140   DATA 74,144,8,173,86,3,141,87,3,208
150   DATA 234,173,85,3,141,87,3,208,226,230
160   DATA 7,173,85,3,141,87,3,202,208,215
170   DATA 96,255,127,128,85,42,213,170,255,127
180   DATA 128,42,85,170,213
```

FLIPPING THE SCREEN UPSIDE DOWN

This program flips a picture upside down instantly by rotating the picture along a horizontal axis.

EXPLANATION

When you run the program HV SCREEN FLIP.A, it saves the binary file HV SCREEN FLIP. Load in this binary file with the following command:

BLOAD HV SCREEN FLIP

To execute this routine, use the command CALL 24576, where 24576 is the starting address of the machine language routine.

If you issue the CALL command again, the original picture will be displayed.

```
5    REM   === HV SCREEN FLIP.A ===
10   HOME
20   FOR X = 0 TO 59: READ V: POKE 24576 + X,V: NEXT
30   PRINT "SAVE TO DISK (Y/N): ";: GET A$: IF A$ = "N" T
HEN  END
40   IF A$ < > "Y" THEN 30
50   PRINT  CHR$ (13); CHR$ (4);"BSAVE HV SCREEN FLIP,A$6
000,L$3C"
100   DATA 169,0,141,60,96,169,192,141,61,96
110   DATA 160,0,32,17,244,165,38,133,6,165
120   DATA 39,133,7,173,60,96,160,0,32,17
130   DATA 244,160,39,177,6,170,177,38,145,6
140   DATA 138,145,38,136,16,243,238,60,96,206
150   DATA 61,96,173,61,96,201,95,208,207,96
```

FLIPPING THE SCREEN LEFT TO RIGHT AND PRESERVING COLOR

This program flips a picture left to right by rotating it around a vertical axis. It does not alter the colors.

EXPLANATION

When you run the program HH SCREEN FLIP.A, it saves the binary HH SCREEN FLIP. Load in this binary file with the following command:

```
BLOAD HH SCREEN FLIP
```

To execute this routine, use the command CALL 24638, where 24638 is the starting address of the machine language routine.

If you issue the CALL command again, the original picture will be displayed.

This routine preserves the original colors, since it does not affect the seven rightmost graphics plot positions.

```
5    REM   === HH SCREEN FLIP.A ===
10   HOME
20   FOR X = 0 TO 115: READ V: POKE 24638 + X,V: NEXT
30   PRINT "SAVE TO DISK (Y/N): ";: GET A$: IF A$ = "N" T
HEN  END
40   IF A$ <  > "Y" THEN 30
50   PRINT  CHR$ (13); CHR$ (4);"BSAVE HH SCREEN FLIP,A$6
03E,L$74"
100  DATA  169,0,141,180,96,141,178,96,168,32
110  DATA  17,244,172,178,96,177,38,32,137,96
120  DATA  169,38,56,237,178,96,168,177,38,170
130  DATA  173,181,96,145,38,138,32,137,96,172
140  DATA  178,96,145,38,200,140,178,96,192,19
150  DATA  208,219,177,38,32,137,96,145,38,160
160  DATA  0,140,178,96,238,180,96,173,180,96
170  DATA  201,192,208,191,96,162,0,142,181,96
180  DATA  74,144,16,141,179,96,189,170,96,24
190  DATA  109,181,96,141,181,96,173,179,96,232
200  DATA  224,8,208,232,173,181,96,96,64,32
210  DATA  16,8,4,2,1,128
```

FLIPPING THE SCREEN LEFT TO RIGHT WITH COMPLEMENTARY COLORS

This program flips an entire picture left to right by rotating it around a vertical axis. The colors (excluding black and white) are switched to their complementary colors.

EXPLANATION

When you run the program HH SCREEN FLIP2.A, it saves the binary file HH SCREEN FLIP2.

Load in this binary file with the following command:

`BLOAD HH SCREEN FLIP2`

To execute this routine, use the command CALL 24638, where 24638 is the starting address of the machine language routine.

If you issue the CALL command again, the original picture will be displayed.

This routine does not affect the black or white colors. However, since it affects the seven rightmost graphics plot positions, blue and orange are swapped and violet and green are swapped.

Since both HH SCREEN FLIP and HH SCREEN FLIP2 occupy the same memory block, only one routine can be used at a time.

```
5    REM  === HH SCREEN FLIP2.A ===
10   HOME
20   FOR X = 0 TO 108: READ V: POKE 24638 + X,V: NEXT
30   PRINT "SAVE TO DISK (Y/N): ";: GET A$: IF A$ = "N" T
HEN  END
40   IF A$ < > "Y" THEN 30
50   PRINT  CHR$ (13); CHR$ (4);"BSAVE HH SCREEN FLIP2,A$
603E,L$6D"
100   DATA 169,0,141,173,96,141,171,96,168,32
110   DATA 17,244,172,171,96,177,38,32,130,96
120   DATA 169,39,56,237,171,96,168,177,38,170
130   DATA 173,174,96,145,38,138,32,130,96,172
140   DATA 171,96,145,38,200,140,171,96,192,20
150   DATA 208,219,160,0,140,171,96,238,173,96
160   DATA 173,173,96,201,192,208,198,96,162,0
170   DATA 142,174,96,74,144,16,141,172,96,189
180   DATA 163,96,24,109,174,96,141,174,96,173
190   DATA 172,96,232,224,8,208,232,173,174,96
200   DATA 96,64,32,16,8,4,2,1,128
```

SETTING UP THE SPECIAL EFFECTS
SCROLLING ROUTINES

The six routines that are used to scroll the screen need to be set up differently than the previous four routines. The machine language scrolling routines are quite lengthy. Therefore, generator routines that create the actual scrolling routines are given. This saves you from entering approximately 8000 bytes of data.

The following directions explain how to set up and use the last six special effects routines that scroll the graphics screen in the four directions: up, down, left, and right.

You need to follow Step A only the first time you enter the programs. Afterwards, start with Step 1.

STEP A: ENTERING THE GENERATOR ROUTINE FOR THE FIRST TIME ONLY

First enter one of the following six Applesoft programs. Save and run the program. When it asks whether you want to save the routine to disk, answer Y if the program has not already been saved. This saves the generator routine, which is the binary file that creates the scrolling routine.

When you run and answer Y
to this Applesoft program:

You will obtain this
binary file:

```
LEFTSCROLL.A           LEFTSCROLL
LEFTSCROLL2.A          LEFTSCROLL2
RIGHTSCROLL.A          RIGHTSCROLL
RIGHTSCROLL2.A         RIGHTSCROLL2
UPSCROLL.A             UPSCROLL
DOWNSCROLL.A           DOWNSCROLL
```

The special effects routine is not yet ready for use. This will be done in Step 2. Go to Step 1 next in order to set up the proper pages. This is necessary before you set up the special effects routine.

STEP 1: SELECTING PAGE 1 OR PAGE 2

Decide which page you want to scroll. Enter HGR to scroll page 1 or HGR2 to scroll page 2. The equivalent POKE commands for setting up page 1 or page 2 mentioned earlier can be substituted for HGR or HGR2.

STEP 2: CREATING A SPECIAL EFFECTS ROUTINE

The special effects routine is not yet ready for use. You must first BRUN the appropriate generator routine. This causes the generator routine to create the special effects routine. For example, the following command will generate the Scroll Left Same Color routine:

```
BRUN LEFTSCROLL2
```

STEP 3: LOADING A HI-RES GRAPHICS PICTURE

Load the hi-res graphics picture into memory using the following statement, where picturename represents the name of the picture:

BLOAD picturename

The picture must be loaded to the same page that you set in Step 1, since only that page will be affected by the scrolling routines.

STEP 4: CALLING A SPECIAL EFFECTS ROUTINE

Call the special effects routine with the command CALL 24758, where 24758 represents the starting address of the routine. The starting address is the same for all six scrolling routines.

The following routines scroll only the page that had been set when the generator routine was called. However, you may load other hi-res graphics pictures on the same page and use the scrolling routines without reloading them.

SCROLLING DIFFERENT PICTURES ON THE SAME PAGE

To scroll another picture on the same page, load your picture on that page. Call the desired scrolling routine by issuing the CALL A command, where A is the starting address of the special effects routine.

SCROLLING ON BOTH PAGES

If you want to use the other hi-res graphics page, then you must set the new page with HGR, HGR2, or the equivalent POKE commands.

If the generator routine is in memory, you do not have to RUN the Applesoft program or BRUN the generator routine again. It will remain in memory until you turn off the computer or load in a different scrolling routine. Issue the CALL A command, where A is the starting address of the particular generator routine. This instructs the computer to execute the generator routine, which creates the scrolling routine.

Table 7-11 gives the starting addresses of the generator routines.

TABLE 7-11. STARTING ADDRESSES OF GENERATOR ROUTINES

Generator Routine	Starting Address
LEFTSCROLL	28672
LEFTSCROLL2	32260
RIGHTSCROLL	28672
RIGHTSCROLL2	32260
UPSCROLL	28672
DOWNSCROLL	28672

The routine is now in memory and ready for use. Use the CALL 24758 command to access the particular scrolling routine.

If you adjust the HIMEM or use the MAXFILES command, the special effects routine may be written over and consequently not function properly. You will then have to return to Step 1.

Scrolling Left with Complementary Colors

This program scrolls a hi-res graphics design from right to left and continues on the right side of the screen. This creates a wraparound effect, since the leftmost 7 bytes become the rightmost 7 bytes. It changes the colors to their complementary colors in the process.

EXPLANATION

To load this routine into memory use the command:

BRUN LEFTSCROLL

Issue the CALL 24758 command each time you want to scroll the screen left 7 plot positions.

Since this program shifts an odd number of positions at a time, the colors flip between their normal and complementary colors. Blue switches with orange, while green switches with violet. Black and white are not affected.

```
5    REM   === LEFTSCROLL.A ===
10   HOME
20   FOR X = 0 TO 247: READ V: POKE 28672 + X,V: NEXT
30   PRINT "SAVE TO DISK (Y/N): ";: GET A$: IF A$ = "N" T
HEN  END
40   IF A$ <  > "Y" THEN 30
50   PRINT  CHR$ (13); CHR$ (4);"BSAVE LEFTSCROLL,A$7000,
L$F8"
100   DATA  169,182,133,6,162,0,160,0,169,96
110   DATA  133,7,32,177,112,32,17,244,160,0
120   DATA  169,173,32,212,112,200,169,141,32,225
130   DATA  112,32,192,112,208,235,169,160,145,6
140   DATA  200,169,0,145,6,32,161,112,140,248
150   DATA  112,162,1,142,249,112,169,185,32,133
160   DATA  112,206,249,112,169,153,32,133,112,238
170   DATA  249,112,238,248,112,173,248,112,201,192
180   DATA  208,230,160,7,185,240,112,145,6,136
190   DATA  16,248,160,7,32,161,112,32,177,112
200   DATA  32,17,244,165,38,24,105,39,133,38
210   DATA  160,0,169,173,32,225,112,200,169,141
220   DATA  32,212,112,32,192,112,208,228,169,96
230   DATA  145,6,96,72,173,248,112,160,0,32
240   DATA  17,244,160,0,104,145,6,200,165,38
250   DATA  24,109,249,112,145,6,200,165,39,145
260   DATA  6,200,24,152,101,6,133,6,165,7
270   DATA  105,0,133,7,160,0,96,169,65,141
280   DATA  250,112,169,110,141,251,112,140,248,112
```

```
290    DATA 152,96,32,161,112,238,250,112,208,3
300    DATA 238,251,112,238,248,112,173,248,112,201
310    DATA 192,96,145,6,200,165,38,145,6,200
320    DATA 165,39,145,6,96,145,6,200,173,250
330    DATA 112,145,6,200,173,251,112,145,6,96
340    DATA 200,192,39,240,3,76,56,101
```

SCROLLING LEFT WITH SAME COLOR

This program scrolls a hi-res graphics picture from right to left to create a wraparound effect. It keeps the same colors as the original picture and scrolls faster than the previous program. The routine scrolls 14 plot positions at a time. Since this is an even number, the colors remain intact.

EXPLANATION

To load this routine into memory use the command:

BRUN LEFTSCROLL2

Issue the CALL 24758 command each time you want to scroll the screen left 14 plot positions.

```
5    REM  === LEFTSCROLL2.A ===
10   HOME
20   FOR X = 0 TO 341: READ V: POKE 32260 + X,V: NEXT
30   PRINT "SAVE TO DISK (Y/N): ";: GET A$: IF A$ = "N" T
HEN  END
40   IF A$ <  > "Y" THEN 30
50   PRINT  CHR$ (13); CHR$ (4);"BSAVE LEFTSCROLL2,A$7E04
,L$156"
100  DATA 169,182,133,6,162,0,160,0,169,96
110  DATA 133,7,169,194,141,90,127,169,123,141
120  DATA 94,127,138,141,93,127,32,252,126,169
130  DATA 130,141,90,127,169,124,141,94,127,169
140  DATA 1,141,93,127,152,170,32,252,126,169
150  DATA 160,145,6,200,169,0,145,6,32,236
160  DATA 126,140,91,127,162,2,142,92,127,169
170  DATA 185,32,208,126,206,92,127,206,92,127
180  DATA 169,153,32,208,126,24,169,3,109,92
190  DATA 127,141,92,127,169,185,32,208,126,206
200  DATA 92,127,206,92,127,169,153,32,208,126
210  DATA 238,92,127,238,91,127,173,91,127,201
220  DATA 192,208,202,160,8,185,81,127,145,6
230  DATA 136,16,248,160,8,32,236,126,169,38
240  DATA 141,93,127,169,194,141,90,127,169,123
250  DATA 141,94,127,152,32,185,126,169,39,141
260  DATA 93,127,169,130,141,90,127,169,124,141
270  DATA 94,127,152,32,185,126,169,96,145,6
280  DATA 96,141,91,127,32,67,127,169,173,32
290  DATA 19,127,200,169,141,32,34,127,32,47
300  DATA 127,208,237,96,72,173,91,127,160,0
310  DATA 32,17,244,160,0,104,145,6,200,165
320  DATA 38,24,109,92,127,145,6,200,165,39
330  DATA 145,6,200,24,152,101,6,133,6,165
340  DATA 7,105,0,133,7,160,0,96,141,91
350  DATA 127,32,67,127,169,173,32,34,127,200
360  DATA 169,141,32,19,127,32,47,127,208,237
370  DATA 96,145,6,200,173,90,127,145,6,200
380  DATA 173,94,127,145,6,96,145,6,200,165
390  DATA 38,145,6,200,165,39,145,6,96,32
```

```
400   DATA 236,126,238,90,127,208,3,238,94,127
410   DATA 238,91,127,173,91,127,201,192,96,32
420   DATA 17,244,160,0,165,38,24,109,93,127
430   DATA 133,38,96,200,200,192,38,240,3,76
440   DATA 184,105
```

SCROLLING RIGHT WITH COMPLEMENTARY COLORS

This program scrolls the screen right 7 plot positions each time it is called. The rightmost 7 bytes become the leftmost 7 bytes, creating a wraparound effect. Since an odd number of positions are scrolled, the colors flip between their complementary and original colors.

EXPLANATION

To load this routine into memory use the command:

BRUN RIGHTSCROLL

Issue the CALL 24758 command each time you want to scroll the screen right 7 plot positions.

```
5    REM   === RIGHTSCROLL.A ===
10   HOME
20   FOR X = 0 TO 245: READ V: POKE 28672 + X,V: NEXT
30   PRINT "SAVE TO DISK (Y/N): ";: GET A$: IF A$ = "N" T
HEN  END
40   IF A$ < > "Y" THEN 30
50   PRINT  CHR$ (13); CHR$ (4);"BSAVE RIGHTSCROLL,A$7000
,L$F6"
100   DATA 169,182,133,6,162,0,160,0,169,96
110   DATA 133,7,32,177,112,32,17,244,165,38
120   DATA 24,105,39,133,38,160,0,169,173,32
130   DATA 212,112,200,169,141,32,225,112,32,192
140   DATA 112,208,228,169,160,145,6,200,169,38
150   DATA 145,6,32,161,112,140,246,112,162,0
160   DATA 142,247,112,169,185,32,133,112,238,247
170   DATA 112,169,153,32,133,112,206,247,112,238
180   DATA 246,112,173,246,112,201,192,208,230,160
190   DATA 7,185,240,112,145,6,136,16,248,160
200   DATA 7,32,161,112,32,177,112,32,17,244
210   DATA 160,0,169,173,32,225,112,200,169,141
220   DATA 32,212,112,32,192,112,208,235,169,96
230   DATA 145,6,96,72,173,246,112,160,0,32
240   DATA 17,244,160,0,104,145,6,200,165,38
250   DATA 24,109,247,112,145,6,200,165,39,145
260   DATA 6,200,24,152,101,6,133,6,165,7
270   DATA 105,0,133,7,160,0,96,169,65,141
280   DATA 248,112,169,110,141,249,112,140,246,112
290   DATA 152,96,32,161,112,238,248,112,208,3
300   DATA 238,249,112,238,246,112,173,246,112,201
310   DATA 192,96,145,6,200,165,38,145,6,200
320   DATA 165,39,145,6,96,145,6,200,173,248
330   DATA 112,145,6,200,173,249,112,145,6,96
340   DATA 136,48,3,76,56,101
```

SCROLLING RIGHT WITH SAME COLOR

This program scrolls the graphics picture from left to right 14 plot positions and wraps around on the left side of the screen. The colors remain intact.

EXPLANATION

To load this routine into memory use the command:

BRUN RIGHTSCROLL2

Issue the CALL 24758 command each time you want to scroll the screen right 14 plot positions.

```
5   REM  === RIGHTSCROLL2.A ===
10  HOME
20  FOR X = 0 TO 339: READ V: POKE 32260 + X,V: NEXT
30  PRINT "SAVE TO DISK (Y/N): ";: GET A$: IF A$ = "N" T
HEN  END
40  IF A$ < > "Y" THEN 30
50  PRINT  CHR$ (13); CHR$ (4);"BSAVE RIGHTSCROLL2,A$7E0
4,L$154"
100  DATA 169,182,133,6,162,0,160,0,169,96
110  DATA 133,7,169,38,141,91,127,169,194,141
120  DATA 88,127,169,123,141,92,127,152,32,252
130  DATA 126,169,39,141,91,127,169,130,141,88
140  DATA 127,169,124,141,92,127,152,32,252,126
150  DATA 169,160,145,6,200,169,36,145,6,32
160  DATA 236,126,140,89,127,162,1,142,90,127
170  DATA 169,185,32,208,126,238,90,127,238,90
180  DATA 127,169,153,32,208,126,56,173,90,127
190  DATA 233,3,141,90,127,169,185,32,208,126
200  DATA 238,90,127,238,90,127,169,153,32,208
210  DATA 126,206,90,127,238,89,127,173,89,127
220  DATA 201,192,208,202,160,6,185,81,127,145
230  DATA 6,136,16,248,160,6,32,236,126,169
240  DATA 194,141,88,127,169,123,141,92,127,152
250  DATA 141,91,127,32,185,126,169,130,141,88
260  DATA 127,169,124,141,92,127,169,1,141,91
270  DATA 127,152,170,32,185,126,169,96,145,6
280  DATA 96,141,89,127,32,67,127,169,173,32
290  DATA 19,127,200,169,141,32,34,127,32,47
300  DATA 127,208,237,96,72,173,89,127,160,0
310  DATA 32,17,244,160,0,104,145,6,200,165
320  DATA 38,24,109,90,127,145,6,200,165,39
330  DATA 145,6,200,24,152,101,6,133,6,165
340  DATA 7,105,0,133,7,160,0,96,141,89
350  DATA 127,32,67,127,169,173,32,34,127,200
360  DATA 169,141,32,19,127,32,47,127,208,237
370  DATA 96,145,6,200,173,88,127,145,6,200
380  DATA 173,92,127,145,6,96,145,6,200,165
```

```
390    DATA 38,145,6,200,165,39,145,6,96,32
400    DATA 236,126,238,88,127,208,3,238,92,127
410    DATA 238,89,127,173,89,127,201,192,96,32
420    DATA 17,244,160,0,165,38,24,109,91,127
430    DATA 133,38,96,136,136,48,3,76,184,105
```

SCROLLING UP

This program scrolls the graphics picture up the screen 1 plot position each time it is called. A wraparound effect is created, since the top byte becomes the bottom byte. Since it only moves one byte at a time, this program scrolls the screen slowly.

EXPLANATION

To load this routine into memory use the command:

BRUN UPSCROLL

Issue the CALL 24758 command each time you want to scroll the screen up 1 plot position at a time.

```
5    REM   === UPSCROLL.A ===
10   HOME
20   FOR X = 0 TO 141: READ V: POKE 28672 + X,V: NEXT
30   PRINT "SAVE TO DISK (Y/N): ";: GET A$: IF A$ = "N" T
HEN  END
40   IF A$ < > "Y" THEN 30
50   PRINT  CHR$ (13); CHR$ (4);"BSAVE UPSCROLL,A$7000,L$
8E"
100   DATA 169,182,133,6,169,96,133,7,165,230
110   DATA 141,123,112,160,7,185,119,112,145,6
120   DATA 136,16,248,169,190,133,6,169,1,141
130   DATA 142,112,169,185,32,81,112,206,142,112
140   DATA 169,153,32,81,112,238,142,112,238,142
150   DATA 112,173,142,112,201,192,208,230,169,191
160   DATA 160,0,32,17,244,165,39,141,132,112
170   DATA 160,14,185,127,112,145,6,136,16,248
180   DATA 96,72,173,142,112,160,0,32,17,244
190   DATA 160,0,104,145,6,200,165,38,145,6
200   DATA 200,165,39,145,6,200,152,24,101,6
210   DATA 133,6,165,7,105,0,133,7,96,160
220   DATA 0,185,0,255,141,255,63,173,255,63
230   DATA 153,208,255,200,192,40,240,3,76,184
240   DATA 96,96
```

This program scrolls the graphics picture down the screen with the bottom-most byte becoming the top. It scrolls the screen down 1 byte or plot position each time it is called. Therefore, this program scrolls the screen slowly.

EXPLANATION

To load this routine into memory use the command:

BRUN DOWNSCROLL

Issue the CALL 24758 command each time you want to scroll the screen down 1 plot position at a time.

```
5    REM  === DOWNSCROLL.A ===
10   HOME
20   FOR X = 0 TO 141: READ V: POKE 28672 + X,V: NEXT
30   PRINT "SAVE TO DISK (Y/N): ";: GET A$: IF A$ = "N" T
HEN  END
40   IF A$ < > "Y" THEN 30
50   PRINT  CHR$ (13); CHR$ (4);"BSAVE DOWNSCROLL,A$7000,
L$8E"
100  DATA 169,182,133,6,169,96,133,7,169,191
110  DATA 160,0,32,17,244,165,39,141,123,112
120  DATA 160,7,185,119,112,145,6,136,16,248
130  DATA 169,190,133,6,169,190,141,142,112,169
140  DATA 185,32,81,112,238,142,112,169,153,32
150  DATA 81,112,206,142,112,206,142,112,173,142
160  DATA 112,201,255,208,230,165,230,141,132,112
170  DATA 160,14,185,127,112,145,6,136,16,248
180  DATA 96,72,173,142,112,160,0,32,17,244
190  DATA 160,0,104,145,6,200,165,38,145,6
200  DATA 200,165,39,145,6,200,152,24,101,6
210  DATA 133,6,165,7,105,0,133,7,96,160
220  DATA 0,185,208,255,141,255,63,173,255,63
230  DATA 153,0,255,200,192,40,240,3,76,184
240  DATA 96,96
```

KEYBOARD DEMONSTRATION OF SPECIAL EFFECTS ROUTINES

This program demonstrates the use of the special effects routines using keyboard control.

EXPLANATION ═══

The program demonstrates four special effects at a time. It loads the special effects routines SCREEN EOR and HV SCREEN FLIP. You can select one of the following scrolling routines: LEFTSCROLL, LEFTSCROLL2, RIGHTSCROLL, RIGHTSCROLL2, UPSCROLL, or DOWNSCROLL. And you can select one of the page flips, either HH SCREEN FLIP or HH SCREEN FLIP2.

The program includes an etch-a-sketch routine to draw a design. If you have a binary picture that you would like to use, then omit lines 30–160 from the program and save the program as HIRES KEYBOARD DEMO 2. Then BLOAD your picture to page 1 and run the program HIRES KEYBOARD DEMO 2.

Line 10 reads in the names of the special effects. Lines 30–160 provide an etch-a-sketch program to draw a design. The space bar allows you to change the color of the dot being HPLOTted. The keys I, J, K, and M move the dot up, left, right, and down, respectively. The keyboard is read on line 70. Lines 80–90 adjust the value of X or Y, depending on the keypress. Line 100 checks the color of the last dot HPLOTted.

The dot is HPLOTted from its old position XP,YP to its new position X,Y at line 110.

There is an adjustment factor for the number of dots you move at a time. Enter any number 1–9 to set this factor at any time in the program. Line 120 checks for a digit 1–9 keystroke and sets the adjustment factor S to your selected number.

The ESC key at line 1030 terminates the etch-a-sketch routine and requests you to select two special routines.

Lines 170–200 request that you specify a scrolling routine, and lines 210–240 request that you specify a flip routine. The routines are loaded into memory above one another, along with the color switch routine and upside down flip at line 250. Line 260 BRUNs the scrolling routine.

Line 270 sets the graphics screen to full screen hi-res graphics without erasing the screen. The keyboard is read at lines 280–300 and the appropriate machine language routine is called.

The space bar, followed by a number from 0 to 6, allows you to change the colors of the hi-res graphics picture. The RETURN key starts the scrolling routine, and any key stops the scrolling. The key Q flips the picture upside down, while the key W flips the picture from side to side. CONTROL C RETURN stops the program.

```
5   REM   === HIRES KEYBOARD DEMO ===
10  FOR X = 1 TO 8: READ S$(X): NEXT X
20  D$ =  CHR$ (13) +  CHR$ (4)
25  REM   --- ETCH A SKETCH ---
30  HGR : HOME : POKE  - 16302,0
40  HC = 6:S = 1:X = 127:Y = 96
50  HCOLOR= HC: HPLOT X,Y
60  POKE  - 16368,0
67  REM   --- READ KEYBOARD ---
70  K =  PEEK ( - 16384): IF K < 128 THEN 70
80  K$ =  CHR$ (K - 128):X = X + (K$ = "K") * S - (K$ = "
J") * S:K = X - (X > 278) * S + (X < 0) * S
90  Y = Y + (K$ = "M") * S - (K$ = "I") * S:Y = Y - (Y >
191) * S + (Y < 0) * S
100 XP =  PEEK (224) +  PEEK (225) * 256:YP =  PEEK (226
)
105  REM   ---PLOT DOT ---
110  HPLOT XP,YP TO X,Y TO X + 1,Y TO XP + 1,YP: HPLOT X
,Y
120  IF  VAL (K$) < 11 AND  VAL (K$) > 0 THEN S =  VAL (
K$)
130  IF  ASC (K$) = 27 THEN  POKE  - 16368,0: GOTO 170
140  IF K$ <  > " " THEN  POKE  - 16368,0: GOTO 70
150 HC = HC + 1:HC = HC - (HC = 8) * 8: HCOLOR= HC
160  POKE  - 16368,0: GOTO 70
165  REM   --- DISPLAY MENU ---
170  TEXT : HOME : VTAB 13
180  FOR X = 1 TO 6: HTAB 7: PRINT "("X") "S$(X): NEXT X
190  PRINT : INPUT "CHOOSE A SCROLLING PROGRAM (1-6) ";P
$
200 P =  VAL (P$): IF P < 1 OR P > 6 THEN  POKE 37, PEEK
 (37) - 2: GOTO 190
210  HOME : VTAB 13
220  FOR X = 1 TO 2: HTAB 7: PRINT "("X") "S$(X + 6): NE
XT
230  PRINT : INPUT "WHICH FLIP (1-2) ";F$
240 F =  VAL (F$): IF F < 1 OR F > 2 THEN  POKE 37, PEEK
 (37) - 2: GOTO 230
245  REM   --- LOAD MACHINE LANGUAGE ROUTINES ---
250  PRINT D$"BLOAD SCREEN EOR": PRINT D$"BLOAD HV SCREE
N FLIP": PRINT D$"BLOAD"S$(F + 6)
260  PRINT D$"BRUN"S$(P)
265  REM   --- DISPLAY HIRES SCREEN ---
270  POKE  - 16304,0: POKE  - 16297,0: POKE  - 16302,0:
POKE  - 16368,0
275  REM   --- READ KEYBOARD ---
280 K =  PEEK ( - 16384): IF K = 141 THEN  CALL 24758
290  IF K = 209 THEN  CALL 24576
300  IF K = 215 THEN  CALL 24638
310  IF  PEEK ( - 16384) <  > 160 THEN 280
320  POKE  - 16301,0: VTAB 21: INPUT "EOR FACTOR (0-6) "
;F
330  CALL 768,F: POKE  - 16302,0: GOTO 280
1000  DATA  LEFTSCROLL,LEFTSCROLL2,RIGHTSCROLL,RIGHTSCRO
LL2
1010  DATA  UPSCROLL,DOWNSCROLL,HH SCREEN FLIP,HH SCREE
N FLIP2
```

PADDLE DEMONSTRATION OF SPECIAL EFFECTS ROUTINES

This program demonstrates the special effects routines using paddle, button, and keyboard control.

EXPLANATION ═══

The program is similar to HIRES KEYBOARD DEMO except it uses paddle, button, and keyboard controls. See the explanation for HIRES KEYBOARD DEMO. The etch-a-sketch uses paddle 0 to change colors rather than the space bar, and the paddles control the movement of the dot rather than the keys I, J, K, and M. There is no adjustment factor for spacing in this program.

The button on paddle 1 terminates the etch-a-sketch program and requests the special effects routines. This is similar to HIRES KEYBOARD DEMO.

The controls differ with the exception of the space bar followed by a number from 0 to 6, which still controls the color switching. The movement of either paddle controls the scrolling. When the paddle reads in the middle range (87-167), the scrolling stops.

Button 0 flips the picture upside down, while button 1 flips the picture from side to side. If you have an Apple IIe/IIc, the open and closed apples function the same as buttons 0 and 1 on the paddles. CONTROL C RETURN stops the program.

```
5    REM   === HIRES PADDLE DEMO ===
10   FOR X = 1 TO 8: READ S$(X): NEXT X
20   D$ =  CHR$ (13) +  CHR$ (4)
25   REM   --- ETCH A SKETCH ---
30   HGR : HOME : POKE  - 16302,0
40   HC = 1: HCOLOR= HC
50   HPLOT   PDL (0) * 278 / 255, PDL (1) * 191 / 255
60   X =  PDL (0) * 278 / 255:Y =  PDL (1) * 191 / 255
70   XP =  PEEK (224) +  PEEK (225) * 256:YP =  PEEK (226)
80   HPLOT   TO X,Y: HPLOT XP + 1,YP TO X + 1,Y: HPLOT X,Y
85   REM   --- READ BUTTONS ---
90   IF  PEEK ( - 16286) > 127 THEN 150
100  IF  PEEK ( - 16287) < 128 THEN P = 0: GOTO 60
110  IF P = 1 THEN 60
120  HC = HC + 1:HC = HC - (HC = 8) * 8: HCOLOR= HC
130  POKE 28, PEEK (228):P = 1
140  GOTO 60
145  REM   --- DISPLAY MENU ---
150  TEXT : HOME : VTAB 13
160  FOR X = 1 TO 6: HTAB 7: PRINT "("X")" "S$(X): NEXT X
170  PRINT : INPUT "CHOOSE A SCROLLING PROGRAM (1-6) ";P
     $
180  P =  VAL (P$): IF P < 1 OR P > 6 THEN  POKE 37, PEEK
     (37) - 2: GOTO 170
190  HOME : VTAB 13
200  FOR X = 1 TO 2: HTAB 7: PRINT "("X")" "S$(X + 6): NE
     XT
210  PRINT : INPUT "WHICH FLIP (1-2) ";F$
220  F =  VAL (F$): IF F < 1 OR F > 2 THEN  POKE 37, PEEK
     (37) - 2: GOTO 210
225  REM   --- LOAD MACHINE LANGUAGE ROUTINES ---
```

```
230   PRINT D$"BLOAD SCREEN EOR": PRINT D$"BLOAD HV SCREE
N FLIP": PRINT D$"BLOAD"S$(F + 6)
240   PRINT D$"BRUN"S$(P)
245   REM   --- DISPLAY HIRES SCREEN ---
250   POKE  - 16304,0: POKE  - 16297,0: POKE  - 16302,0:
POKE  - 16368,0
255   REM   --- READ PADDLES/BUTTONS/KEYBOARD ---
260   IF   PDL (0) < 87 OR   PDL (0) > 167 OR   PDL (1) < 87
 OR   PDL (1) > 167 THEN   CALL 24758
270   IF   PEEK ( - 16286) > 127 THEN   CALL 24638
280   IF   PEEK ( - 16287) > 127 THEN   CALL 24576
290   IF   PEEK ( - 16384) < > 160 THEN 260
300   POKE  - 16301,0: VTAB 21: INPUT "EOR FACTOR (0-6) "
;F
310   CALL 768,F: POKE  - 16302,0: GOTO 260
1000   DATA   LEFTSCROLL,LEFTSCROLL2,RIGHTSCROLL,RIGHTSCRO
LL2
1010   DATA   UPSCROLL,DOWNSCROLL,HH SCREEN FLIP,HH SCREEN
 FLIP2
```

SPIRAL DISPLAY OF SCREEN

This routine displays the high resolution graphics screen in a spiral that moves in a counterclockwise direction.

EXPLANATION

The routine takes the picture from page 1 and spirals it onto page 2, starting at the center of the screen.

DATA statements are used to enter the directions for a machine language program. These instructions are poked into memory starting at address 24576. Run the program and answer Y to save it, if it has not already been saved. This creates a binary file.

When you wish to use this routine, load in a hi-res graphics image to page 1 with the following command, where picturename is the name of the binary file:

```
BLOAD picturename,A$2000
```

Then BLOAD the spiral routine with the command:

```
BLOAD SPIRAL DISPLAY
```

Issue the HGR2 command or the equivalent pokes to set page 2. Use the command CALL 24576 to access the machine language routine.

This routine cannot be used with the scrolling or page flipping routines, since they occupy the same memory locations.

You can adjust the speed of this spiraling routine by poking in two additional values. Enter these two commands, where H represents the counter for an outer loop and L represents the counter for an inner loop. The values of L and H can be in the range 0–255, where 0 equals a count of 256. This routine is initially set up so H = 4 and L = 0. By entering the following two POKE commands, you change the values of H and L.

```
POKE 24776,H
POKE 24781,L
```

To obtain the starting values again, enter the following two POKE commands:

```
POKE 24776,4
POKE 24781,0
```

```
5    REM  === SPIRAL DISPLAY.A ===
10   HOME
20   FOR X = 0 TO 259: READ V: POKE 24576 + X,V: NEXT
30   PRINT "SAVE TO DISK (Y/N): ";: GET A$: IF A$ = "N" T
HEN  END
40   IF A$ < > "Y" THEN 30
50   PRINT  CHR$ (13); CHR$ (4);"BSAVE SPIRAL DISPLAY,A$6
000,L$103"
100   DATA 169,32,133,230,169,0,141,5,97,141
110   DATA 6,97,160,0,32,17,244,172,6,97
120   DATA 165,38,153,10,97,165,39,153,38,97
130   DATA 238,6,97,24,173,5,97,105,8,141
140   DATA 5,97,201,192,144,222,169,28,141,8
150   DATA 97,169,11,141,7,97,169,1,141,4
160   DATA 97,169,17,141,9,97,32,153,96,32
170   DATA 233,96,206,8,97,32,153,96,32,249
180   DATA 96,208,245,32,233,96,238,7,97,32
190   DATA 153,96,32,239,96,208,245,238,4,97
200   DATA 238,9,97,173,9,97,201,40,208,3
210   DATA 76,215,96,32,233,96,238,8,97,32
220   DATA 153,96,32,249,96,208,245,32,233,96
230   DATA 206,7,97,32,153,96,32,239,96,208
240   DATA 245,238,4,97,238,9,97,32,233,96
250   DATA 76,72,96,172,7,97,185,10,97,133
260   DATA 6,133,8,185,38,97,133,7,24,105
270   DATA 32,133,9,172,8,97,162,7,177,6
280   DATA 145,8,24,165,7,105,4,133,7,24
290   DATA 165,9,105,4,133,9,202,16,235,169
300   DATA 4,141,66,97,160,0,136,208,253,206
310   DATA 66,97,208,248,96,206,9,97,32,233
320   DATA 96,238,8,97,32,153,96,32,249,96
330   DATA 208,245,96,169,0,141,3,97,96,238
340   DATA 3,97,173,3,97,205,4,97,96,238
350   DATA 3,97,173,3,97,205,9,97,96,0
```

CIRCLES, SINES, COSINES, AND DESIGNS

The Apple computer can generate numerous interesting designs, images, illusions, and portraits of people. Many beautiful designs can be obtained by cyclical repetition of math functions with slight variations between cycles. Art shows now include computer-generated art as another form of creative expression.

The sine and cosine are built-in trigonometric functions that can produce sine waves, circles, spirals, and other geometric designs. The sine wave can be used for a border in high resolution graphics or to display your name or message in text. A variation of the circle routine can produce ellipses and spirals.

Computer art can be generated by combinations of the sine and cosine functions to produce designs that resemble flowers, spheres, and spirals.

The following programs give suggested values for the variables. After running the programs with the suggested values, try changing them to obtain additional designs.

It is advisable to read the first several pages of this chapter, including the explanation of the Circle program, in order to understand sine and cosine functions, amplitude, frequency, and the adjustment factor. These variables are used in most of the programs but are only explained thoroughly in the beginning of the chapter.

DEGREES AND RADIANS

The computer uses radians rather than degrees to measure angles. This shows the conversion between degrees and radians.

EXPLANATION

We use degrees to measure angles, but the computer uses radians. A complete revolution of a circle is 360° or 2π radians, where $\pi = 3.14159$.

$$2\pi \text{ radians} = 360°$$

$$\frac{2\pi}{360} \text{ radians} = 1 \text{ degree} \qquad 1 \text{ radian} = \frac{360}{2\pi} \text{ degrees}$$

$$\frac{\pi}{180} \text{ radians} = 1 \text{ degree} \qquad 1 \text{ radian} = \frac{180}{\pi} \text{ degrees}$$

CONVERSION

To convert from degrees to radians, multiply degrees by $\pi/180$:

$$RAD = DEG * \pi / 180$$

To convert from radians to degrees, multiply radians by $180/\pi$:

$$DEG = RAD * 180 / \pi$$

SINE AND COSINE

This graphically illustrates the built-in functions of sine and cosine waves.

EXPLANATION

The following diagrams illustrate the sine and cosine wave functions.

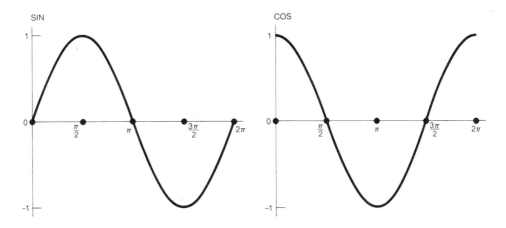

As the argument (value within parentheses) goes from 0 to 2π radians, the values of the sine and cosine functions range from 1 to -1, as shown in Table 8-1.

TABLE 8-1. VALUES OF SINE AND COSINE

Angle in radians	COS(A)	SIN(A)
$\pi/2$	0	1
π	-1	0
$3\pi/2$	0	-1
2π	1	0

FREQUENCY

Frequency represents how often the sine wave is completed as A goes from 0 to 2π radians.

The following figures represent a frequency of 1, 2, and 3.

Frequency = 1   Frequency = 2   Frequency = 3

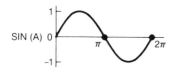

Y = SIN (A)   Y = SIN (2*A)   Y = SIN (3*A)

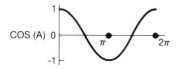

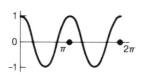

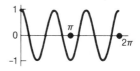

X = COS (A)   X = COS (2*A)   X = COS (3*A)

Amplitude

Multiplying the sine and cosine functions by AM, where AM represents the value of the amplitude, adjusts the functions so the amplitude ranges from AM to −AM. AM can be considered a scaling factor. This is illustrated by the figures below.

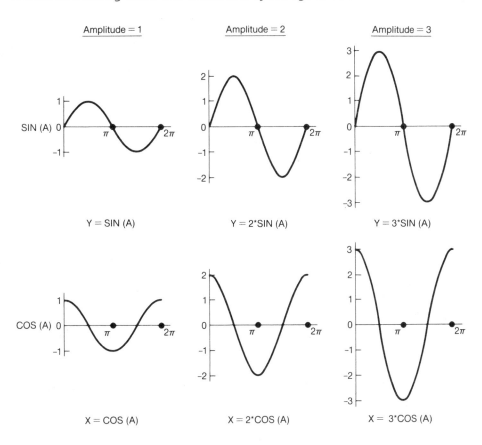

SINE WAVES

VERTICAL STAR SINE WAVE

This program prints an asterisk or star on the text screen in a sine wave formation. This sine wave moves down the screen rather than across, since the axis of the sine wave is vertical rather than horizontal.

EXPLANATION

The sine function is usually viewed moving across the screen. This program rotates the function 90° so it will snake down the screen while it prints an asterisk. A curve is completed as A goes from 0 to 2π radians. This is called a cycle. N controls the number of cycles.

The variables are:

PI	Value of π
N	Number of cycles
S	Step size
AM	Amplitude or scaling factor
XC	Center of sine wave on text screen
Z	Counter for delay loop
A	Value of angle from 0 to N $\times$ 2π radians
X	Tabbing value

Since the sine of an angle can only have values from 1 to -1, you must expand its scale in order to see its shape. AM represents the amplitude and adjusts the scaling. To obtain a range that contains the maximum number of points on the text screen, let AM = 19. When you multiply the sine value by AM in line 90, you expand the range from -1 through 1 to a new range of -19 through 19. This range, including 0, takes 39 print positions.

Since you cannot tab a negative number or plot a negative value, you must add a factor to bring the values of the sine wave within tabbing or plotting limits. XC represents the desired center. When you add XC in line 90, where XC = 20, you bring the range from -19 through 19 to a new adjusted range of 1—39. This shifts the center from 0 to XC or 20. You now have the tabbing range across the screen.

The step size S in line 70 determines the number of points plotted along the curve. A larger step size means fewer points, and a smaller step size means more points.

```
5   REM  === STAR SINE WAVE ===
10 PI = 3.14159
20 N = 4:S = .2:AM = 19:XC = 20
30  TEXT : HOME
40  HTAB (15): VTAB (12): PRINT "SINE WAVE"
50  FOR Z = 1 TO 500: NEXT Z
60  HOME
70  FOR A = 0 TO N * PI STEP S
80 X = AM *  SIN (A) + XC
90  PRINT  TAB( X);"*"
100  FOR Z = 1 TO 50: NEXT Z
110  NEXT A
199  END
```

SINE WAVE

1. Change the number of cycles graphed by changing the value of N.
2. Change the number of points plotted by changing the step sizes.
3. Change what is printed from an asterisk to another symbol, your name, or a message. You may have to change the scale factor AM from 19 to another number, and change the X center XC from 20 to another number to enable your message to fit on the screen.

SINE WAVE A BORDER IN HGR

This program draws a sine wave border around the screen in high resolution graphics.

EXPLANATION

A straight line border is drawn at line 40. Then two subroutines are used to draw the sine waves. The subroutine at 1000–1060 draws the sine wave down the screen, while the subroutine at 2000–2060 draws the sine wave across the screen.

The variables are set in lines 50–160 for each sine wave and the appropriate subroutine is executed.

The variables are:

N	Number of cycles
INC	Step size
XC	Center on X-axis
YC	Center on Y-axis
AM	Amplitude or scaling factor
F	Frequency
X	Value on X-axis
Y	Value on Y-axis
XS	Increment or step size on X-axis
YS	Increment or step size on Y-axis
A	Value of angle from 0 to 2π radians

The variable AM represents the amplitude and adjusts the range of the values of the sine wave from $-AM$ to AM. The variable F stands for the frequency and adjusts how often the sine wave is completed as A varies from 0 to 2π radians.

Since the origin of the hi-res screen is in the upper left corner, you will have to add a constant to the horizontal and vertical values in order to position the center of the figure on the screen at the desired location. XC adjusts the horizontal position, while YC adjusts the vertical position.

XS determines the increment or step size on the X-axis as the sine function moves across the screen, while YS does the same on the Y-axis as the function moves down the screen.

N determines the number of cycles of the sine function that will be drawn. Different values of N are used for the X-axis and Y-axis and these values must be adjusted if you change the frequency F.

```
5    REM   === SINE WAVE BORDER ===
10 PI = 3.14159
20   HGR2
30   HCOLOR= 3
35   REM   --- BORDER ---
40   HPLOT 0,0 TO 279,0 TO 279,191 TO 0,191 TO 0,0
45   REM   --- SINE WAVES ---
50 N = 14:INC = .5:XC = 10:AM = 5
60 F = .5:YS = 1:Y = 5
70   GOSUB 1000"SINE DOWN"
80 N = 21:INC = .5:YC = 10:AM = 5
90 F = .5:XS = 1:X = 5
100   GOSUB 2000"SINE ACROSS"
110 N = 14:INC = .5:XC = 270:AM = 5
```

```
120 F = .5:YS = 1:Y = 5
130  GOSUB 1000"SINE DOWN"
140 N = 21:INC = .5:YC = 180:AM = 5
150 F = .5:XS = 1:X = 5
160  GOSUB 2000"SINE ACROSS"
499  END
995  REM  === DOWN ===
1000  HPLOT XC + AM *  SIN (0),0
1010  FOR A = 0 TO N * 2 * PI STEP INC
1020 X = AM *  SIN (A * F) + XC
1030 Y = Y + YS
1040  HPLOT  TO X,Y
1050  NEXT A
1060  RETURN
1995  REM  === ACROSS ===
2000  HPLOT 0,AM *  SIN (0) + YC
2010  FOR A = 0 TO N * 2 * PI STEP INC
2020 X = X + XS
2030 Y = AM *  SIN (A * F) + YC
2040  HPLOT  TO X,Y
2050  NEXT A
2060  RETURN
```

SAMPLE OUTPUT

MODIFICATION

To change the border, you can change the step size INC, the amplitude AM, the frequency F, and the number of cycles N to other values.

CIRCLES

CIRCLES USING TRIGONOMETRIC METHOD

This program draws a circle using the trigonometric method.

EXPLANATION ══

There are various ways of drawing a circle—estimation method, algebraic method, and trigonometric method. This program uses the latter technique.

The variables are:

PI	Value of π
AF	Adjustment factor for circle/ellipse
R	Radius or amplitude of sine and cosine functions
XC	Center on X-axis
YC	Center on Y-axis
A	Value of angle from 0 to 2π radians
INC	Step size or increment
X	Distance on X-axis
Y	Distance on Y-axis

The value of X is determined by the cosine function, while the value of Y is determined by the sine function. COS(A) represents the horizontal distance from the center of the circle; SIN(A) represents the vertical distance from the center of the circle.

The variable A represents the angle in radians. The value of A ranges from 0 to 2π radians, where 2π represents one complete rotation of the circle and INC is the step size.

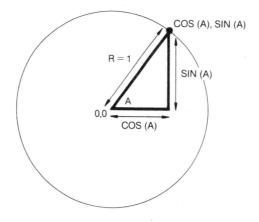

The value of INC determines the number of points that will be plotted. Table 8-2 indicates the number of points plotted for various values of INC. Add one additional point for the starting point.

TABLE 8-2. INC PLOTTED POINTS		
Value of INC	Number of points plotted	
INC = .1	$10 \times 2 \times 3.14 = 10 \times 6.28 = 62.8$	$= 62+1 = 63$ points
INC = .5	$2 \times 2 \times 3.14 = 2 \times 6.28 = 12.56$	$= 12+1 = 13$ points
INC = .01	$100 \times 2 \times 3.14 = 100 \times 6.28 = 628+1 = 629$ points	

In order to adjust the radius of the circle to the desired value, multipy the functions by R, where R represents the amplitude.

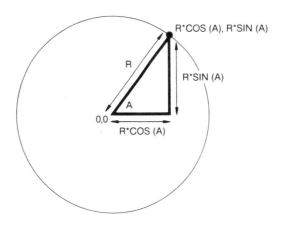

The variables XC and YC shift the center of the circle from the upper left corner of the screen 0,0 to the center of your choice XC,YC.

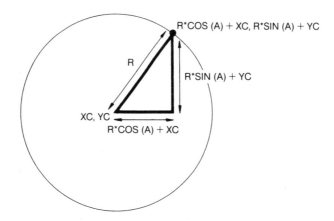

Since the screen is not a square, the circles appear as ellipses or flattened circles. On a printer, however, they would appear as circles. To make them appear as circles on the screen, an adjustment factor AF is used to multiply the cosine function. You may have to change the values of the adjustment factor to accommodate the adjustment of your TV screen or monitor. Try values such as 1.13, 1.15, or 1.18.

The value of R✱COS(A)✱AF+XC represents the distance on the X-axis, while the value of R✱SIN(A)+YC represents the value on the Y-axis.

The first point is HPLOTted. The remaining points on the circumference are connected to the preceding point. The last point is connected to the first point to complete the circle.

```
5   REM   === CIRCLE ===
10  PI = 3.14159
20  AF = 1.17
30  HGR : POKE  - 16302,0
40  HCOLOR= 3
50  R = 80:XC = 140:YC = 96:INC = .1
60  GOSUB 1000"DRAW CIRCLE"
999   END
1000  HPLOT R * AF *  COS (0) + XC,R *  SIN (0) + YC
1010  FOR A = 0 TO 2 * PI STEP INC
1020  HPLOT  TO R * AF *  COS (A) + XC,R *  SIN (A) + YC
1025 J = J + 1
1030  NEXT A
1040  HPLOT  TO R * AF *  COS (0) + XC,R *  SIN (0) + YC
1050  RETURN
```

1. Try changing the value of the radius, where 95 is the maximum value.
2. Change the increment INC to other values such as .7, .9, or .5.
3. You can get different shaped ellipses by changing the value of AF to .5 or 2. Adjust the value of the radius accordingly.
4. Input the values for the variables. Change line 50 and add lines 7, 45, 52, and 54. Line 7 avoids the range error message and program termination when an illegal value for X or Y is HPLOTted.

```
7 ONERR GOTO 45
```

or

```
7 ONERR GOTO 999
```

```
45 TEXT: HOME
50 INPUT "ENTER THE RADIUS ";R
52 INPUT "ENTER THE CENTER FOR X AND Y AXIS "; XC, YC
54 INPUT "ENTER THE INCREMENT ";INC
```

SPOKES

This program draws spokes emanating from the center to the circumference of a circle.

EXPLANATION

This program is a variation of the Circle program. Instead of connecting each point on the circumference to each other, it connects each point on the circumference to a point in the center XC,YC of the circle.

The variables are:

PI	Value of π
AF	Adjustment factor for circle/ellipse
R	Radius of circle or amplitude
XC	Center on X-axis
YC	Center on Y-axis
A	Value of angle from 0 to 2π radians
INC	Step size or increment
X	Distance on X-axis
Y	Distance on Y-axis

See the explanation of the Circle program for a description of this program.

```
5   REM  === CIRCLE/SPOKES ===
10 PI = 3.14159
20 AF = 1.17
30  HGR : POKE  - 16302,0
40  HCOLOR= 3
50 R = 80:XC = 140:YC = 96:INC = .1
60  GOSUB 1000"DRAW CIRCLE/SPOKES"
999  END
1000  HPLOT R * AF *  COS (0) + XC,R *  SIN (0) + YC
1010  FOR A = 0 TO 2 * PI STEP INC
1020  HPLOT XC,YC TO R * AF *  COS (A) + XC,R *  SIN (A)
 + YC
1030  NEXT A
1040  RETURN
```

SAMPLE OUTPUT

AF = .75

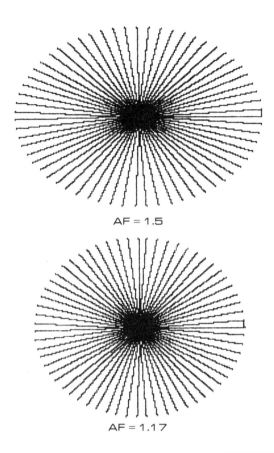

AF = 1.5

AF = 1.17

MODIFICATIONS

1. Change the adjustment factor AF to get an elliptical figure.
2. Change the center of the spoke to a point other than the center of the screen. You need to add a line 35, which may be one of the following:

```
35 X = 0:Y = 0
```

or

```
35 X = 20:Y = 130
```

or

```
35 X = 100:Y = 60
```

or

```
35 X = 140:Y = 0
```

Then change line 1020 to:

```
1020 HPLOT X,Y TO R * COS(A) * XF + XC,R * SIN(A) + YC
```

where X and Y represent a point within the circle or outside the circle. The values of X and Y do not have to be equal to XC and YC, respectively.

DRAWING CIRCLE FASTER WITH ARRAYS

This program uses arrays to store the calculated values of the circle in order to draw the circle quickly.

EXPLANATION

The computer does calculations quickly—almost always faster than we could even with the aid of a calculator. But it still takes some time to make the calculations. If you calculate as you draw, the drawing will be slow.

The program first calculates the values and, when all the values are calculated and stored, it draws the circle. This program is a modification of the program that draws a circle.

The variables are:

PI   Value of π
N   Number of points
S   Step size
R   Radius or amplitude of sine and cosine functions
AF   Adjustment factor for circle/ellipse
XC   Center on X-axis
YC   Center on Y-axis
X(N)   Value on X-axis
Y(N)   Value on Y-axis
A   Value of angle as it ranges from 0 to 2π radians

Subroutine 1000–1050 stores the X and Y values as array elements. Line 100 lets you position the circle at the center of your choice XC,YC. Lines 110–150 draw the circle using the array elements that have already been calculated. Line 110 draws the starting point, while line 150 connects the last point or endpoint to the starting point.

```
5    REM   === DRAW CIRCLE FASTER ===
10   DIM X(63),Y(63)
20   TEXT : HOME
30 PI = 3.14159
40   VTAB 8: HTAB 17: PRINT "CIRCLE"
50   VTAB 12: HTAB 11: INVERSE : PRINT "ONE MOMENT PLEASE
": NORMAL
60 N = 0:S = .1:R = 95:AF = 1.17
70   GOSUB 1000"SET UP ARRAYS"
75   REM   --- DRAW CIRCLE ---
80   HGR : POKE  - 16302,0
90   HCOLOR= 3
100 XC = 140:YC = 96
110   HPLOT X(1) + XC,Y(1) + YC
115   REM   --- DRAW CIRCLE ---
120   FOR C = 1 TO N
130   HPLOT  TO X(C) + XC,Y(C) + YC
140   NEXT C
150   HPLOT  TO X(1) + XC,Y(1) + YC
160   HPLOT  TO X(1) + XC,Y(1) + YC
199   END
995   REM   --- SET UP ARRAYS WITH X,Y ---
1000  FOR A = 0 TO 2 * PI STEP S
1010 N = N + 1
1020 X(N) =  INT ( COS (A) * R * AF)
1030 Y(N) =  INT ( SIN (A) * R)
1040  NEXT A
1050  RETURN
```

STRING CIRCLE OF N POINTS

This program draws a string circle of N points as N ranges from 1 to 15.

EXPLANATION

The program uses string art to draw a quasi-circle. It is a modification of the Circle program.

The set of variables are:

PI	Value of π
ND	Number of designs
R	Radius of design
AF	Adjustment factor for circular design rather than elliptical shape
XC	Center on X-axis
YC	Center on Y-axis
N	Counter for number of designs
C	Value of angle from 0 to 2π radians
F	Counter that determines frequency of the sine and cosine functions
A	Angle C in radians times frequency F
J, K	Counter for endpoints
X(J),X(K)	Array elements for X value
Y(J),Y(K)	Array elements for Y value
Z	Delay counter

This program uses arrays to store the values so the designs can be drawn quickly. Lines 70–110 set up the arrays X( ) and Y( ) with the cosine and sine values that represent the values of the X and Y coordinates for N designs.

The loop at 140–170 plots a circle of N points, where N ranges from 1 to 15, since ND = 15.

Even values for N create a circle pattern in the center of the design, while with odd values for N the strings cross through the center of the design.

```
5   REM === STRING CIRCLE N POINTS ===
10  DIM X(30),Y(30)
15  REM --- INITIALIZATION ---
20 PI = 3.14159
30 ND = 15:R = 95:AF = 1.17
40 XC = 140:YC = 96
45  REM --- SET UP ARRAYS ---
50  FOR N = 1 TO ND
60 C = 2 * PI / N
70  FOR F = 0 TO N - 1
80 A = C * F
90 X(F) = R * AF *  COS (A) + XC
100 Y(F) = R *  SIN (A) + YC
110  NEXT F
120  HGR2
130  HCOLOR= 3
135  REM --- DRAW CIRCLE N POINTS ---
140  FOR J = 0 TO N - 1
150  FOR K = 0 TO N - 1
160  HPLOT X(J),Y(J) TO X(K),Y(K)
```

```
170   NEXT K,J
180   FOR Z = 1 TO 500: NEXT Z
190   NEXT N
199   END
```

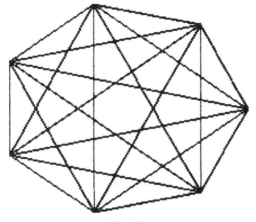

N = 7

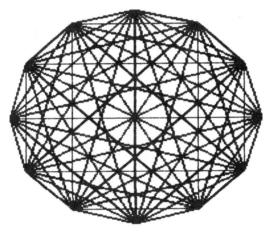

N = 12

MODIFICATIONS ═══════════════════════════════════

1. Change the value of ND, which determines the number of designs.
2. Change the adjustment factor AF to get an elliptical design.

CIRCLE FILL 1

This program draws a circle and fills it in.

EXPLANATION

The program uses trigonometric functions to determine the values of the X and Y coordinates. It is a modification of the Circle program.

The set of variables are:

PI   Value of π
S   Step size
XC   Center on X-axis
YC   Center on Y-axis
R   Radius or amplitude of sine and cosine functions
AF   Adjustment factor for circle/ellipse
A   Value of angle in range of 0 to 2π radians
X   Value on X-axis
Y   Value on Y-axis

A line is drawn from the center of the circle XC,YC to a point on the radius with a small step size S = .01. This fills in the circle as the radius swings around.

```
5    REM === CIRCLE FILL 1 ===
10 PI = 3.14159
20   HGR : POKE  - 16302,0
30 S = .01:XC = 140:YC = 96:R = 50:AF = 1.17
40   HCOLOR= 3: POKE  - 16302,0
50   FOR A = 0 TO 2 * PI STEP S
60 X = R * AF *   COS (A)
70 Y = R *   SIN (A)
80   HPLOT XC,YC TO X + XC,Y + YC
90   NEXT A
99   END
```

SAMPLE OUTPUT

CIRCLE FILL 2

This program also draws a circle and fills it in.

EXPLANATION ═══

The Pythagorean theorem is used to draw this circle. The Pythagorean theorem states that the square of the hypotenuse of the right triangle is equal to the sum of the squares of the other two sides.

Right triangle:

$$c^2 = a^2 + b^2$$

Circle triangle:

$$R^2 = X^2 + Y^2$$
$$Y^2 = R^2 - X^2$$
$$Y = \sqrt{R - X}$$

The set of variables are:

XC	Center on X-axis
YC	Center on Y-axis
R	Radius or amplitude of sine and cosine functions
AF	Adjustment factor to create circle/ellipse
X	Value on X-axis
Y	Value on Y-axis

This circle is filled in in a zig-zag manner.

```
5   REM === CIRCLE FILL 2 ===
10  XC = 140:YC = 80:R = 50:AF = 1.17
20   HGR : POKE  - 16302,0
30   HCOLOR= 3: POKE  - 16302,0
40   HPLOT ( - R * AF) + XC,YC
60  FOR X =  - R TO R STEP 1 / AF
70  Y =  SQR (R ^ 2 - X ^ 2)
80   HPLOT  TO AF * X + XC,YC - Y
90   HPLOT  TO AF * X + XC,YC + Y
100   NEXT X
199   END
```

SAMPLE OUTPUT ═══

DESIGNS USING SINE AND COSINE

The following programs use the sine and cosine functions to draw geometric designs.

FLOWER MAKER

This program draws flowers of varying petal size.

EXPLANATION

The program is a modification of the Circle program. Two nested loops are used. The outer loop 50–120 determines the radius that affects the size of the petals. The inner loop 60–120 draws the modified circle.

The set of variables are:

PI	Value of π
F	Frequency of sine and cosine functions
XC	Center on X-axis
YC	Center on Y-axis
AF	Adjustment factor for circle/ellipse
R	Counter that determines radius
A	Angle that ranges from 0 to 2π
AM	Amplitude of cosine and sine functions
X	Value on X-axis
Y	Value on Y-axis

The amplitude AM of the cosine and sine functions is determined in line 70. The amplitude changes each time the angle changes. The angle A varies from 0 to 2π in 1° increments. Recall that $\pi/180$ radians is equivalent to 1°.

Line 100 determines if the point to be plotted is the first point or any of the remaining points. The HPLOT command is used only with the first point, while the HPLOT TO command is used with the remaining points.

```
5    REM   === FLOWER MAKER ===
10   HGR2
20   HCOLOR= 7
30 PI = 3.14159
40 F = 1:XC = 140:YC = 96:AF = 1.17
45   REM   --- DRAW PETALS ---
50   FOR R = 20 TO 96 STEP 20
60   FOR A = 0 TO 2 * PI STEP PI / 180
70 AM = R *  COS (4 * F * A)
80 X = AM * AF *  COS (F * A)
90 Y = AM *  SIN (F * A)
100   IF A = 0 THEN  HPLOT X + XC,Y + YC
110   HPLOT  TO X + XC,Y + YC
120   NEXT : NEXT
199   END
```

1. Change the constant in line 70 from 4 to 2.
2. Change the step size in line 50.
3. Change the frequency F in line 40.

SAMPLE OUTPUT ═══════════════════════════════════════

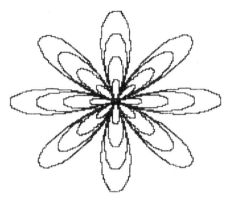

```
50 FOR R = 20 TO 96 STEP 20
70 AM = R * COS (4*F*A)
```

```
50 FOR R = 20 TO 96 STEP 10
70 AM = R * COS (4*F*A)
```

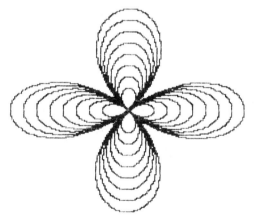

```
50 FOR R = 20 TO 96 STEP 10
70 AM = R * COS (2*F*A)
```

SPHERICAL DESIGN

This program draws a spherical design that resembles the globe.

EXPLANATION

Two spiral patterns intertwine to give a global effect. The spirals move outward and then inward.

The set of variables are:

PI   Value of π
RX   Radius on X-axis
RY   Radius on Y-axis
AM   Amplitude of sine function
XF   Frequency of cosine function
YF   Frequency of sine function
XC   Center on X-axis
YC   Center on Y-axis
N   Number of completed cycles
Z   Increment to value of Y
S   Factor that adjusts the step size for drawing the design
A   Value of angle in radians from 0 to 2π radians

Two user-defined functions define the values for X and Y. FN C(A) defines the cosine function, while FN S(A) defines the sine function. The third function, FN Z(A), is used to modify the value of Y.

RX * SIN(A/(N*2)) represents the amplitude of the cosine in line 50, while RY * SIN(A/(N*2)) represents the amplitude of the sine function in line 60.

```
5   REM   === SPHERICAL ===
7   REM   --- INITIALIZATION ---
10  PI = 3.14159
20  RX = 100:RY = 50:AM = .2:XF = 2:YF = 2
30  XC = 140:YC = 70:N = 7:Z = 0:S = 32
35  REM   --- DEFINE FUNCTIONS ---
40  DEF  FN C(A) = RX *  SIN (A / (N * 2))  *  COS (XF *
A) + XC
50  DEF  FN S(A) = RY *  SIN (A / (N * 2))  *  SIN (YF *
A) + YC
60  DEF  FN Z(A) = AM *  SIN (A / (N * 2))
75  REM   --- DRAW SPHERICAL DESIGN ---
80  HGR : POKE  - 16302,0
90  HCOLOR= 3
100  HPLOT XC,YC
110  FOR A = 0 TO N * 2 * PI STEP PI / S
120  X =  FN C(A):Y =  FN S(A):Z = Z +  FN Z(A)
130  HPLOT  TO X,Y + Z
140  NEXT A
199  END
```

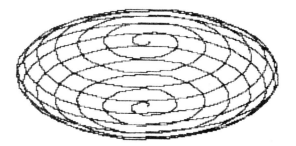

MODIFICATIONS

1. Modify the values of AM, RX and RY, XF and YF, N, and S to obtain different spheres. The values of XC and YC may have to also be modified to center the new spherical design.
2. If you change line 130 to the following statement, you will get a spiral.

```
130 HPLOT TO X,Y
```

LISSAJOUS PATTERNS

This program generates Lissajous patterns.

EXPLANATION

This program is a modification of the program that draws circles and ellipses. The frequency of the sine and cosine differ, whereas with the circle/ellipse program the frequency is the same for both functions.

The set of parameters are:

R	Radius
PI	Value of π computed by arctangent function
AF	Adjustment factor for circle/ellipse shape
XC	Center on X-axis
YC	Center on Y-axis
A	Frequency for cosine function
B	Frequency for sine function
N	Number of rotations
ANG	Angle that ranges $0-2\pi$ radians called theta
X	Value on X-axis
Y	Value of Y-axis
Z	Counter for delay loop

The angle ANG varies from 0 to 2π radians in increments of 2° ($2*\pi/180$). Remember that $\pi/180$ is equivalent to 1°. N cycles are generated.

R represents the radius and determines the amplitude for the cosine and sine functions on lines 110–120. The variables A and B determine the frequency of the cosine and sine functions, respectively. A adjusts the speed up and down on the X-axis, while B adjusts the speed back and forth on the Y-axis. When A = B, a circle or ellipse is drawn depending on the value of AF. If AF = 1.17, then square/circular designs will be drawn instead of rectangular/elliptical designs.

Line 90 HPLOTs the first point, while line 130 uses the HPLOT TO command to connect the remaining points.

The value of π was calculated by the computer instead of being assigned a value. The trigonometric function arctangent ATN( ) can be used to compute the value of π. Here is how this is done.

$$360° = 2\pi \text{ radians}$$
$$180° = \pi \text{ radians}$$
$$90° = \pi/2 \text{ radians}$$
$$45° = \pi/4 \text{ radians}$$

Conversion from degrees to radians

TAN(45°) = 1	(trig fact)
TAN($\pi/4$) = 1	(substitution)
ATN(1) = $\pi/4$	(trig fact)
ATN(1)*4 = π	(computation)

The CALL command on line 150 rings a bell when the design is finished.

```
5    REM === LISSAJOUS PATTERNS ===
10   ONERR  GOTO 199
20 PI =   ATN (1) * 4
30 R = 90:AF = 1.5:XC = 140:YC = 96
40   TEXT : HOME : VTAB 20
50   INPUT "ENTER A AND B ";A,B
60   INPUT "ENTER NUMBER OF CYCLES ";N
65   REM  --- DRAW DESIGN ---
70   HGR : POKE  - 16302,0
80   HCOLOR= 3
90   HPLOT R * AF *  COS (A * 0) + XC,R *  SIN (B * 0) +
YC
100   FOR ANG = 0 TO N * 2 * PI STEP 2 * PI / 180
110 X = R * AF *  COS (A * ANG) + XC
120 Y = R *  SIN (B * ANG) + YC
130   HPLOT  TO X,Y
140   NEXT ANG
150   CALL  - 1052
160   GET A$: GOTO 40
199   END
```

SAMPLE OUTPUT ══

Table 8-3 lists a few of the designs that can be generated by the program Lissajous Patterns.

TABLE 8-3. LISSAJOUS DESIGNS			
Design	A	B	N
Playpen	3	7	1
	5	13	1
	6	13	1
Spring	7	2	1
	10	2	1
	13	2	1
3-D Net	3.5	7.5	2
	9	10	1
	13	17	1
Ribbons	3.1	7.3	1

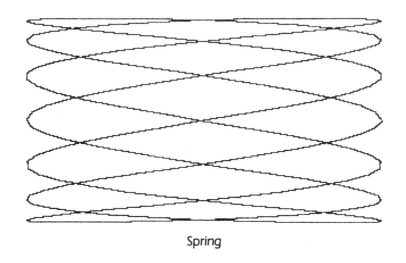

Spring

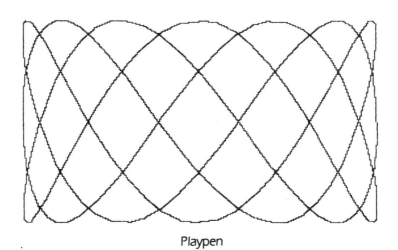

Playpen

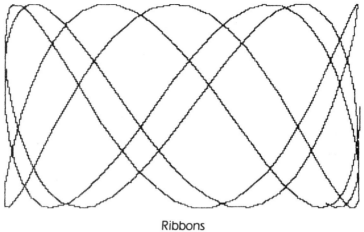

Ribbons

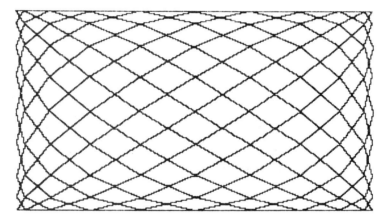

3-D Net

MODIFICATIONS

1. Change the value of the adjustment factor AF to obtain the circular/elliptical or square/rectangular designs.
2. Change the value of the radius R for a smaller design.

SUPEROSE

This program draws a great variety of designs made with curves.

EXPLANATION

The program is a modification of Lissajous Patterns. Both the amplitude and frequency of the functions differ, whereas in the Lissajous Patterns program only the frequency varied. In Lissajous Patterns, the amplitude of the functions was the radius, whereas in this program the amplitude is determined by the radius and sine function and changes throughout the program.

Think of a pen mounted on a rotating arm of varying length. The radius or location of the pen is a function of the angle A. If the radius remains constant a circle is drawn.

The set of variables are:

PI	Value of π
R	Radius
AF	Adjustment factor to get circle/ellipse shape
XC	Center on X-axis
YC	Center on Y-axis
A	Frequency for cosine function
B	Frequency for sine function
EF	Envelope factor: determines number of petals
ANG	Value of angle from 0 to 2π radians
AM	Amplitude or adjusted radius
X	Value on X-axis
Y	Value on Y-axis

A and B determine the frequency of the cosine and sine functions, respectively, on lines 130 and 140. When A = B, a circle or ellipse is drawn depending on the value of AF.

The envelope factor EF controls the frequency for the sine function in line 90. When EF is odd, you will get EF leaves or petals, whereas an even EF yields 2*EF leaves or petals.

Line 100 HPLOTs the first point. The remaining points are connected with the command HPLOT TO in line 150.

AM represents the amplitude and is a function of the radius R and the sine function with a frequency of EF. Throughout the loop 110–160 the value of the amplitude varies.

The program rings a bell at line 170 when the design is complete.

```
5   REM === SUPEROSE ===
10  ONERR  GOTO 199
20 PI = 3.14159
30 R = 90:AF = 1.17:XC = 140:YC = 96
40  TEXT : HOME : VTAB 20
50  INPUT "ENTER A AND B SUCH THAT A<=B ";A,B
60  INPUT "ENTER ENVELOPE FACTOR ";EF
65  REM  --- DRAW DESIGN ---
70  HGR : POKE  - 16302,0
80  HCOLOR= 3
90 AM = R *  SIN (EF * 0)
100  HPLOT AM * AF *  COS (A * 0) + XC,AM *  SIN (B * 0)
 + YC
110  FOR ANG = 0 TO 2 * PI STEP 2 * PI / 180
120 AM = R *  SIN (EF * ANG)
130 X = AM * AF *  COS (A * ANG) + XC
140 Y = AM *  SIN (B * ANG) + YC
150  HPLOT  TO X,Y
160  NEXT ANG
170  CALL  - 1052
180  GET A$: GOTO 40
199  END
```

SAMPLE OUTPUT ══

Table 8-4 lists a few of the many designs that the Superose program can generate.

TABLE 8-4. SUPEROSE DESIGNS

Design	A	B	EF	Special Characteristics
Flower	1	1	4	8 petals
	1	1	5	5 petals
	1	1	6	12 petals
	1	1	7	7 petals
	1	1	8	16 petals
Star	100	100	1	
	100	100	2	
	100	100	3	
	200	200	2	
	300	300	3	
Dragonfly	1	5	20	
	1	5	30	
Ant	4	5	3	
Bunny	1	3	3	
Butterfly	5	10	1	
	1	2	3	
Lotus	3	3	2	
	4	4	3	

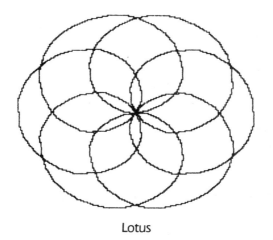

Lotus

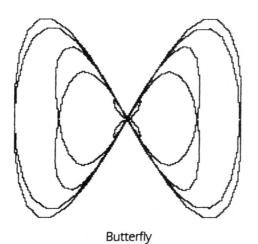

Butterfly

Star-Triangle

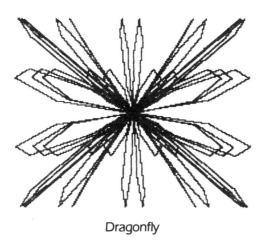

Dragonfly

MODIFICATIONS

1. Vary the value of R to adjust the size of the design, where 90 is the maximum radius that can be used.
2. Change the variable AF, which adjusts the circle/ellipse factor as in the previous Circle programs.

SPIRAL DESIGN

This program draws a solid background in a random color and a spiral design that varies.

EXPLANATION

The spiral design varies from a circular spiral to a triangular star-like spiral, while the direction varies from clockwise to counterclockwise.

The set of variables is:

PI   Value of π
XC   Center on X-axis
YC   Center on Y-axis
PT   Number of points
S   Step size for drawing background
N   Number of complete rotations of spiral design
XM   Midpoint of X-axis
YM   Midpoint of Y-axis
R   Radius of the design
AF   Adjustment factor for circular/elliptical design
C   Random color
B   Counter for background
ST   Step size for drawing spiral
A   Value of angle in radians from 0 to 2π radians
X   Value on X-axis
Y   Value on Y-axis
BL   Counter for drawing spiral design in black

Lines 50–70 draw the background. Line 80 determines the step size for the spiral design. The loop from 90 to 160 draws a black spiral design and a white spiral design. Lines 120–130 draw the black spiral, while lines 140–150 draw the white spiral design.

Line 170 waits for a keypress. If the ESC key is pressed, then the design ends. Any other key enables the next random design to be drawn.

```
5    REM   === SPIRAL DESIGN ===
7    REM   --- INITIALIZATION ---
10 PI = 3.14159
20 XC = 140:YC = 96:PT = 105:S = 2:N = 30
30 XM = 140:YM = 96:R = 50:AF = 1.17
40   HGR2
45   REM   --- BACKGROUND ---
50 C =   INT ( RND (1) * 6) + 1: HCOLOR= C
60   IF C = 0 OR C = 4 THEN 80
70   FOR B = 0 TO 191 STEP S: HPLOT 0,B TO 279,B: NEXT B
75   REM   --- SPIRAL DESIGN ROUTINE ---
80 ST =   INT ( RND (1) * 300) + 50
90   FOR A = 0 TO N * 2 * PI STEP ST * (2 * PI / 360)
100 X = R * AF * A / PT *   COS (A) + XC
110 Y = R * A / PT *   SIN (A) + YC
115   REM   --- BLACK SPIRAL ---
120   HCOLOR= 0
130   FOR BL = 1 TO A / 22: HPLOT XM + BL,YM + BL TO X +
BL,Y + BL: NEXT BL
```

```
140    HCOLOR= 3
150    HPLOT XM,YM TO X,Y:XM = X:YM = Y
160    NEXT A
165    REM  --- WAIT FOR KEYPRESS ---
170    WAIT  - 16384,128
180 K =  PEEK ( - 16384): IF K - 128 = 27 THEN 299
190    POKE  - 16368,0
200    GOTO 20
299    END
```

MODIFICATIONS

1. Omit the background by deleting lines 55-80.
2. Omit drawing the spiral design in black by deleting lines 130-140.
3. Add an ONERR GOTO statement at line 9 if you input variables.

```
9 ONERR GOTO 199
```

SAMPLE OUTPUT

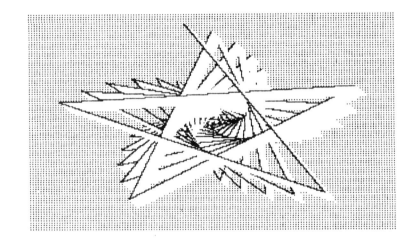

SLIDE SHOWS

A slide show can be used to display your graphics pictures. This chapter introduces five slide show programs, each of which can be modified to suit your needs.

The first slide show program links your graphics and text programs together to make a presentation or display. The next program uses text files so you can readily change the order of the programs of your slide show.

The third slide show displays low, high, or mixed low and high resolution pictures. A menu gives the viewer the choice of the standard presentation of the pictures or the opportunity to view individual pictures.

The last two programs use page flipping to display low and high resolution graphics pictures, respectively.

The speed of the show can be under control of the program or the user. For program control, a delay loop can be used to pace the viewing of the pictures.

User control can be achieved with the use of the keyboard or paddle buttons or both.

The slide show ends automatically when the last picture is viewed, while allowing the user to stop the show at any time throughout the program.

Bells or clicks can be made after the picture has been loaded. While waiting for a program to load, the program name or number can be displayed. If a text window is available, the title or description of the picture can be displayed.

The first two slide shows use programs in Applesoft BASIC. The last three shows require the pictures to be saved as binary files. To use the last three programs, save three or more pictures in lo-res graphics and three or more pictures in hi-res graphics.

APPLESOFT PROGRAMS

LINKING LO- AND HI-RES
(POOR MAN'S SLIDE SHOW)

This program allows you to run a slide show with your graphics programs, mixing both high and low resolution programs.

EXPLANATION

At the end of each program, whether it be text or lo-res or hi-res graphics, enter a command to RUN the next program. When you run a program from a program, you must first issue a CONTROL D by using CHR$(4).

Assume that the programs to be connected are: DESIGN 1, DESIGN 2, DESIGN 3, etc.

At the end of your program enter the following lines. The line numbering may be different for your program.

```
5 REM === DESIGN 1 ===
997 HOME: VTAB 23: PRINT "PRESS RETURN TO CONTINUE ";
998 GET A$
999 PRINT CHR$(13)+CHR$(4)"RUN DESIGN 2"
```

At the end of DESIGN 2, enter a command to RUN DESIGN 3. Continue until all the programs have been chained or linked together.

Each text program should begin with the TEXT command to clear the screen from the graphics mode and set the standard window dimensions.

The last program can end the program or be linked to the first program for a continual display.

MODIFICATIONS

1. Instead of the GET command at line 998, you can enter a delay statement to pause between pictures. Adjust the speed of the delay loop to suit your viewing needs. Or ask the viewer for a slow, moderate, or fast viewing and use a variable in place of 3000 on line 998.

```
998 FOR X = 1 TO 3000:NEXT Z
999 PRINT CHR$(4) "RUN DESIGN 2"
```

2. You can use the buttons on the paddle to control the pause between pictures.

```
998 IF PEEK (-16287) >128 THEN PRINT CHR$(4) "RUN DESIGN 2"
999 GOTO 998
```

SAVING A TEXT PAGE

The following statements allow you to save a text page. In Chapters 5 and 6 you were shown how to save a low and high resolution graphics picture.

EXPLANATION ══════════════════════════════════

You may have a text page with the text attractively displayed with a border or inverse or flashing characters. This can be saved as a binary file and loaded when needed. This is useful for a title page.

If you have a text page that you would like to save, then save it with either of the following statements where filename is any legal name.

In the immediate mode you can use:

```
BSAVE filename,A$400,L$400
```

or

```
BSAVE filename,A1024,L1024
```

In a program you can use:

```
900 PRINT CHR$(4) "BSAVE filename,A$400,L$400"
```

or

```
900 PRINT CHR$(4) "BSAVE filename,A1024,L1024"
```

RETRIEVING A TEXT PAGE

This statement shows you how to retrieve a text page that has been saved as a binary file.

EXPLANATION ══════════════════════════════════

Enter this statement when you want to retrieve a text page:

```
BLOAD filename
```

or

```
50 PRINT CHR$(4) "BLOAD filename"
```

SWITCHING TO GR AFTER HGR2

This helps avoid the problem of switching from a high resolution graphics picture on page 2 to a low resolution graphics picture on page 1.

BACKGROUND

If you load a lo-res graphics picture on page 1 after viewing a hi-res picture on page 2, you will view page 2 of lo-res graphics. If you list the program you will see the listing of the lo-res program, yet cannot view the lo-res graphics picture on the screen. Page 2 has been set by the HGR2 command or its equivalent POKE commands. You want to view page 1.

EXPLANATION

There are two methods to view the lo-resolution graphics design on page 1 after running a program that uses page 2 of hi-res graphics. Either enter the command TEXT or POKE −16300,0 between the HGR2 and GR commands. The POKE command switches to page 1.

```
10 TEXT: GR
20 (continue with low resolution graphics)
```

or

```
10 POKE − 16300,0: GR
20 (continue with low resolution graphics)
```

This program will demonstrate a flip from a simple program in hi-res graphics on page 2 to a lo-res graphics picture on page 1. Omit line 30 to see why it is needed.

```
5   REM  === HGR2 -> GR ===
10  HGR2 : HCOLOR= 3: HPLOT 0,0 TO 279,159
20  GET A$
30  POKE  - 16300,0
40  GR : HOME : COLOR= 1
50  VLIN 0,39 AT 20: HLIN 0,39 AT 20
99  END
```

EXECING A TEXT FILE WITH A DELAY STATEMENT

This presents an easier and more flexible method of presenting a slide show.

EXPLANATION

This program sets up a text file that contains the names of the programs to be included in your slide show.

Enter the names of your programs starting at line 50. Save this program as SLIDE EXEC STARTER and run it. A text file called SLIDES is created. Then enter EXEC SLIDES, and the computer takes over the presentation.

The advantage of this method is that you can see the program being printed or plotted. You do not need to BSAVE the pictures, and you can easily change the order and the programs by changing the text file.

If you change the arrangement of the program in SLIDE EXEC STARTER and want to keep this version also, then change the name of the text file from SLIDES to another name.

```
5   REM  === SLIDE EXEC STARTER ===
10   PRINT  CHR$ (4)"OPEN SLIDES"
20   PRINT  CHR$ (4)"DELETE SLIDES"
30   PRINT  CHR$ (4)"OPEN SLIDES"
40   PRINT  CHR$ (4)"WRITE SLIDES"
50   PRINT  "RUN SPIRAL IN/COLOR OUT/BLACK"
60   PRINT  "RUN STAR SINE WAVE"
70   PRINT  "RUN DRAW CIRCLE FASTER"
80   PRINT  CHR$ (4)"CLOSE SLIDES"
99   END
```

MODIFICATION

You can add a delay to your program by typing in the following program and saving it with the DELAY or any other legal filename of your choice.

```
5   REM  === DELAY ===
10   FOR Z = 1 TO 500: NEXT Z
```

Then enter the following lines to run the delay program between each text or graphics program.

```
55 PRINT CHR$(4)"RUN DELAY"
65 PRINT CHR$(4)"RUN DELAY"
75 PRINT CHR$(4)"RUN DELAY"
```

The slide show program with delays then becomes:

```
5   REM  === SLIDE EXEC STARTER/DELAY ===
10   PRINT  CHR$ (4)"OPEN SLIDES"
20   PRINT  CHR$ (4)"DELETE SLIDES"
30   PRINT  CHR$ (4)"OPEN SLIDES"
40   PRINT  CHR$ (4)"WRITE SLIDES"
50   PRINT  "RUN SPIRAL INWARD CLOCKWISE"
55   PRINT  "RUN DELAY"
60   PRINT  "RUN STAR SINE WAVE"
65   PRINT  "RUN DELAY"
70   PRINT  "RUN DRAW CIRCLE FASTER"
75   PRINT  "RUN DELAY"
80   PRINT  CHR$ (4)"CLOSE SLIDES"
99   END
```

BINARY FILES

LO- AND HI-RES PICTURES USING MENU AND STROBE

This program sets up a slide show of low and high resolution graphics pictures that have been saved as binary files. A menu is provided to allow the viewer to see the standard presentation or an individual picture.

EXPLANATION

This program requires that you save your graphics pictures as binary files. Lo-res graphics pictures take 6 sectors on the disk, whereas hi-res binary files take 34 sectors.

Lines 20–40 enter the names of the pictures into array FS(X) and store the type of graphics (low or high) in TS(X). GR represents low resolution graphics, and HGR represents high resolution graphics.

The pictures are loaded in the order that they appear in the DATA statements. You can easily change the order by rearranging the items in the DATA statements.

A menu lists the picturenames in two columns under the headings GR and HGR. Lines 50–150 set up the menu and decide in which column the picturename should be printed.

The viewer has the option of viewing the programs in the order in which they are stored in the DATA statements or viewing an individual picture.

Lines 160–200 obtain the viewer's choice and determine the routine to execute. Lines 210–270 allow the viewer to see an individual picture. Lines 280–320 present the standard order. The subroutine at lines 1000–1020 sets up the graphics screen and loads the picture. The POKE commands on line 1010 set up page 1 and full screen graphics, respectively.

Line 1020 does not include the array element FS(X) in quotes. FS(X) represents the string element that holds the name of the picture and is not the name of the picture itself.

After the last picture is viewed in the standard format, the program returns to the menu. The subroutine at lines 2000–2030 strobes the keyboard. While viewing the pictures whether in individual or standard format, an ESC keypress terminates the program, whereas pressing any other key continues the slide show.

To use the program for your own slide shows, enter the names of your binary files and their type: GR or HGR in the DATA statements starting at line 3010. On line 3000, insert the number of pictures in your slide show. These pictures must first be saved as binary files. Refer to Chapters 5 and 6 on how to BSAVE and BLOAD files. You can use both low and high resolution pictures in this slide show.

```
5    REM   === MENU SLIDE SHOW ===
10   ONERR   GOTO 399
15   REM   --- READ IN ARRAY ELEMENTS ---
20   READ N: DIM F$(N),T$(N)
30   FOR X = 1 TO N: READ F$(X),T$(X)
40   NEXT X
45   REM   --- PRINT MENU ---
50   TEXT : HOME : POKE 48,32
60   HLIN 0,39 AT 1: HLIN 0,39 AT 47
70   VLIN 0,47 AT 0: VLIN 0,47 AT 39
80   POKE 32,1: POKE 33,38: POKE 34,1: POKE 35,22
90   HOME : VTAB 3: PRINT  TAB( 8)"<<< GRAPHIC PICTURES >
>>"
```

```
100  VTAB 5: INVERSE : VTAB 5: INVERSE : HTAB 3: PRINT "
 GR ";: HTAB 20: PRINT " HGR ": NORMAL
110  VTAB 7: FOR X = 1 TO N: IF T$(X) = "GR" THEN  PRINT
 TAB( 3) LEFT$ (F$(X),15)
120  NEXT X
130  VTAB 7: FOR X = 1 TO N: IF T$(X) = "HGR" THEN  HTAB
 20: PRINT  LEFT$ (F$(X),15)
140  NEXT X
150  VTAB 20: CALL  - 958: PRINT  TAB( 3)"S)TANDARD  I)N
DIVIDUAL  Q)UIT ";
155  REM  --- EVALUATE RESPONSE ---
160  GET A$: PRINT A$
170  IF A$ = "Q" THEN 399
180  IF A$ = "S" THEN 280
190  IF A$ = "I" THEN 210
200  GOTO 150
205  REM  --- INDIVIDUAL PICTURES ---
210  VTAB 21: CALL  - 958: HTAB 3
220  INPUT "NAME OF THE PICTURE:";P$
230  FOR T = 1 TO N: IF  LEFT$ (F$(T),15) = P$ THEN X =
T:T = N: GOTO 260
240  NEXT T
250  GOTO 210
260  TEXT : HOME : GOSUB 1000: GOSUB 2000
270  GOTO 50
275  REM  --- STANDARD PRESENTATION ---
280  HOME
290  FOR X = 1 TO N
300  GOSUB 1000: GOSUB 2000
310  NEXT X
320  GOTO 50
399  TEXT : HOME : VTAB 12: HTAB 14: PRINT "T H E   E N
D": END
995  REM  --- SET GRAPHIC SCREEN/LOAD PICTURE ---
1000  IF T$(X) = "GR" THEN  GR : HOME : PRINT  CHR$ (13)
 + CHR$ (4);"BLOAD";F$(X): RETURN
1010  IF T$(X) = "HGR" THEN  HGR : POKE 16300,0: POKE  -
 16302,0
1020  PRINT  CHR$ (13) + CHR$ (4)"BLOAD";F$(X);",A$2000
": RETURN
1995  REM  --- STROBE KEYBOARD ---
2000  POKE  - 16368,0
2010 K =  PEEK ( - 16384): IF K < 128 THEN 2010
2020  IF K - 128 = 27 THEN 399
2030  RETURN
2995  REM  --- NAMES AND TYPES OF PICTURES ---
3000  DATA 6 : REM  NUMBER OF PICTURES
3010  DATA  A LETTER OF THE ALPHABET,GR,FLOWER,HGR
3020  DATA  MOSAIC,GR,NET 3-D,HGR
3030  DATA  RECTANGLES,GR,DRAGONFLY,HGR
```

1. Change the keyboard strobe to a delay statement for the standard presentation. Change line 300 to read the following, where 500 represents the amount of delay:

```
300 GOSUB 1000: FOR Z = 1 TO 500:NEXT Z
```

2. Add a bell when the picture is loaded by changing line 1020 to:

```
1020 PRINT CHR$(13) + CHR$(4);"BLOAD";F$(X);
     ",A$2000":CALL -198:RETURN
```

CALL −1052 can be used in place of CALL −198.

LO-RES SLIDE SHOW USING PAGE FLIPPING

This program provides a smoother slide show for low resolution graphics pictures by using page flipping either by user or program control.

BACKGROUND

There are two pages for lo-res graphics—page 1 and page 2. A page is simply a portion of memory needed to hold a screen of graphics or text. Pages 1 and 2 of lo-res graphics start at different memory locations. Page 1 starts at address 1024 (in decimal) or $400 (in hexadecimal), and page 2 starts at address 2048 (in decimal) or $800 (in hexadecimal). Both pages are 1024 bytes long or $400 in hexadecimal. See the memory map in Appendix B.

Page 1 of lo-res graphics and the text page occupy the same memory location: address 1024 (decimal) or $400 (hexadecimal). When you type TEXT after a graphics program, the computer is interpreting the graphics instructions and returns an interesting screen display of text characters in standard, inverse, and flashing mode.

Page 2 of lo-res graphics occupies the same memory locations as your Applesoft BASIC program.

LO-RES SLIDE SHOW STARTER

To use page flipping with low resolution graphics pictures, you must relocate your Applesoft program that provides the slide show routines. You can locate it above page 2 of text starting at memory location 3073. See the memory map in Appendix B.

There must be a starter program before the slide show program to set two memory locations so your slide program does not run into page 2 of low resolution graphics/text. Memory location 104 holds the starting page of the program address (3072/256=12). The term page, in this context, refers to a block of 256 bytes of memory. A zero is placed in location 3072 to place the start of the slide show program at 3073.

Enter the starter program and save it as LORES SLIDE SHOW STARTER or any other legal filename of your choice. Then type in the second program, LORES SLIDE SHOW, using the names of your own binary files that you have previously BSAVEd.

Any time you want to make a change to LORES SLIDE SHOW, be sure to run LORES SLIDE SHOW STARTER first. This will load the LORES SLIDE SHOW program above page 2 of lo-res graphics. If you fail to do this and enter the program directly, make changes, and run the program, you will lose the program. Page 2 of lo-res graphics will write over your program when you run the page flipping program.

```
5   REM  === LORES SLIDE SHOW STARTER ===
10  POKE 104,12
20  POKE 3072,0
30  PRINT  CHR$ (4);"RUN LORES SLIDE SHOW"
99  END
```

LO-RES SLIDE SHOW

In the previous program, MENU SLIDE SHOW, you saw the picture being loaded onto the screen. This program uses page flipping and loads a picture onto one page while you are viewing the other page.

This slide show starts by loading and displaying the first graphics picture on page 1. While you are viewing this picture, the next picture is loaded onto page 2.

Then the programs alternate between page 1 and page 2. While you are viewing page 1, page 2 is being loaded. While you are viewing page 2, page 1 is being loaded. This continues until you have exhausted the supply of pictures.

To inform the computer that it should display the contents of page 1 or 2, you need to use the appropriate POKE command on lines 1000 and 2000. POKE −16300,0 displays the contents of page 1, and POKE −16299,0 displays the contents of page 2. You must precede this with the command for lo-res graphics (either the familiar GR command or POKE −16298,0).

The mixed text/graphics mode is set on lines 1000 and 2000. This program allows only mixed text/graphics pictures; you cannot use full screen graphics pictures. However, you cannot add text to the bottom of the screen, since it is difficult to display text in the window on page 2. If you want the title with a picture, then you must save the picture with the title.

Line 20 reads the names of the pictures into an array N$( ). TN represents the total number of pictures to be displayed.

Lines 40–260 set up the type of control for the slide show. The viewer has a choice of user control or program control. If the viewer selects program control, then he has a choice of speeds. If the viewer chooses user control, he has a choice of keyboard or paddle control. With keyboard control the space bar advances the slide show and the ESC key returns to the menu. With paddle control, the button on paddle 0 or 1 advances to the next picture and the ESC key returns to the menu. On the Apple IIe/IIc, either the open or closed apple can be used in place of the buttons on paddle 0 or 1.

Line 270 initializes the page P, picture number N, first time flag F, and end flag E. Lines 280–290 load the picture to the proper page so pages are alternated throughout the program. Line 300 branches to line 320 if F equals 0 and continues with line 310 if F equals 1.

Depending on the page P, line 310 sets up either page 1 or 2. Line 310 is used only once, when F = 1. Line 320 presents keyboard/paddle control starting at subroutine 3000 or program control starting at subroutine 4000, depending on the value of A, where A can be 1, 2, or 3 as determined in line 100.

The command POP is used in lines 3040, 3080, and 3110 to "pop" the return address for the GOSUB commands from the stack. POP is used when you branch to another line rather than returning with the RETURN command.

Line 330 checks for the last picture. Lines 340–360 set up the alternate page, advance to the next picture, and check if all the pictures have been displayed.

Insert the names of your lo-res graphics pictures in line 4010 and the number of pictures in line 4000.

Remember that the program LORES SLIDE SHOW STARTER must be run first, i.e., do not run the LORES SLIDE SHOW first.

```
5   REM  === LORES SLIDE SHOW ===
10  D$ =  CHR$ (13) +  CHR$ (4)
20  READ TN: DIM N$(TN): FOR X = 1 TO TN: READ N$(X): NE
XT X
30  TEXT : HOME
35  REM  --- DETERMINE USER/PROGRAM CONTROL ---
40  PRINT  TAB( 11)"<<< SLIDE SHOW >>>"
50  VTAB 5: PRINT "WOULD YOU LIKE THE SHOW TO BE UNDER:"
: PRINT : PRINT
60  PRINT  TAB( 10)"1. USER CONTROL"
70  PRINT : PRINT  TAB( 10)"2. PROGRAM CONTROL"
80  PRINT : PRINT  TAB( 10)"3. QUIT PROGRAM"
90  VTAB 14: PRINT "SELECT # ";
100  GET A$:A =  VAL (A$)
110  IF A < 1 OR A > 3 OR A <  >  INT (A) THEN  PRINT :
GOTO 90
120  PRINT A
130  VTAB 5: CALL  - 958
140  ON A GOTO 150,210,499
145  REM  --- SET UP USER CONTROL ---
150  PRINT "K(KEYBOARD OR P)PADDLES ";
160  GET A$: IF A$ <  > "K" AND A$ <  > "P" THEN 160
170  PRINT A$
180  IF A$ = "K" THEN UC = 1
190  IF A$ = "P" THEN UC = 2
200  GOTO 270
205  REM  --- SET UP PROGRAM CONTROL ---
210  PRINT "ENTER AMOUNT OF DELAY:": PRINT : PRINT
220  PRINT  TAB( 10)"FAST (1-150)": PRINT
230  PRINT  TAB( 10)"MODERATE (151-750)": PRINT
240  PRINT  TAB( 10)"SLOW (751-1500)": PRINT
250  INPUT "SELECT # ";T
260  IF T < 1 OR T > 1500 THEN  VTAB 14: CALL  - 958: GO
TO 250
265  REM  --- LOAD PICTURES ---
270  P = 2:N = 1:F = 1:E = 0
280  IF P = 1 THEN  PRINT D$;"BLOAD";N$(N);",A$400"
290  IF P = 2 THEN  PRINT D$;"BLOAD";N$(N);",A$800"
300  IF  NOT F THEN 320
310  ON P GOSUB 1000,2000:P = 1:N = N + 1:F = 0: GOTO 28
0
320  ON A GOSUB 3000,3100
330  IF E = 1 THEN 30
340  ON P GOSUB 1000,2000
350  P = 3 - P:N = N + 1
360  IF N = TN + 1 THEN E = 1: FOR Z = 1 TO 100: NEXT Z:
 GOTO 320
370  GOTO 280
499  TEXT : HOME : END
995  REM  --- DISPLAY PAGE 1 ---
1000  POKE  - 16304,0: POKE  - 16300,0: POKE  - 16298,0:
 POKE  - 16301,0: RETURN
1995  REM  --- DISPLAY PAGE 2 ---
2000  POKE  - 16304,0: POKE  - 16299,0: POKE  - 16298,0:
 POKE  - 16301,0: RETURN
```

(continued on next page)

```
2995    REM   --- KEYBOARD/PADDLE CONTROL ---
3000    ON UC GOTO 3010,3060
3005    REM   --- CHECK KEYBOARD ---
3010    POKE  - 16368,0
3020 K =  PEEK ( - 16384): IF K < 128 THEN 3020
3030    IF K = 160 THEN  RETURN
3040    IF K = 155 THEN  POP : GOTO 30
3050    GOTO 3010
3055    REM   --- CHECK PADDLES ---
3060    POKE  - 16368,0
3070    IF  PEEK ( - 16286) > 127 OR  PEEK ( - 16287) > 12
7 THEN  RETURN
3080    IF  PEEK ( - 16384) = 155 THEN  POP : GOTO 30
3090    GOTO 3070
3095    REM   --- CHECK FOR ESC KEYPRESS ---
3100    POKE  - 16368,0
3110    FOR X = 1 TO T: IF  PEEK ( - 16384) = 155 THEN X =
T: POP : GOTO 30
3120    NEXT X: RETURN
4000    DATA  3: REM  NUMBER OF PICTURES
4010    DATA  RECTANGLES,L,MOSAIC
```

HI-RES SLIDE SHOW USING PAGE FLIPPING
(FORWARD AND REVERSE)

This program lets you view a slide show of your high resolution pictures with either paddle button control or keyboard control.

EXPLANATION

The program is similar to the slide show for lo-res graphics in that page flipping is used for a smooth effect. However, you do not need a starter program because page 1 and page 2 of hi-res graphics and your Applesoft program do not share the same memory.

The program displays a menu of the pictures available. The S key starts the slide show. Page flipping is used to load another picture while one is being viewed.

Button 1 displays the next picture, while button 0 displays the previous picture. The space bar returns to the text page and displays the name of the picture that was just viewed in inverse mode. The ESC key returns the original menu and allows the viewer to restart the program or quit.

If you have an Apple IIe/IIc, you can use either button 0 and 1 or the open and closed apple keys. If you do not have paddles or a joystick, the left and right arrow keys can be used instead of buttons 0 and 1.

Line 10 stores the values from DATA statement 5000 for the vertical and horizontal lines on the menu text screen. Line 20 stores the names of the binary files in an array F$( ). Lines 30–140 set up the main menu. Line 70 sets the border, while line 90 freezes the screen. Lines 100–130 determine the tabbing for the binary file names and print only the left 12 characters of the filename.

The subroutine at lines 150–160 gets the response and executes the routine at 170–230 to start the slide show if an S was pressed and exits the program with a Q keypress.

The routine at lines 240–250 checks for reverse direction, while the routine at lines 260–270 checks for the ESC key or space bar. Lines 280–290 check for the forward direction.

Lines 300–350 advance to the next picture. The first time through the loop, when $T = 1$, the program loads the first two pictures. X holds the number of the picture in memory, but not currently displayed. $D = 1$ indicates the last picture has been reached.

Line 200 directs the computer to load the picture to the proper page. P holds the page, where $P = 1$ indicates page 1 and $P = 2$ indicates page 2.

Line 330 determines if the last picture has been displayed. D is initialized as 0 at line 220 and is set to 1 at line 330 when the last picture has been displayed.

Line 340 checks the value of U and reverses direction of the slide show presentation when $U = 1$.

Lines 360–499 hold the quit routine. The command CALL −1036 moves the cursor right one position.

The subroutine at line 1000 displays page 1, while 2000 displays page 2, and line 3000 displays the text page. The routine at lines 4000–4050 displays the name of the picture in inverse mode when the space bar is pressed.

```
5    REM   === HIRES SLIDE SHOW ===
10   FOR X = 0 TO 5: READ V(X): NEXT X
20   READ N: DIM F$(N): FOR X = 1 TO N: READ F$(X): NEXT
X
25   REM   --- MENU ---
30   TEXT : HOME
40   POKE 48,42: FOR X = 0 TO 5: HLIN 0,39 AT V(X): NEXT
X
50   VLIN 0,47 AT 0: VLIN 0,47 AT 39
60   VTAB 3: HTAB 15: PRINT "SLIDE SHOW"
70   HLIN 0,11 AT 4: HLIN 0,11 AT 5: HLIN 26,39 AT 4: HLI
N 26,39 AT 5
80   VTAB 7: HTAB 12: PRINT "GRAPHICS PICTURES":
90   POKE 32,2: POKE 33,36: POKE 34,8: POKE 35,22
100   HOME : FOR X = 1 TO N
110   VTAB 9 + X - (X - .5 > N / 2) * N / 2
120   HTAB 8 + 15 * (X - .5 > N / 2)
130   PRINT  LEFT$ (F$(X),12): NEXT X
140   GOSUB 3000"TEXT"
145   REM   --- GET RESPONSE ---
150   VTAB 20: CALL  - 958: HTAB 12: PRINT "S)TART  Q)UIT
: ";: GET A$: PRINT A$
160   ON A$ = "Q" GOTO 360: ON A$ = "S" GOTO 170: GOTO 15
0
165   REM   --- START SLIDE SHOW ---
170   POKE  - 16368,0:X = 1:T = 1
180   IF X / 2 =  INT (X / 2) THEN A$ = "4000":P = 2: GOT
O 200
190 A$ = "2000":P = 1
200   PRINT  CHR$ (13); CHR$ (4);"BLOAD";F$(X);",A$";A$
210   IF  NOT T THEN 240
220 T = 0:D = 0
230   GOTO 300
235   REM   --- CHECK REVERSE DIRECTON ---
240   IF (( PEEK ( - 16287) > 127 AND  PEEK ( - 16286) <
128) OR  PEEK ( - 16384) = 136) AND X > 2 THEN X = X - 2
:T = 1:U = 1: GOTO 180
250   IF U = 1 THEN U = 0: GOTO 180
255   REM   --- CHECK FOR ESC/SPACE BAR ---
260   IF  PEEK ( - 16384) = 155 THEN 100
270   IF  PEEK ( - 16384) = 160 THEN  GOSUB 4000
275   REM   --- CHECK FOR FORWARD DIRECTION ---
280   IF ( PEEK ( - 16286) > 127 AND  PEEK ( - 16287) < 1
28) OR  PEEK ( - 16384) = 149 THEN  GOTO 300
290   GOTO 240
300   IF D = 1 THEN  GOSUB 3000: GOTO 100
310   ON P GOSUB 1000,2000
320 X = X + 1
330   IF X = N + 1 THEN D = 1: POKE  - 16368,0:P = (X / 2
=  INT (X / 2)) * 2 + (X / 2 <  >  INT (X / 2)): GOTO 2
40
340   POKE  - 16368,0: IF U = 1 THEN 240
350   GOTO 180
355   REM   --- QUIT ROUTINE ---
360   TEXT : HOME : VTAB 13: HTAB 14
370 A$ = "T H E  E N D": FOR X = 1 TO  LEN (A$): IF  MID
$ (A$,X,1) = " " THEN  CALL  - 1036: NEXT X: GOTO 390
```

```
380   INVERSE : PRINT  MID$ (A$,X,1);: NEXT X
390   NORMAL
499   END
995   REM  --- DISPLAY PAGE 1 ---
1000  POKE  - 16304,0: POKE  - 16297,0: POKE  - 16302,0:
 POKE  - 16300,0: RETURN
1995  REM  --- DISPLAY PAGE 2 ---
2000  POKE  - 16304,0: POKE  - 16297,0: POKE  - 16302,0:
 POKE  - 16299,0: RETURN
2995  REM  --- DISPLAY TEXT ---
3000  POKE  - 16303,0: POKE  - 16300,0: RETURN
3995  REM  --- DISPLAY NAME OF PICTURE ---
4000  HOME : FOR Z = 1 TO N: VTAB 9 + Z - (Z - .5 > N /
 2) * N / 2: HTAB 8 + 15 * (Z - .5 > N / 2)
4010  IF X - 1 = Z THEN  INVERSE : PRINT F$(Z): NORMAL
4020  IF X - 1 < > Z THEN  PRINT F$(Z)
4030  NEXT Z: GOSUB 3000"TEXT"
4040  VTAB 20: PRINT "PRESS ANY KEY TO CONTINUE:";: POKE
 - 16368,0: GET A$: ON P GOSUB 2000,1000
4050  RETURN
4995  REM  --- DATA FOR TEXT DISPLAY ---
5000  DATA 0,1,8,9,46,47
6000  DATA  4: REM  NUMBER OF PICTURES
6010  DATA  LOTUS,FLOWER,NET 3-D,DRAGONFLY
```

BELLS, CLICKS, SOUNDS, AND TUNES

Simple sound can be obtained with the G-bell and by peeking a particular location to click the speaker.

Bells can be embedded within a message, and the speaker can be clicked after each character is printed to simulate a typewriter or ticker tape machine.

For a greater variety of sound, you need to enter a machine language routine that can click the speaker more quickly to generate tones. You control the frequency, or pitch, and the duration, or length of tone. There are several machine language tone-generating routines. One of these routines will be introduced in this chapter.

Ascending or descending tunes can easily be obtained. If you can read music, you can enter songs. The frequencies and durations for the following songs will be given: theme from Star Wars, "Charge," Beethoven's Ninth Symphony, "Mary Had a Little Lamb," "Twinkle Twinkle Little Star," Brahms' Lullaby, and "Take Me Out to the Ball Game."

You will benefit most from the section on musical tunes if you follow the programs in sequence. Each program introduces a new concept and uses the ideas presented in previous programs as well.

BELLS

This subroutine embeds bells within a message.

EXPLANATION

You can add G-bells to your program, but if you edit the line, the bells are erased or eliminated. In place of CONTROL G you can use CHR$(7) or call a machine routine that is permanently stored in ROM with the CALL −198 command or its equivalent CALL 65338.

Both subroutines start at line 1000, take the message M$ apart, and ring a bell after each character is printed.

MESSAGE WITH BELLS 1

This program uses CHR$(7) to represent a bell. The SPEED command is used to slow down the printing of A$.

```
5   REM    === MESSAGE WITH BELLS 1 ===
10   HOME
20 A$ = "THIS IS THE END ... GOOD-BYE"
55   VTAB 12
60   HTAB 20 -  LEN (A$) / 2
70   GOSUB 1000
99   END
995   REM   --- BELL ROUTINE ---
1000 BL$ =  CHR$ (7)
1010  SPEED= 200
1020  FOR X = 1 TO  LEN (A$)
1030  PRINT  MID$ (A$,X,1);
1040  IF  MID$ (A$,X,1) =  CHR$ (32) THEN 1060
1050  PRINT BL$;
1060  NEXT X
1070  PRINT
1080  SPEED= 255
1090  RETURN
```

MESSAGE WITH BELLS 2

This program uses CALL −198 to ring the bell. You can replace this CALL command with its equivalent CALL −1052.

```
5   REM    === MESSAGE WITH BELLS 2 ===
10   HOME
20   A$ = "THIS IS THE END ... GOOD-BYE"
55   VTAB 12
60   HTAB 20 -  LEN (A$) / 2
70   GOSUB 1000
99   END
995   REM   --- BELL ROUTINE ---
1000   FOR X = 1 TO  LEN (A$)
1010   PRINT  MID$ (A$,X,1);
1020   IF  MID$ (A$,X,1) =  CHR$ (32) THEN 1050
1030   CALL   - 198
1040   FOR Z = 1 TO 10: NEXT Z
1050   NEXT X: PRINT : RETURN
```

CLICKS

ALARM

This program makes an alarm sound.

EXPLANATION

When you PEEK memory location −16336 or its equivalent, 49000, you toggle the speaker. The toggle is like a light switch—every other toggle clicks the speaker to produce a sound. To get 10 clicks, the speaker must be toggled 2*10 or 20 times.

The speaker is clicked at lines 30 and 40 to produce the alarm sound.

```
5   REM   === ALARM ===
10  S =   - 16336
20   FOR X = 1 TO 10
30  B =  PEEK (S) -  PEEK (S) +  PEEK (S)
40   FOR Z = 1 TO 50:B =  PEEK (S): NEXT Z
50   NEXT X
99   END
```

TYPEWRITER

This program simulates the sound of a typewriter as characters are printed to the screen.

EXPLANATION

The subroutine at lines 1000–1070 takes the message A$ apart. After each nonblank character is printed, the speaker is toggled 4 times to produce 2 clicks. The variable H represents the starting tab position that centers the A$ message.

```
5   REM  === TYPEWRITER ===
10  A$ = "I AM AN APPLE II COMPUTER"
20   HOME
30  H = (40 -  LEN (A$)) / 2 + 1
40   GOSUB 1000
50   VTAB 22
99   END
995  REM  --- CLICK SPEAKER AS PRINT CHARACTER ---
1000  SPEED= 50
1010  HTAB H
1020  FOR X = 1 TO  LEN (A$)
1030  PRINT  MID$ (A$,X,1);
1040  IF  MID$ (A$,X,1) =  CHR$ (32) THEN 1070
1050  FOR T = 1 TO 4:S =  PEEK ( - 16336): NEXT T
1060  FOR Z = 1 TO 55: NEXT Z
1070  NEXT X
1080  SPEED= 255
1090  RETURN
```

MODIFICATION

Delete the delay statement at line 1060 for a different effect.

TICKER TAPE

This program simulates a ticker tape machine. It prints out a message with sound effects.

EXPLANATION

A border is printed at line 50 to simulate a strip of tape. A$ represents the message to be printed. The message is continually printed within the border.

If the message is less than 40 characters, line 70 pads it with dots to obtain a message of 40 characters. Line 80 pads five additional dots to the end of the message to separate the end of message from the beginning.

Lines 90–110 print the first 40 characters and click the speaker. The routine at 1000–1010 clicks the speaker N times, where N is a random number from 2 to 10. SP is defined in line 30 as −16336. Lines 120–180 continue printing the message and clicking the speaker. Any keypress will terminate the program. The keyboard is strobed in line 160.

```
5    REM   === TICKER TAPE ===
10   POKE  - 16368,0
20 SP =  - 16336
30 S$ = ":"
40   TEXT : HOME
45   REM   --- DRAW TAPE ---
50   INVERSE : VTAB 10: FOR X = 1 TO 2: FOR Y = 1 TO 40:
PRINT S$;: NEXT Y: PRINT : PRINT : PRINT : NEXT X: NORMA
L
60 A$ = "I HOPE THAT YOU HAVE ENJOYED THE TIPS AND TRICK
S"
65   REM   --- PAD A$ WITH PERIODS ---
70   IF  LEN (A$) < 40 THEN  FOR X = 1 TO 40 -  LEN (A$):
A$ = A$ + ".": NEXT X
80 A$ = A$ + "....."
85   REM   --- PRINT MESSAGE ROUTINE ---
90   FOR X = 1 TO 40: VTAB 12: HTAB 41 - X: PRINT  LEFT$
(A$,X)
100  GOSUB 1000
110  NEXT X
120  FOR X = 1 TO  LEN (A$)
130  VTAB 12
140 Z$ =  MID$ (A$,X, LEN (A$) - 1) +  MID$ (A$,1,X - 1)
150  PRINT  LEFT$ (Z$,40)
160 K =  PEEK ( - 16384): IF K > 128 THEN 190
170  GOSUB 1000
180  NEXT X: GOTO 120
190  POKE  - 16368,0: HOME : VTAB 12: HTAB 18: PRINT "BY
E"
199  END
995  REM   --- CLICK SPEAKER ---
1000  FOR N = 1 TO  INT ( RND (1) * 11) + 2:S =  PEEK (S
P): FOR Z = 1 TO 25: NEXT Z: NEXT N
1010  RETURN
```

MODIFICATIONS

1. Change the speaker subroutine so the speaker is clicked twice each time the subroutine is accessed:

```
1000 FOR N = 1 TO 2:S = PEEK(SP):S = PEEK(SP):FOR Z = 1 TO
     25:NEXT Z,N
1010 RETURN
```

2. A SPEED command can be added to the program at lines 115 and 195:

```
115 SPEED = 50

195 SPEED = 255
```

SOUND

MACHINE LANGUAGE TONE GENERATOR

There are a limited number of sounds available from the G-bell and from peeking location −16336. For a greater variety of sound and musical tunes you can use a routine in BASIC that will generate a machine language routine. There are various machine language routines to generate sound. One such routine is presented in the following programs.

You can use the machine language routine in your BASIC programs by setting two variables—frequency and duration—and then issuing a CALL command.

The frequency refers to the pitch and is represented in the following programs by F, where F can range from 1 to 255, with 255 representing the lowest pitch and 1 the highest pitch. Duration refers to the length of time the tone is played and is represented by D, where D ranges from a value of 1 to 255, with 255 the longest duration and 1 the shortest.

The sounds generated by the G-bell and by peeking location −16336 are limited to low frequency sounds. With a machine language program you can obtain a higher frequency resulting in a greater range of sounds. Poke in the values for frequency and duration and call the subroutine, and you have a sound. Put this in a loop that pokes a pattern of frequencies and durations and you have music.

Although many memory locations are dedicated to particular functions, there are several unused or free locations in which to place your own machine language routines. The following music generator routine is stored at address 770–790. Address 768 holds the frequency, address 769 stores the duration, and the CALL 770 command accesses the routine. The routine is not relocatable. If you want to use a different memory location for the music program, you will have to use a different machine language program.

ASCENDING/DESCENDING

This program uses the machine language sound routine to generate ascending and descending tones.

EXPLANATION

The machine language routine is poked into memory at lines 10–30, starting at address 770. The values of the DATA statements represent instructions in machine language.

Lines 60, 80, and 100 let you enter the beginning, ending, and step size. The values are checked in lines 70 and 90 to verify that they are within the limits 1–255. Line 110 determines if the step is positive or negative. The duration is entered in line 130 and checked in line 140.

The routine at lines 160–180 plays the sequence of sounds.

The frequency is determined by the counter F as F ranges from ST to EN in increments of INC. When the value of the frequency F increases, the pitch decreases, and when the value of the F decreases, the pitch increases.

```
5    REM  === ASCENDING/DESCENDING ===
7    REM  --- POKE IN MACHINE LANGUAGE TONE GENERATOR ---
10   FOR L = 770 TO 790: READ V: POKE L,V: NEXT L
20   DATA   173,48,192,136,208,5,206,1,3,240,9
30   DATA   202,208,245,174,0,3,76,2,3,96
35   REM  --- USER ENTERS VALUES FOR LOOP ---
40   HOME
50   HTAB 18: PRINT "MUSIC": VTAB 6
60   INPUT "ENTER STARTING VALUE (1-255) ";ST
70   IF ST < 1 OR ST > 255 THEN 60
80   INPUT "ENTER ENDING VALUE (1-255) ";EN
90   IF EN < 1 OR EN > 255 THEN 80
100  INPUT "ENTER STEP SIZE ";INC
110  IF INC >  ABS (EN - ST) THEN 100
120  IF ST > EN THEN INC =  - INC
130  INPUT "ENTER DURATION VALUE  (1-255) ";D
140  IF D < 1 OR D > 255 THEN 130
150  PRINT : PRINT
155  REM  --- PLAY TONES ---
160  FOR F = ST TO EN STEP INC
170  POKE 768,F: POKE 769,D: CALL 770
180  NEXT F
190  PRINT "PRESS ANY TO CONTINUE-SPACE BAR TO END ";
200  GET R$: IF R$ =  CHR$ (32) THEN 299
210  GOTO 40
299  END
```

MODIFICATIONS

Run the program several times with different values for the starting, ending, and increment variables. When you find a sequence of sounds that you like, set up a loop and use that sequence in your program.

MENU WITH SOUND EFFECTS FOR WRONG RESPONSE

This program displays a menu and plays a set of tones when an illegal response is made.

EXPLANATION ═══

The program demonstrates one way to use the sound routine to produce random sound effects.

Lines 10–30 poke the machine language into memory. Lines 40–50 read the names of the programs available. The menu is printed at lines 60–110.

The subroutine starting at line 1000 selects a random number from 34 to 255 to represent the frequency. It assigns a duration of 64 and plays the set of tones when an illegal entry is made.

Line 130 captures the keypress. Line 140 checks for invalid entries. If an invalid entry is made, the subroutine at 1000 is called and the program waits for the user to make another entry. When a valid entry is made, the program runs the program associated with that number.

Line 2000 contains the number of programs available. Line 2010 holds the Quit option, while lines 2020–2030 store the names of the programs available.

To use this program, enter the number and names of your programs in lines 2000 and 2020–2030, respectively.

```
5    REM   === MENU WITH SOUND EFFECTS ===
7    REM   --- POKE IN MACHINE LANGUAGE TONE GENERATOR ---
10   FOR L = 770 TO 790: READ V: POKE L,V: NEXT L
20   DATA   173,48,192,136,208,5,206,1,3,240,9
30   DATA   202,208,245,174,0,3,76,2,3,96
35   REM   --- DISPLAY MENU ---
40   READ N: DIM A$(N)
50   FOR X = 0 TO N - 1: READ A$(X): NEXT X
60   HOME : VTAB 5:H = 10
70   INVERSE : HTAB 5: PRINT "<<< PROGRAMS AVAILABLE >>>"
: NORMAL
80   VTAB 8
90   FOR X = 0 TO N - 1
100  HTAB H: PRINT X;") ";A$(X): PRINT
110  NEXT X
115  REM   --- GET RESPONSE ---
120  HTAB H - 7: CALL  - 868: PRINT "SELECT:";
130  GET R$:R =  VAL (R$)
140  IF R > N - 1 OR  ASC (R$) < 48 OR  ASC (R$) > 57 TH
EN   VTAB  PEEK (37) + 1: HTAB H: FLASH : PRINT "ILLEGAL
ENTRY ": NORMAL : GOSUB 1000: FOR Z = 1 TO 100: NEXT Z:
VTAB  PEEK (37): GOTO 120
150  VTAB 18: HTAB H: PRINT R$
160  IF R = 0 THEN 199
170  PRINT  CHR$ (4)"RUN"A$(R)
199  TEXT : HOME : END
995  REM   --- PLAY RANDOM SET OF TONES ---
1000  FOR S = 1 TO 3:F =  INT ( RND (1) * 222) + 34: POK
E 768,F: POKE 769,40: CALL 770: NEXT S
```

```
1010   RETURN
2000   DATA  5
2010   DATA  QUIT
2020   DATA  TICKER TAPE,ASCENDING/DESCENDING
2030   DATA  STAR WARS,CHARGE!
```

FREQUENCY CHART

Table 10-1 lists the values for F that correspond to the frequency of musical notes.

	Note	F
TABLE 10-1.		
FREQUENCY		
CHART		
Octave 1	C	255
	C# or Db	241
	D	227
	D# or Eb	214
	E	202
	F	191
	F# or Gb	180
	G	170
	G# or Ab	161
	A	152
	A# or Bb	143
	B	135
Octave 2	middle C	128
	C# or Db	121
	D	114
	D# or Eb	108
	E	102
	F	96
	F# or Gb	91
	G	85
	G# or Ab	81
	A	76
	A# or Bb	72
	B	68
Octave 3	C	64
	C# or Bb	60
	D	57
	D# or Eb	54
	E	51
	F	48
	F# or Gb	45
	G	43
	G# or Ab	40
	A	38
	A# or Bb	36
	B	34

EQUIVALENT PIANO POKES FOR FREQUENCY

	B	34
36	Bb – A#	
	A	38
40	Ab – G#	
	G	43
45	Gb – F#	
	F	48
	E	51
54	Eb – D#	
	D	57
60	Db – C#	
	C	64
	B	68
72	Bb – A#	
	A	76
81	Ab – G#	
	G	85
91	Gb – F#	
	F	96
	E	102
108	Eb – D#	
	D	114
121	Db – C#	
middle	C	128
	B	135
143	Bb – A#	
	A	152
161	Ab – G#	
	G	170
180	Gb – F#	
	F	191
	E	202
214	Eb – D#	
	D	227
241	Db – C#	
	C	255

DURATION CHART

Table 10-2 indicates the values for D that correspond to the duration of different notes.

TABLE 10-2.
DURATION CHART

Length of Note	D
Whole note	255
Dotted half note	192
Half note	127
Dotted quarter note	96
Quarter note	64
Dotted eighth note	48
Eighth note	32
Dotted sixteenth note	24
Triplet	21
Sixteenth note	16

PLAYING A TUNE

DATA STATEMENTS TO HOLD FREQUENCY AND DURATION

The following programs store the values for the frequency and duration in DATA statements.

Since the computer reads the DATA statements in the order in which they appear in the program, the order is important, especially if your program contains other DATA statements.

The DATA statements can be placed anywhere in a program (beginning, middle, or end); however, they must be placed in the order in which they will be read. The data for the machine language sound generator routine must precede the data that contain the frequency and duration.

CHANGING TEMPO (THEME FROM STAR WARS)

The following program plays the theme from Star Wars and allows you to change the tempo.

EXPLANATION

The machine language routine is poked into memory at line 10. The values for the machine language tone generator are at lines 1000–1010. Line 2000 holds the number of notes to be played. The values in the DATA statements on lines 2010–2030 represent the values for frequency and duration, respectively.

To enter your own song, use Table 10-1 and Table 10-2 to determine the values for the frequency and duration of the notes. If you want to change the tempo, you can multiply the duration value by a number such as 2, 3, or 3.5. This was done on line 70.

However, a problem arises when you try to use a duration greater than 255. The computer will respond with a range error message. Line 80 checks for a value greater than 255 and stores the value in variable DU (duration). It then sets a flag FL equal to 1 and sets the duration D to the maximum 255.

Line 100 checks the value of the flag FL. If the value is 1, the program sets a delay loop of length DU − 255.

```
5    REM  === STAR WARS ===
10   FOR L = 770 TO 790: READ V: POKE L,V: NEXT L
20   TEXT : HOME
30   VTAB 12: HTAB 14: PRINT "** STAR WARS **"
40   READ N
50   FOR X = 1 TO N
60   READ F,D
70 D = D * 3
80   IF D > 255 THEN DU = D:FL = 1:D = 255
90   POKE 768,F: POKE 769,D: CALL 770
100   IF FL = 1 THEN  FOR Z = 1 TO DU - 255: NEXT Z:FL =
0
110   NEXT X
199   END
995   REM --- SOUND ROUTINE DATA ---
1000   DATA    173,48,192,136,208,5,206,1,3,240,9
1010   DATA   202,208,245,174,0,3,76,2,3,96
1995   REM   --- FREQUENCY, DURATION ---
2000   DATA 42: REM   NUMBER OF NOTES
2010   DATA   170,21,170,21,170,21,128,127,85,127,96,21,10
2,21,114,21,64,127,85,64,96,21,102,21,114,21
2020   DATA    64,127,85,64,96,21,102,21,96,21,114,127,170
,21,170,21,170,21,128,127,85,127,96,21,102,21,114,21
2030   DATA 64,127,85,64,96,21,102,21,114,21,64,127,85,64
,96,21,102,21,114,21,128,64,128,21,128,21,128,21,128,64
```

ADDING A REST ("CHARGE!")

This shows you how to add a rest to your song.

EXPLANATION

If you want to add a rest, add a piece of dummy data and check for that value during the program. When the computer reads the dummy data on line 90, it sets up a delay loop so the computer will pause to simulate a rest. The ending value of the delay loop will be the value of the duration. It takes the duration value and doubles it to arrive at the rest. If you want a longer rest, change the 2 in line 90 to a larger number.

This program uses a dummy value of a negative number to flag the rest. Use Table 10-3 to enter the values for the duration that will determine the type of rest.

TABLE 10-3. RESTS

Type of Rest	Duration Value
Whole	255
Half	127
Quarter	64
Eighth	32
Sixteenth	16

```
5    REM  === CHARGE! ===
7    REM --- POKE IN MACHINE LANGUAGE TONE GENERATOR ---
10   FOR L = 770 TO 790: READ V: POKE L,V: NEXT L
20   DATA   173,48,192,136,208,5,206,1,3,240,9
30   DATA   202,208,245,174,0,3,76,2,3,96
40   HOME
50   HTAB 18: PRINT  TAB( 18)"CHARGE!"
55   REM  --- PLAY SONG ---
60   READ T
70   FOR X = 1 TO T
80   READ F,D
90   IF F < 0 THEN  FOR Z = 1 TO 2 * D: NEXT Z: GOTO 160
100  D = D * 1
110   IF D > 255 THEN DU = D:FL = 1:D = 255
120   POKE 768,F
130   POKE 769,D
140   CALL 770
150   IF FL = 1 THEN  FOR Z = 1 TO DU - 255: NEXT Z:FL =
0
160   NEXT X
199   END
995   REM --- FREQUENCY AND DURATION OF TUNE ---
1000   DATA  7 : REM  NUMBER OF NOTES
1010   DATA  128,64,96,64,76,64,64,64
1020   DATA  -1,96
1030   DATA  76,64,64,255
```

CALL MUSIC OR CALL SOUND

This presents a statement to use CALL MUSIC or CALL SOUND in place of CALL 768.

EXPLANATION

When you call a machine language routine by name, be sure to use a name that does not contain any reserved words. TONE contains the reserved word ON and therefore cannot be used in this case.

Make the following changes to set up variables such as MUSIC or SOUND to be equal to 770 and then CALL the variable name rather than its value.

Add line 35 and change line 140:

```
35 MUSIC = 770

140 CALL MUSIC
```

or

```
35 SOUND = 770

140 CALL SOUND
```

ONE ARRAY TO STORE TUNE (BEETHOVEN'S 9TH)

This program uses an array to store a tune to be used throughout your program. This is useful when the program has other DATA statements. It is also convenient when the same tune is to be played more than once in your program. The tune is "Ode to Joy" from Beethoven's Ninth Symphony.

EXPLANATION

The arrays F (X) and D (X) hold the values for the frequency and duration, respectively. Be sure that the first set of DATA statements contains the machine language routine, since the computer reads the DATA statements in the order in which they physically appear in the program.

The DATA statements at lines 20 and 30 hold the machine language routine, while the statements at 1000–1040 store the number of notes and the frequency and duration of each note of the song.

Line 130 issues the command CALL MUSIC, since MUSIC has been assigned the value 770 in line 40.

```
5    REM    === BEETHOVEN'S 9TH ===
7    REM    --- POKE IN MACHINE LANGUAGE TONE GENERATOR ---
10   FOR L = 770 TO 790: READ V: POKE L,V: NEXT L
20   DATA   173,48,192,136,208,5,206,1,3,240,9
30   DATA   202,208,245,174,0,3,76,2,3,96
40  MUSIC = 770
50   TEXT : HOME
60   HTAB 12: PRINT "BEETHOVEN'S 9TH"
65   REM    --- READ FREQUENCY/DURATION INTO ARRAY ---
70   READ N: DIM F(N),D(N)
80   FOR X = 1 TO N: READ F(X),D(X): NEXT X
85   REM    --- PLAY TUNE ---
90   FOR X = 1 TO N
100  IF F(X) < 0 THEN  FOR Z = 1 TO 2 * D(X): NEXT Z: GO
TO 150
110  D(X) = D(X) * 2
120  IF D(X) > 255 THEN DU = D(X):FL = 1:D(X) = 255
130  POKE 768,F(X): POKE 769,D(X): CALL MUSIC
140  IF FL = 1 THEN  FOR Z = 1 TO DU - 255: NEXT Z:FL =
0
150  NEXT X
199  END
995  REM --- FREQUENCY AND DURATION OF TUNE ---
1000  DATA 63: REM   NUMBER OF NOTES
1010  DATA 102,64,102,64,96,64,85,64,85,64,96,64,102,64,
114,64,128,64,128,64,114,64,102,64,102,96,114,32,114,127
1020  DATA 102,64,102,64,96,64,85,64,85,64,96,64,102,64,
114,64,128,64,128,64,114,64,102,64,114,96,128,32,128,127
```

```
1030   DATA 114,64,114,64,102,64,128,64,114,64,102,32,96,
32,102,64,128,64,114,64,102,32,96,32,102,64,114,64,128,6
4,114,64,170,64,102,64
1040   DATA 102,64,102,64,96,64,85,64,85,64,96,64,102,64,
114,64,128,64,128,64,114,64,102,64,114,96,128,32,128,127
```

MULTIPLE ARRAYS TO STORE TUNE
("MARY" AND "TWINKLE")

This program shows you how to store two songs in arrays and play either song. This is useful if you want to play the songs in any sequence and not the order listed in the DATA statements.

EXPLANATION

When you have several tunes to play at various points in a program, use different arrays to store the tunes at the start of the program and use the appropriate array when needed.

The arrays FM( ) and DM( ) store the frequency and duration for "Mary Had a Little Lamb"; the variable NM holds the number of notes for that song. The arrays FT( ) and DT( ) store the frequency and duration for "Twinkle, Twinkle Little Star," with NT holding the number of notes.

The loop at lines 50–60 sets up the array with the notes of "Mary Had a Little Lamb," while the loop at lines 70–80 sets up the array with the notes from "Twinkle, Twinkle Little Star."

This program sets up a menu of the two songs available and lets the user enter the number of the song or a 0 to quit the program. Lines 90–130 set up the menu and line 140 accepts the viewer's selection.

Line 150 checks for the zero entry to quit the program. Line 160 instructs the computer to execute the subroutine that plays the song requested. After the song is played, the program returns to the menu.

This is an example of how you can use arrays to play two different tunes. Your program may play one tune for a correct answer and another tune for an incorrect answer. You could have your program select the tunes to coordinate the graphics pictures with the music. For example, if you are showing scenes of different countries or cities, you might want an appropriate tune. If your program involves different teams in football or the Olympics, you might want to play the appropriate theme, college song, or national anthem.

```
5   REM   === MARY AND TWINKLE ===
10   TEXT : HOME : PRINT  TAB( 18)"MUSIC"
15   REM     --- POKE IN MACHINE LANGUAGE TONE GENERATOR ---
20   FOR L = 770 TO 790: READ V: POKE L,V: NEXT L
30   DATA   173,48,192,136,208,5,206,1,3,240,9
40   DATA   202,208,245,174,0,3,76,2,3,96
45   REM     --- READ FREQUENCY/DURATION INTO ARRAY ---
47   REM     --- READ MARY ---
50   READ NM: DIM FM(NM),DM(NM)
60   FOR X = 1 TO NM: READ FM(X),DM(X): NEXT X
65   REM   --- READ TWINKLE ---
70   READ NT: DIM FT(NT),DT(NT)
80   FOR X = 1 TO NT: READ FT(X),DT(X): NEXT X
85   REM   --- PRINT MENU ---
90   TEXT : HOME
100   PRINT  TAB( 18)"MUSIC": PRINT : PRINT
110   PRINT "0. QUIT PROGRAM": PRINT
120   PRINT "1. MARY HAD A LITTLE LAMB": PRINT
130   PRINT "2. TWINKLE TWINKLE LITTLE STAR": PRINT : PRI
```

```
NT : PRINT
140   INPUT "ENTER THE NUMBER OF THE SONG ";NS
150   IF NS = 0 THEN 299
160   ON NS GOSUB 1000,2000
170   GOTO 90
299   END
995   REM   --- PLAY MARY ---
1000  FOR X = 1 TO NM
1010  IF FM(X) < 0 THEN  FOR Z = 1 TO DM(X): NEXT X: GOT
O 1060
1020 DM(X) = 2 * DM(X)
1030  IF DM(X) > 255 THEN DU = DM(X):FL = 1:DM(X) = 255
1040  IF FL = 1 THEN  FOR Z = 1 TO DU - 255: NEXT Z:FL =
 0
1050  POKE 768,FM(X): POKE 769,DM(X): CALL 770
1060  NEXT X
1070  RETURN
1995  REM   --- PLAY TWINKLE ---
2000  FOR X = 1 TO NT
2010  IF FT(X) < 0 THEN  FOR Z = 1 TO DT(X): NEXT X: GOT
O 2060
2020 DT(X) = 2 * DT(X)
2030  IF DT(X) > 255 THEN DU = DT(X):FL = 1:DT(X) = 255
2040  IF FL = 1 THEN  FOR Z = 1 TO DU - 255: NEXT Z:FL =
 0
2050  POKE 768,FT(X): POKE 769,DT(X): CALL 770
2060  NEXT X
2070  RETURN
4993  REM --- FREQUENCY AND DURATION OF TUNE ---
4995  REM   --- MARY HAD A LITTLE LAMB ---
5000  DATA  26: REM  NUMBER OF NOTES
5010  DATA 102,64,114,64,128,64,114,64,102,64,102,64,102
,127
5020  DATA 114,64,114,64,114,128
5030  DATA 102,64,85,64,85,127
5040  DATA 102,64,114,64,128,64,114,64,102,64,102,64,102
,64,102,64
5050  DATA 114,64,114,64,102,64,114,64,128,127
5995  REM   --- TWINKLE TWINKLE LITTLE STAR ---
6000  DATA  42: REM  NUMBER OF NOTES
6010  DATA  128,64,128,64,85,64,85,64,76,64,76,64,85,127
6020  DATA  96,64,96,64,102,64,102,64,114,64,114,64,128,
127
6030  DATA  85,64,85,64,96,64,96,64,102,64,102,64,114,12
7
6040  DATA  85,64,85,64,96,64,96,64,102,64,102,64,114,12
7
6050  DATA  128,64,128,64,85,64,85,64,76,64,76,64,85,127
6060  DATA  96,64,96,64,102,64,102,64,114,64,114,64,128,
127
```

MODIFICATION

The naming of the arrays is up to you. The arrays F1( ), D1( ), F2( ), D2( ), and F3( ), D3( ) can be used to store the frequency and duration, respectively, for the different tunes. The variables N1, N2, and N3 can represent the number of notes for each tune.

CHANGING PITCH (BRAHMS' LULLABY)

This program lets you change the pitch of a song. The tune is Brahms' Lullaby.

EXPLANATION

The program allows you to change the pitch of a song by changing the adjustment factor AF. The range of the values of AF vary with different programs.

Assign an adjustment factor AF, where AF ranges from a negative number to a positive number, such as −5 through 5. If AF = 0, then the original pitch will be played. If the value of AF is a negative number, then the pitch will be lower, while a positive value of AF will result in a higher pitch.

Line 50 calculates the pitch factor based on the value of AF in line 40. The value of 2^{12} represents the ratio between the frequencies of two adjacent notes. AF represents the number of half tones of change. PF represents the ratio of the original note and the adjusted note.

```
5    REM   === BRAHM'S LULLABY ===
7    REM   --- POKE IN MACHINE LANGUAGE TONE GENERATOR ---
10   FOR L = 770 TO 790: READ V: POKE L,V: NEXT L
20   TEXT : HOME
30   VTAB 12: HTAB 11: PRINT "** BRAHM'S LULLABY **"
40   AF = 2: REM   ADJUSTMENT FACTOR FOR PITCH
50   PF = 2 ^ ((1 / 12) * ( - AF))
55   REM   --- READ FREQUENCY/DURATION INTO ARRY ---
60   READ N: DIM F(N),D(N)
70   FOR X = 1 TO N: READ F(X),D(X)
80 F(X) = PF * F(X): IF F(X) > 255 THEN  PRINT "TRY A SM
ALLER AF": GOTO 199
90   NEXT X
95   REM   --- PLAY SONG ---
100   FOR X = 1 TO N
110   IF F(X) < 0 THEN  FOR Z = 1 TO 2 * D(X): NEXT Z: GO
TO 160
120 D(X) = 3 * D(X)
130   IF D(X) > 255 THEN DU = D(X):FL = 1:D(X) = 255
140   POKE 768,F(X): POKE 769,D(X): CALL 770
150   IF FL = 1 THEN  FOR Z = 1 TO DU - 255: NEXT Z:FL =
0
160   NEXT X
199   END
995   REM --- SOUND ROUTINE DATA ---
1000   DATA   173,48,192,136,208,5,206,1,3,240,9
1010   DATA   202,208,245,174,0,3,76,2,3,96
1995   REM   --- FREQUENCY, DURATION ---
2000   DATA   54: REM   NUMBER OF NOTES
2010   DATA   102,32,102,32,85,127,102,32,102,32,85,127,10
2,32,85,32
2020   DATA   64,64,68,64,76,64,76,64,85,64,114,32,102,32
2030   DATA   96,64,114,64,114,32,102,32,96,127,114,32,96
,32
2040   DATA   68,32,76,32,85,64,68,64,64,127,128,32,128,32
```

```
2050   DATA   64,127,76,32,96,32,85,127,102,32,128,32
2060   DATA   96,64,85,64,76,64,102,64,85,64,128,32,128,32
2070   DATA    64,127,76,32,96,32,85,127,102,32,128,32
2080   DATA   96,21,85,21,96,21,102,64,114,64,128,127
```

SAVING THE MACHINE LANGUAGE
TONE GENERATOR ROUTINE

This statement demonstrates how to save the machine language generator as a binary file, which allows you to use the tone generator without having to include it in every program. This is useful for a game, quiz, or adventure game.

EXPLANATION

Run one of the programs with the tone generator to get the routine in memory. The following statement saves the machine language routine with a BSAVE command. It uses the filename SOUND GENERATOR, although you could replace that name with any legal filename of your choice. You can express the address and length in either decimal or hexadecimal notation.

```
BSAVE SOUND GENERATOR,A770,L21
```

or

```
BSAVE SOUND GENERATOR,A$302,L$15
```

ACCESSING THE TONE ROUTINE
("TAKE ME OUT TO THE BALL GAME")

This statement shows you how to access the machine language tone generator that has been saved as a binary file and play the song "Take Me Out to the Ball Game."

EXPLANATION

The tone generator routine saved as SOUND GENERATOR is BLOADed in line 30. The frequency and duration are stored in arrays. The adjusted tune is played at lines 100–160.

The binary file SOUND GENERATOR must be on every disk that has programs that access it.

```
5    REM   === BALL GAME ===
10   TEXT : HOME
20   VTAB 12: HTAB 3: PRINT "** TAKE ME OUT TO THE BALL G
AME **"
30   PRINT CHR$ (4)"BLOAD SOUND GENERATOR"
35 MUSIC = 770
40 AF =  - 2: REM   ADJUSTMENT FACTOR FOR PITCH
50 PF = 2 ^ ((1 / 12) * ( - AF))
55   REM   --- READ FREQUENCY/DURATION INTO ARRAY ---
60   READ N: DIM F(N),D(N)
70   FOR X = 1 TO N: READ F(X),D(X)
80 F(X) = PF * F(X): IF F(X) > 255 THEN  PRINT "TRY A LA
RGER AF": GOTO 199
90   NEXT X
95   REM   --- PLAY SONG
100  FOR X = 1 TO N
110  IF F(X) < 0 THEN  FOR Z = 1 TO D(X): NEXT Z: GOTO 1
60
120 D(X) = 1 * D(X)
130  IF D(X) > 255 THEN DU = D(X):FL = 1:D(X) = 255
140  POKE 768,F(X): POKE 769,D(X): CALL MUSIC
150  IF FL = 1 THEN  FOR Z = 1 TO DU - 255: NEXT Z:FL =
0
160  NEXT X
199  END
995  REM   --- FREQUENCY, DURATION ---
1000  DATA 62: REM   NUMBER OF NOTES
1010  DATA 128,127,64,64,76,64,85,64,102,64,85,192,114,1
92
1020  DATA 128,127,64,64,76,64,85,64,102,64,85,319,81,64
1030  DATA 76,64,81,64,76,64,102,64,96,64,85,64,76,127,9
6,64,114,192
1040  DATA  76,127,76,64,76,64,68,64,64,64,57,64,68,64,7
6,64,85,64,102,64,114,64
1050  DATA 128,127,64,64,76,64,85,64,102,64,85,192,114,1
92
1060  DATA 128,64,128,64,114,64,102,64,96,64,85,64,76,19
2,-1,64,76,64,68,64
1070  DATA  64,192,64,192,64,64,68,64,76,64,85,64,91,64,
85,64
1080  DATA 76,192,68,192,64,192
```

ASCII CODES

ASCII Code	Keystroke	Screen Display	ASCII Code	Keystroke	Screen Display
		ASCII CHARACTER CODES FOR APPLE II/II PLUS			
0	CTRL @		32	space bar	space
1	CTRL A		33	!	!
2	CTRL B		34	"	"
3	CTRL C		35	#	#
4	CTRL D		36	S	S
5	CTRL E		37	%	%
6	CTRL F		38	&	&
7	CTRL G	Bell	39	'	'
8	CTRL H	Backspace or ←	40	(	(
9	CTRL I		41	)	)
10	CTRL J	Linefeed	42	*	*
11	CTRL K		43	+	+
12	CTRL L		44	,	,
13	CTRL M	Carriage return	45	−	−
14	CTRL N		46	.	.
15	CTRL O		47	/	/
16	CTRL P		48	0	0
17	CTRL Q		49	1	1
18	CTRL R		50	2	2
19	CTRL S		51	3	3
20	CTRL T		52	4	4
21	CTRL U	Forward space or →	53	5	5
22	CTRL V		54	6	6
23	CTRL W		55	7	7
24	CTRL X	Line cancel	56	8	8
25	CTRL Y		57	9	9
26	CTRL Z		58	:	:
27	ESC key		59	;	;
28	na		60	<	<
29	CTRL SHIFT M		61	=	=
30	CTRL ^		62	>	>
31	na		63	?	?

na = not available

ASCII CHARACTER CODES FOR
APPLE II/II PLUS (CONT.)

ASCII Code	Keystroke	Screen Display	ASCII Code	Keystroke	Screen Display
64	@	@	96	na	
65	A	A	97	na	!
66	B	B	98	na	"
67	C	C	99	na	#
68	D	D	100	na	$
69	E	E	101	na	%
70	F	F	102	na	&
71	G	G	103	na	'
72	H	H	104	na	(
73	I	I	105	na	)
74	J	J	106	na	*
75	K	K	107	na	+
76	L	L	108	na	,
77	M	M	109	na	—
78	N	N	110	na	.
79	O	O	111	na	/
80	P	P	112	na	0
81	Q	Q	113	na	1
82	R	R	114	na	2
83	S	S	115	na	3
84	T	T	116	na	4
85	U	U	117	na	5
86	V	V	118	na	6
87	W	W	119	na	7
88	X	X	120	na	8
89	Y	Y	121	na	9
90	Z	Z	122	na	:
91	na	[	123	na	;
92	na	\	124	na	<
93	SHIFT M	]	125	na	=
94	^	^	126	na	>
95	na	—	127	na	?

na = not available.

ASCII CHARACTER CODES FOR APPLE IIe/IIc

ASCII Code	Keystroke	Screen Display	ASCII Code	Keystroke	Screen Display
0	CTRL @		32	space bar	space
1	CTRL A		33	!	!
2	CTRL B		34	"	"
3	CTRL C		35	#	#
4	CTRL D		36	$	$
5	CTRL E		37	%	%
6	CTRL F		38	&	&
7	CTRL G	Bell	39	'	'
8	CTRL H	Backspace or ←	40	(	(
9	CTRL I	TAB key	41	)	)
10	CTRL J	Linefeed or ↓	42	*	*
11	CTRL K	↑	43	+	+
12	CTRL L		44	,	,
13	CTRL M	Carriage return	45	—	—
14	CTRL N		46	.	.
15	CTRL O		47	/	/
16	CTRL P		48	0	0
17	CTRL Q		49	1	1
18	CTRL R		50	2	2
19	CTRL S		51	3	3
20	CTRL T		52	4	4
21	CTRL U	Forward space or →	53	5	5
22	CTRL V		54	6	6
23	CTRL W		55	7	7
24	CTRL X	Line cancel	56	8	8
25	CTRL Y		57	9	9
26	CTRL Z		58	:	:
27	ESC key		59	;	;
28	na		60	<	<
29	CTRL SHIFT M		61	=	=
30	CTRL ^		62	>	>
31	na		63	?	?

na = not available

ASCII CHARACTER CODES FOR
APPLE IIe/IIc (CONT.)

ASCII Code	Keystroke	Screen Display	ASCII Code	Keystroke	Screen Display
64	@	@	96	\	\
65	A	A	97	a	a
66	B	B	98	b	b
67	C	C	99	c	c
68	D	D	100	d	d
69	E	E	101	e	e
70	F	F	102	f	f
71	G	G	103	g	g
72	H	H	104	h	h
73	I	I	105	i	i
74	J	J	106	j	j
75	K	K	107	k	k
76	L	L	108	l	l
77	M	M	109	m	m
78	N	N	110	n	n
79	O	O	111	o	o
80	P	P	112	p	p
81	Q	Q	113	q	q
82	R	R	114	r	r
83	S	S	115	s	s
84	T	T	116	t	t
85	U	U	117	u	u
86	V	V	118	v	v
87	W	W	119	w	w
88	X	X	120	x	x
89	Y	Y	121	y	y
90	Z	Z	122	z	z
91	[	[	123	{	{
92	\	\	124	|	|
93	SHIFT M	]	125	}	}
94	^	^	126	~	~
95	—	—	127	Delete key	▓

na = not available.

The following chart is a simplified version of the Apple's memory map. It indicates the addresses that hold graphics, text, and Applesoft programs, along with free memory that you can use for your own machine language routines. It assumes 64K of memory and Applesoft in ROM. If you have 48K of memory with Applesoft in ROM, the same map can be used, except that the addresses above 49151 are not available.

MEMORY MAP		
Address in Decimal	Function	Address in Hexadecimal
65535		$FFFF
	INT BASIC/FP BASIC (only with 64K)	
49152		$C000
49151		$BFFF
	Disk operating system (DOS)	
38400		$9600
38399		$95FF
	Unused	
24576		$6000
24575		$5FFF
	Hi-res graphics page 2	
16384		$4000
16383		$3FFF
	Hi-res graphics page 1	
8192		$2000
8191		$1FFF
	Unused	
3072		$C00
3071		$BFF
	Text/lo-res graphics page 2 Start of Applesoft program	
2048		$800
2047		$7FF
	Text/lo-res graphics page 1	
1024		$400
1023		$3FF
	DOS vectors	
960		$3C0
959		$3BF
	Unused	
768		$300
767		$2FF
	System functions	
0		$0

COLOR CHARTS

The following two charts represent the colors available in low and high resolution graphics, respectively.

LOW RESOLUTION GRAPHICS COLOR

Number	Color	Number	Color
0	Black	8	Brown
1	Red	9	Orange
2	Dark blue	10	Gray
3	Purple	11	Pink
4	Dark green	12	Light green
5	Gray	13	Yellow
6	Medium blue	14	Aqua
7	Light blue	15	White

HIGH RESOLUTION GRAPHICS COLORS

Number	Color
0	Black
1	Green
2	Violet
3	White
4	Black
5	Orange/red
6	Blue
7	White

PEEK, POKE, AND CALL COMMANDS

MEMORY LOCATIONS

A 64K Apple computer has 65536 possible memory addresses numbered 0–65535.

The memory locations are expressed as either a positive number from 0 to 65535 or as an equivalent negative number. The negative address is often used when the address is greater than 32767.

To convert a positive number to its equivalent negative number subtract 65536 from it.

$$positive\ number - 65536 = negative\ address$$
$$49152 - 65536 = -16384$$
$$49152\ is\ equivalent\ to\ -16384$$

To convert a negative number to its positive equivalent, add 65536 to it.

$$negative\ address + 65536 = positive\ address$$
$$-16384 + 65536 = 65536 - 16384 = 49152$$
$$-16384\ is\ equivalent\ to\ 49152$$

PEEK

The PEEK command allows you to examine the contents of a memory address. The general form is the following command, where A represents the address: PEEK(A).

PEEK(A) is equivalent to PEEK(A − 65536) and returns the contents of memory location A or A − 65536.

POKE

The POKE command allows you to change the contents of a memory location. The general form is the following command, where A represents the address and V the value to be entered: POKE A,V.

POKE A,V is equivalent to POKE A − 65536,V and pokes the value V into location A or A − 65536.

CALL

The CALL command transfers control from BASIC to a machine language subroutine that starts at the memory location accessed. This subroutine can be a routine resident in ROM or one you create and store in RAM such as the Sound Generator routine.

The general format of the CALL command is the following command, where A is the starting address of the machine language subroutine: CALL A.

CALL A is equivalent to CALL A − 65536 and accesses the machine language subroutine that starts at memory location A.

The following charts present some of the commonly used PEEK, POKE, and CALL commands. The list is not complete but represents the commands used in this book.

Command	Equivalent	Explanation
		Page Zero
28		Last HCOLOR value
		CALL −3082 fills hi-res screen if
		POKE 28,V is used where:
		0=0 127=3 213=6
		42=1 128=4 255=7
		85=2 170=5
32		Left edge of text window 0–39
33		Width of text window 1–40
34		Top edge of text window 0–23
35		Bottom edge of text window 1–24
36		Horizontal cursor position 0–39
37		Vertical cursor position 0–23
48		Lo-res color value * 17
		Holds ASCII value of text character if
		GR, HLIN, or VLIN was used in text mode where:
		0–63 Inverse character
		64–127 Flashing character
		128–191 Standard character
50		Text output format where:
		POKE 50,63 Inverse
		POKE 50,127:POKE 243,64 Flash
		POKE 50,255 Normal
		POKE 50,128 Invisible listing/catalog
		POKE 50,255 Normal listing/catalog
123–124		Program line where DATA is read
125–126		Memory address of DATA
214		RUN flag
		POKE 214,255 disables CTRL C and
		interprets any command as RUN
216		ONERR flag
		POKE 216,0 cancels ONERR
222		Returns error code (see Tables 2-1 and 2-2)
224–225		X-coordinate of last HPLOT .
		high byte in 225
		low byte in 224
226		Y-coordinate of last HPLOT
228		Last HCOLOR value where:
		0=0 127=3 213=6
		42=1 128=4 255=7
		85=2 170=5
230		Hi-res plotting page where:
		32=Page 1 64=Page 2

Command	Equivalent	Explanation
		DOS
1010–1012		RESET vector
		POKE 1010,102:POKE 1011,213:POKE 1012,112
		makes RESET RUN program (can disable with CTRL C)
		POKE 1012,1 makes RESET boot disk
1013–1015		& vector
		& = CATALOG:
		POKE 1013,76:POKE 1014,110:POKE 1015,165
		& = LIST:
		POKE 1013,76:POKE 1014,165:POKE 1015,214
		& = RUN:
		POKE 1013,76:POKE 1014,18:POKE 1015,217
40286–7	−25250/−25249	POKE −25250,105:POKE −25249,0
		traps and disables CTRL C
43624		Disk drive number
45999–46010		Disk volume heading
		Keyboard
49152	−16384	Holds ASCII value of keypress + 128
		POKE −16384,0 resets keyboard reader
49168	−16368	POKE −16368,0 clears high bit of keyboard reader
		Display Soft Switches
		POKE address,V or K = PEEK(address)
49232	−16304	Sets graphics mode
49233	−16303	Sets text mode
49234	−16302	Sets full screen graphics
49235	−16301	Sets mixed text/graphics mode
49236	−16300	Sets page 1
49237	−16299	Sets page 2
49238	−16298	Sets lo-res mode
49239	−16297	Sets hi-res mode
		Speaker
49250	−16336	X = PEEK(−16336) clicks speaker
		Paddles
49249	−16286	X = PEEK(−16286) reads button on paddle 0
		where X > 127 if button pressed
49250	−16287	X = PEEK(−16287) reads button on paddle 1
		where X > 127 if button pressed

COMMONLY USED CALL COMMANDS

Command	Equivalent	Explanation
64353	−1184	Prints Apple II at top of screen
64484	−1052	Rings bell
64500	−1036	Moves cursor right
		Same as ESC K
64528	−1008	Moves cursor left
		Same as ESC J or CTRL H
64538	−998	Moves cursor up
		Same as ESC I
64578	−958	Clears from cursor to bottom of page
		Same as ESC F
64600	−936	Clears text screen
		Same at HOME and ESC @
64614	−922	Moves cursor down
		Same as ESC M
64624	−912	Scrolls up one line by issuing linefeed
64661	−875	Clears entire text line
64668	−868	Clears text line from cursor to right edge of screen window
		Same as ESC E
64780	−756	Waits for keypress
64858	−678	Waits for carriage return
64860	−676	Rings bell and waits for carriage return
65381	−155	Enters monitor with bell
65385	−151	Enters monitor with no bell

SUMMARY OF COMMANDS TO SAVE GRAPHICS OR TEXT

The following commands can be used in the immediate mode or in a program, where *filename* is the name of the file being saved.

Save high resolution graphics page 1:

```
BSAVE filename,A$2000,L$2000
BSAVE filename,A8192,L8192
```

Save high resolution graphics page 2:

```
BSAVE filename,A$4000,L$2000
BSAVE filename,A16384,L8192
```

Save low resolution graphics page 1:

```
BSAVE filename,A$400,L$400
BSAVE filename,A1024,L1024
```

Save low resolution graphics page 2:

```
BSAVE filename,A$800,L$400
BSAVE filename,A2048,L1024
```

Save primary text page:

```
BSAVE filename,A$400,L$400
BSAVE filename,A1024,L1024
```